श्रीरमणपरावद्योपनिषद्

SRI RAMANAPARAVIDYOPANISHAD

THE SUPREME SCIENCE
AS TAUGHT BY SRI RAMANA

by 'WHO'
(K. LAKSHMANA SARMA)

SRI RAMANASRAMAM
TIRUVANNAMALAI
INDIA

© Sri Ramanasramam
Tiruvannamalai

First Edition : *2006 — 1000 copies*
Second Edition : 2016
1000 copies

CC No. 1126

ISBN: 978-81-8288-058-0

Price: ₹ 130

Published by:
V.S. Ramanan
President
Sri Ramanasramam
Tiruvannamalai 606 603
Tamil Nadu
INDIA
Email : *ashram@gururamana.org*
Web : *www.sriramanamaharshi.org*

Typeset at:
Sri Ramanasramam

Printed by:
Sudarsan Graphics Pvt. Ltd.,
Chennai 600 017
Tamil Nadu, INDIA

PUBLISHER'S NOTE

In the last stanza of "Ulladu Narpadu – Anubandham" (Forty Verses on Reality – Supplement), Bhagavan Sri Ramana Maharshi concluded that this work is the essence of Vedanta. In like manner, Sri K. Lakshmana Sarma composed in Sanskrit *Sri Ramanaparavidyopanishad*, which is also Vedanta Saram, the Supreme Science of the Self as taught by Sri Ramana.

Sri Ramanaparavidyopanishad was first serialized from 1956 to 1961 in the *Call Divine*, a monthly English journal that highlighted the life and teachings of Sri Ramana Maharshi. The Archives Department of Sri Ramanasramam, which has been significantly expanded and developed during the last five years, has collected the full series of articles to produce this book as an Archival publication.

After a thorough study of the text, its translation and commentary, Sri "SAMVID" has laboured to ensure its correctness, and also presented the Preface to this treatise. We are very grateful for his dedicated assistance in bringing out this publication.

Sri Ramanaparavidyopanishad is offered as our humble presentation at the Feet of Bhagavan on the occasion of his fifty-sixth Aradhana anniversary.

25-4-2006
Aradhana Day

PREFACE

Here is a remarkable work called by the Author "SRIRAMANAPARAVIDYOPANISHAD — The Supreme Science as taught by Sri Ramana." The Author Sri Lakshmana Sarma ('WHO'), who was born in the same year as Bhagavan Sri Ramana, was fortunate to have spent more than Twenty years in close association with Bhagavan. During this period, he imbibed the teachings of Bhagavan, made a deep study of it with his background of Vedantic Knowledge and even had the privilege of learning personally from Bhagavan the full import of 'Ulladu Narpadu', the Tamil composition of Bhagavan containing an exposition of the nature of the Ultimate Reality and its Realization in the brief compass of forty verses. The wisdom contained in this exalted work and the oral teachings given by Bhagavan from time to time, which Sri Lakshmana Sarma was convinced as being identical with the teachings of the Upanishads or the Vedanta, was ably and logically presented in the excellent work "MAHAYOGA or The Upanishadic Lore in the Light of the Teachings of Bhagavan Sri Ramana", first published in 1937. The present work serialized in 42 instalments during 1956-61 in the journal "Call Divine" dedicated to Bhagavan's teachings, somehow was not published in book form till date.

This work is as complete a treatise on the teachings of Bhagavan as Mahayoga was. The only differences are:

1. It is a poetic work in Sanskrit consisting of 701 Verses composed in mellifluous Upajati Metre.

2. Though it is not divided into chapters or subjects as MAHAYOGA was, it contains a concise, complete, authentic and logical exposition of the philosophical background of Bhagavan's Teachings together with the Practice shown by Bhagavan for the Realization of the Self or the Ultimate Reality.

3. While Mahayoga contains, in addition to the gist of Bhagavan's Works and Teachings, the author's own expositions of the various topics dealt with, the present work almost entirely consists of Bhagavan's Teachings expressed through his various works and talks with devotees; but they have been presented concisely and precisely in sweet Sanskrit language in poetic form.

4. One can easily discern the logical flow of the subjects and their explanations from beginning to end, making the work a complete guide to every sadhaka who wishes to pursue the direct path of Self-enquiry for Enlightenment.

The uncompromising conviction of Sri Sarma on the identity of Upanishadic (or Vedantic) teachings and their path to Self-realization (as expounded by Sri Sankaracharya) with Bhagavan's own teachings and Realization, is powerfully brought out in this Sanskrit composition. In fact, this work accomplishes the same purpose in respect of Bhagavan's teachings as Vivekachudamani of Sri Sankaracharya achieves in respect of the teachings of the Upanishads.

Rightly has it been called "Sriramanaparavidyopanishad" which can be paraphrased as "The True Knowledge concerning the Supreme Spirit or the Ultimate Reality as taught by Sri Ramana". Science, as understood by modern language, is a branch of knowledge involving systematized observation and experiment. Here, the word "Science" has been used for the observation made by the inward turning of the mind to find one's own True Nature and the practical realization of the Truth that is the Self through such Quest. The diving within to accomplish this purpose, after the restraint of all thought-constructs through such Quest, is the only practical method taught by Bhagavan for Self-realization and Liberation.

The value of this work which has been presented by Sri Sarma with clarity, completeness and precision can be apprcciatcd by any Sadhaka who rcads this wonderful work and makes it a part of his daily svadhyaya (or scriptural study). It will be superfluous to add anything to this preface over and above what Sri Sarma has expounded with such clarity and precision in this work. May the community of Sadhakas be enlightened by going through this exalted work and understanding and practising the Teachings contained in it. Sri Sarma's own Translations and explanations, which are short and to the point, will enable the readers to comprehend fully the entire Teachings.

SAMVID.

ABOUT THE AUTHOR

Sri K. Lakshmana Sarma was born in 1879 at Pudukkottai (the same year in which Bhagavan Sri Ramana was born). He passed Intermediate studies at Pudukkottai, obtained a Degree of Bachelor of Arts at Tiruchirappalli and obtained a Law Degree in Madras. From his early school days he evinced much interest in Sanskrit and attained proficiency in the language.

Sri Sarma worked as a civil lawyer for the Government and as an Official Receiver. He was also a courageous social reformer and from 1918 was committed to Mahatma Gandhi's Freedom Movement. While residing in Pondicherry from 1920-25, he developed and promoted the system of Nature Cure, of which he became a respected authority. His *magnum opus* on the subject, *Practical Nature Cure,* is a standard Text book. He also founded the English monthly, *The Life Natural*.

In 1927 Sri Sarma came into the fold of Bhagavan Sri Ramana. Revering him as the embodiment of both Lord Dakshinamurti and Sri Sankaracharya, he surrendered to him completely. He lived with Bhagavan for more than twenty years, during which period, under the Master's guidance, he delved deeply into his teachings.

Once he pleaded with Bhagavan about his inability to understand classical Tamil in order to appreciate his work "Ulladu Narpadu". Then Bhagavan taught him the elements of classical Tamil language, while learning one verse at a time. Sri Sarma composed verses in Sanskrit and submitted them to Bhagavan for his approval. If his approval was not forthcoming, he would continue to recast the entire verse to ensure correctness and consent. Bhagavan once commended his efforts and remarked that it was a great *tapas* for him to go on revising his translation any number of times until Bhagavan's approval was obtained.

Sri Lakshmana Sarma preferred the pen-name of 'WHO', so as to leave open the choice as to who was the writer, Bhagavan or himself – so surrendered was he to the Master. He has authored the famous work *Maha Yoga*, which contains the teachings of Sri Ramana Maharshi. This popular book has been translated into many languages the world over. Other books authored by Sri Sarma are *Sri Ramana Hridayam/Revelation* and *Guru Ramana Vachanamala* in Sanskrit and English and a Tamil commentary on "Ulladu Narpadu". The present work *Sri Ramana Paravidyopanishad* is essentially Vedanta Saram, the Supreme Science of the Self as taught by Sri Ramana Maharshi.

Sri Lakshmana Sarma, after a long life of dedication, passed away at the ripe age of 85 in 1965.

ॐ

श्रीरमणपरविद्योपनिषद्

om

śrīramaṇaparavidyopaniṣad

OM

The Supreme Science as Taught by Sri Ramana

BENEDICTORY VERSE

अहंस्वरूपेण समस्तजन्तोर्विभान्तमन्तर्विभुमप्रमेयम् ।
गुरुं गुरूणामजमादिदेवं वन्दामहे श्रीरमणं दयाब्धिम् ॥

ahaṁsvarūpeṇa samastajantorvibhāntamantarvibhumaprameyam |
guruṁ gurūṇāmajamādidevaṁ vandāmahe śrīramaṇaṁ dayābdhim ||

We bow our heads to the Holy Ramana, the
Ocean of Grace, the Infinite, Incommensurable,
Unborn Primal Divinity, Guru of all Gurus,
shining in the Hearts of all creatures as 'I'.

In this verse the essence of the teaching is indicated.
Devotion and self-surrender to the One Real Being, the Real

Self of all creatures, is shown to be the means of attaining the Goal of Life, which may be here stated as re-integration with that Being, separateness from Him being the original sin and the cause of all evil.

Herein is also expressed the saving Truth, the unity of the three apparently distinct entities, namely God, the Guru and the Real Self, which was explained in an ancient work, the Manasollasa, a commentary by Sri Sureshwaracharya on Sri Dakshinamurti Stotra by Bhagavan Sri Sankaracharya:

1.   ईश्वरो गुरुरात्मेति मूर्तिभेदविभागिने ।
     व्योमवद् व्याप्तदेहाय दक्षिणामूर्तये नमः ॥

īśvaro gururātmeti mūrtibhedavibhāgine |
vyomavad vyāptadehāya dakṣiṇāmūrtaye namaḥ ||

'Homage to Sri Dakshinamurti, manifest in three forms as God, the Guru and the Real Self, whose form is infinite as the sky'. Dakshinamurti was the name of God when He appeared as the Primal Guru and taught the sacred mystery of the Supreme State, by Silence, to the four sages, Sanaka, Sanandana, Sanatana and Sanatkumara. Bhagavan Sri Ramana Maharshi has said that these three are the three stages of Divine Grace; first God, then the Guru, and lastly the Real Self.

The subject of this revelation is next stated.

2. माण्डूक्यमुख्योपनिषत्सु दिष्टा ज्ञानाभिधा या सहजात्मनिष्ठा ।
ससाधना तेन निजानुभूत्या सन्दर्शिता सा प्रतिपाद्यतेऽत्र ॥

māṇḍūkyamukhyopaniṣatsu diṣṭā jñānābhidhā yā sahajātmaniṣṭhā |
sasādhanā tena nijānubhūtyā sandarśitā sā pratipādyate'tra ||

Herein is expounded the Teaching about the Natural State of the Real Self, known as Right Awareness, which was taught in the Mandukya and other Upanishads, and has (now) been taught by that same (Divine Guru), along with the means thereto, as experienced by Himself.

Both the ancient Upanishads and these new Upanishads have been given out by the same Teacher; for all sages and gurus are *One*, identical with the Supreme Being, the Self of all.

It is to be noted that the state of Deliverance, the goal of all aspirants, is styled the Natural State, because even now we are all in that State, our sense of being in other states being an illusion.

Bhagavan Sri Ramana Maharshi took on a human form and even went through the Sadhana (means of reaching the goal), so that he could teach us by his own experience.

How one becomes a disciple is next briefly described.

3. समीक्ष्य सांसारिकजीवनस्य दुःखात्मतां कामभयाश्रयत्वात् ।
द्वाभ्यां विमुक्तं गुरुमेत्य बुद्धं विमुक्तिमार्गं प्रणिपत्य पृच्छेत् ॥

samīkṣya sāṃsārikajīvanasya duḥkhātmatāṃ kāmabhayāśrayatvāt |
dvābhyāṃ vimuktaṃ gurumetya buddhaṃ vimuktimārgaṃ
praṇipatya pṛcchet ||

Becoming keenly aware that worldly life is full of misery, because it is infested with desire and fear, one should approach a guru who is a sage, being free from those bad forces, and after doing reverence to His Holy Feet, should question him about how to become free.

Only one whose attachments to the worldly life have been weakened by the realization that true and lasting Happiness is not to be had in this worldly life, that actually it is full of misery, because of subjection to desires and fear which never cease, only changing their forms, is ripe for discipleship. Such a one should seek out a *competent* Guru, who is free from the bondage being a Sage abiding always in the Natural State. Reverence to the Guru is imperative, because the ego, which is the seed of all evil, has to be got rid of in due course, not pampered.

The next two verses give the teaching in brief:

4. ब्रूयात् स बुद्धः परमं रहस्यं समस्तबुद्धानुभवप्रसिद्धम् ।
    जानासि चेत् स्वं न तवास्ति दुःखं दुःखी भवेस्त्वं यदि
    वेत्सि न स्वम् ॥

brūyāt sa buddhaḥ paramaṁ rahasyaṁ samastabuddhānubhavaprasiddham |
jānāsi cet svaṁ na tavāsti duḥkhaṁ duḥkhī bhavestvaṁ yadi vetsi na svam ||

The Sage will give out in reply the supreme secret, confirmed by the experience of all the sages: "If thou knowest Thyself, there is no suffering for thee. If thou sufferest, (it means only that) thou knowest not Thyself".

5. यतः सुषुप्तौ न तवास्ति दुःखं त्वयीदमारोपितमेव नान्यत् ।
जिज्ञासया स्वं समवेत्य सत्यं निजस्वरूपे सुखरूप आस्स्व ॥

yataḥ suṣuptau na tavāsti duḥkhaṁ tvayīdamāropitameva nānyat |
jijñāsayā svaṁ samavetya satyaṁ nijasvarūpe sukharūpa āssva ||

"Since you have no suffering in deep sleep, this suffering is only falsely ascribed to thy Self. Realize the Truth of Thyself by the resolve to know it and thereafter remain in thy own true Nature, which is Bliss".

The Real Self transcends the mind and is therefore unaffected by pleasure and pain. These are in and of the mind alone. The proof of this is that these are experienced only when the mind is functioning — as in waking and dream — and not when the mind is still, as in deep sleep. To be free from suffering, the only means, therefore, is to become aware of one's Real Self by the Quest taught by the Bhagavan Guru. The Self does not need to be *made* happy. He is himself happiness. This very teaching in brief appear, in the Tamil book, Kaivalya Navanitham (कैवल्यनवनीतम्) — the butter of the Advaitic State – and Bhagavan Sri Ramana Maharshi gave it out as the essence of his own teaching.

Is that all? What about the contents of the Upanishads and the rest of the sacred lore?

6. अर्थोऽयमेवं गुरुणोपदिष्टः सारः समस्तश्रुतिशीर्षवाचाम् ।
अस्योपदेशस्य हि विस्तरेण व्याख्यैव सर्वा निगमान्तवाणी ॥

artho'yamevaṁ guruṇopadiṣṭaḥ sāraḥ samastaśrutiśīrṣavācām |
asyopadeśasya hi vistareṇa vyākhyaiva sarvā nigamāntavāṇī ||

This teaching of the Guru is the very essence of all the Upanishads. All the texts of the latter are just commentaries on this teaching.

The Teaching is given in a slightly more detailed form in the verses that follow.

7.   ज्ञानस्वरूपं निजसत्यमेकं स्वयंप्रकाशं हृदि सत्यमस्ति ।
संशान्तचित्तेन हृदि स्थितिर्या सा तस्य बोधोऽपि विमुक्तिभावः ॥

jñānasvarūpaṁ nijasatyamekaṁ svayamprakāśaṁ hṛdi satyamasti |
saṁśāntacittena hṛdi sthitiryā sā tasya bodho'pi vimuktibhāvaḥ ||

In the Heart there dwells the Reality which is Pure Consciousness, the Real Self. To be in the Heart, with the mind quiescent, is the Knowledge (Awarenss) of Him, and also the State of Deliverance.

The State of Deliverance is just the mind-free state, wherein the Real Self, the Dweller in the Heart, is realized as such.

The real Self is not the dutiful little, apparent self, called the 'soul'. What then is he? The answer follows.

8.   आत्मस्वरूपा हृदि भासमाना सदैकरूपा विमला चितिश्च ।
ब्रह्माभिधानं जगतोऽखिलस्याप्याधारसत्यं द्वयमेकमेव ॥

ātmasvarūpā hṛdi bhāsamānā sadaikarūpā vimalā citiśca |
brahmābhidhānaṁ jagato'khilasyāpyādhārasatyaṁ dvayamekameva ||

That pure Consciousness, which is the Real Self shining in the heart, ever the same (without change), and the basic substratum — namely Brahman — of the whole universe, are both one and the same.

That is the meaning intended to be conveyed by the sacred texts of the Upanishads, which say that the Supreme Being Himself entered the body as the soul, — while giving a popular account of what is known as "creation". Really there was no creation, except what will be explained presently.

9. आधारसत्ये विमले तु तस्मिन् निजस्वरूपे मनसोपक्लृप्तम् ।
अविद्यया विश्वममुं निमील्य भाति स्वयं सत्यवदज्ञतायाम् ॥

ādhārasatye vimale tu tasmin nijasvarūpe manasopakḷptam |
avidyayā viśvamamuṁ nimīlya bhāti svayaṁ satyavadajñatāyām ||

But the world-appearance, superimposed by the mind, because of its Ignorance, upon that substratum, — which is the Truth of the Self, — conceals that Reality and itself shines as real (in its own light), so long as there is Ignorance.

Ignorance and mind are inseparable; where there is mind, there alone is ignorance; where there is no mind, neither is there Ignorance, since in the mind-free state the Real Self is not concealed. This explains why the Real Self is not known to men in general.

An analogy is given in the next verse in order to help understand the above.

10. निमील्य रज्जुं भुजगः स्वयं सन् मन्दान्धकारे सति भाति यद्वत् ।
आत्मानमेवं भुवनं निमील्य भाति स्वयं सत्यवदज्ञतायाम् ॥

nimīlya rajjuṁ bhujagaḥ svayaṁ san mandāndhakāre sati bhāti yadvat |
ātmānamevaṁ bhuvanaṁ nimīlya bhāti svayaṁ satyavadajñātāyām ||

As in dim light the (illusory) snake, concealing the real rope, is taken as real in its own sight, so the world, concealing the Self, appears as real in its own sight, in the state of ignorance.

The notion of the Self that develops because of this basic ignorance is next described.

11. अविद्ययाऽऽत्मा वपुषा मितश्च सुखी च दुःखी भवपाशबद्धः ।
प्रतीयतेऽज्ञोऽपि पृथक् परस्मादात्मा तु साक्षात्पर एव नान्यः ॥

avidyayā"tmā vapuṣā mitaśca sukhī ca duḥkhī bhavapāśabaddhaḥ |
pratīyate'jño'pi pṛthak parasmādātmā tu sākṣātpara eva nānyaḥ ||

Because of ignorance, the Self is believed to be limited to the body, enjoying and suffering, bound by bonds of desire to the world, ignorant and distinct from the Supreme Being. Really the Self is identical with Him, not other.

This mistaken view of one's own Self is the starting point of all the evil, known as Samsara, which means the necessity of being born and dying in an endless cycle. But all this is unreal, as explained in the very first verse of the *Ekatma Panchakam* (The Five Verses on the One Self), in which it is said that mistaking the body as the Self, the cycle of births and deaths, Self Realization and becoming the Self are all a dream, like a world tour in a dream.

12.	संसारिता स्वस्य ततो मृषैव बुध्येत तन्निर्मनने पदे तु ।
	"नह्यस्त्यविद्या मनसोऽतिरिक्ता मनोह्यविद्या भवबन्धरूपा" ॥

saṁsāritā svasya tato mṛṣaiva budhyeta tannirmanane pade tu |
"nahyastyavidyā manaso'tiriktā manohyavidyā bhavabandharūpā" ||

Hence this world-wandering of the self is just a myth. But this can be verified only in the mind-free State. "Apart from the mind there is no ignorance; the mind itself is Ignorance, which is bondage to life in the world".

The latter half of the verse is a quotation from the *Viveka Chudamani* of Sri Sankaracharya.

The analogy of the rope-snake is here repeated to explain this wrong notion of the Self.

13.	वीक्ष्याहिमीक्षेत यथा न रज्जुं विश्वं सजीवेश्वरमात्मरूपे ।
	अविद्यायाऽऽरोपितमीक्षमाणो न वीक्षते स्वं परमार्थसत्यम् ॥

vīkṣyāhimīkṣeta yathā na rajjuṁ viśvaṁ sajīveśvaramātmarūpe |
avidyayā''ropitamīkṣamāṇo na vīkṣate svaṁ paramārthasatyam ||

As one seeing the false snake fails to see the real rope, so, seeing the world — wherein are included the Personal God and the individual soul — does not see the Real Self as He really is, i.e., as the Supreme Reality (Brahman).

How long will this effect of Ignorance continue?

14.   निमीलितः स्वो भवितैव तावद्यावत् स्वतः सत्यमिदं विभाति ।
तथा न भायान्मनसि प्रणष्टे नाशाय तस्मान्मनसो यतेत ॥

nimīlitaḥ svo bhavitaiva tāvadyāvat svataḥ satyamidaṁ vibhāti |
tathā na bhāyānmanasi praṇaṣṭe nāśāya tasmānmanaso yateta ||

The Self will remain concealed so long as the
world is taken as real. It will cease to be so taken,
when the mind is once for all extinguished; hence
one must strive for extinguishing the mind.

The world-appearance being the obstacle to right
awareness of the Self and the mind being the cause of the world-
appearance, the cure of this evil is by attaining the Mind-free
State, which is done by the quest, briefly described presently.

15.   निमीलितं स्वं मनसा तमेनं मिथ्याप्रपञ्चप्रविकल्पनेन ।
स्वान्वेषणेनात्मनि निष्ठितः सन्नुन्मील्य तस्मिन्प्रविलापयेद्यः ॥

nimīlitaṁ svaṁ manasā tamenaṁ mithyāprapañcapravikalpanena |
svānveṣaṇenātmani niṣṭhitaḥ sannunmīlya tasminpravilāpayedyaḥ ||

16.   मनोऽप्यविद्यामखिलं प्रपञ्चं तेनानुभूयेत निजं स्वरूपम् ।
संसारहीनं निरुपाधिकं च ब्रह्मात्मकं केवलमद्वितीयम् ॥

mano'pyavidyāmakhilaṁ prapañcaṁ tenānubhūyeta nijaṁ svarūpam |
saṁsārahīnaṁ nirupādhikaṁ ca brahmātmakaṁ kevalamadvitīyam ||

He who, seeking the Self — concealed, as
shown above, by the mind by projecting on him

the illusory world appearance — becomes firmly established in the True State as that Self, thus uncovering that Self and dissolving the mind, the Ignorance and the whole world into Him, will enjoy his own true Self, which is without Samsara, not covered by the vehicles, identical with the Brahman, alone and without a second.

The full significance of this revelation will be understood in due course, in the course of this book.

An alternative to the Quest is the path of Devotion to God culminating in Self-surrender, which also leads ultimately to the same goal; this is indicated in the next two verses.

17.　भीत्याऽथवा जन्ममृतिप्रवाहात् प्रपद्यते चेच्छरणं महेशम्।
नश्येदविद्या कृपयैव तस्य तदा स्थितः स्यान्निजसत्यभावे॥

bhītyā'thavā janmamṛtipravāhāt prapadyate ceccharaṇaṁ maheśam |
naśyedavidyā kṛpayaiva tasya tadā sthitaḥ syānnijasatyabhāve ||

Or if one, from fear of the flood of births and deaths, takes refuge in God, then ignorance will cease by His Grace alone, and then he will become established in the true state of the Self.

This self-surrender is the final stage of the practice of devotion, which is dealt with in the next verse.

18.　भक्त्या परस्मै स्वनिवेदनं यत् प्रपत्तिमेतां निगदन्ति सन्तः।
तद्भक्तिरीशे नवधोपदिष्टा कार्या मुमुक्षोः श्रवणादिरूपा॥

bhaktyā parasmai svanivedanaṁ yat prapattimetāṁ nigadanti santaḥ |
tadbhaktirīśe navadhopadiṣṭā kāryā mumukṣoḥ śravaṇādirūpā ||

The wise call by the name 'self-surrender' the offering of oneself to God through devotion. Hence the seeker of deliverance must practise Devotion to God, which is described as ninefold, consisting of listening and the rest.

Here reference is made to a verse in Srimad Bhagavata:

श्रवणं कीर्तनं विष्णोः स्मरणं पादसेवनम् ।
अर्चनं वन्दनं दास्यं सख्यमात्मनिवेदनम् ॥

śravaṇaṁ kīrtanaṁ viṣṇoḥ smaraṇaṁ pādasevanam |
arcanaṁ vandanaṁ dāsyaṁ sakhyamātmanivedanam ||

"Listening to tales of God's glory, telling and remembering them, cleaving to His Feet, worship, obeisance, acts of service, cherishing Him as friend, and offering of oneself to Him".

A few of the different names of the Supreme State are next given:-

19. निष्ठाऽचला सा निजसत्यभावे ज्ञानं विमुक्तिः सहजा स्थितिश्च ।
स्थितोऽचलस्तत्र पदे परस्मिन् निरस्तमोहो भवति प्रबुद्धः ॥

niṣṭhā'calā sā nijasatyabhāve jñānaṁ vimuktiḥ sahajā sthitiśca |
sthito'calastatra pade parasmin nirastamoho bhavati prabuddhaḥ ||

That State, wherein one remains immovable in one's true nature (as the Real Self) is (itself called) Right Awareness, Deliverance and the

Natural State. He that dwells immovably in that Supreme State, free from delusion, is the Awakened One (Prabuddha).

The Significance of the last-given term will appear when we come to study the contrast between the three stages of life in bondage with the socalled fourth state, which is beyond. The natural state is socalled because it transcends the three stages, viz., waking, dream and deep sleep.

The term 'Prabuddha' is the same as the term 'Buddha', which means 'a Sage'.

The physical body may and often does survive the attainment of the Supreme State. How this can be is next explained.

20. निष्ठां परां तामधिगम्य बुद्धो जीवच्छरीरोऽपि विमुक्त एव ।
करोत्यहन्तां ममतां न देहे बुद्धो ह्यतोऽसावशरीर एव ॥

niṣṭhāṁ parāṁ tāmadhigamya buddho jīvacchariro'pi vimukta eva |
karotyahantāṁ mamatāṁ na dehe buddho hyato'sāvaśarīra eva ||

The Sage who has attained that Supreme State is Free, even though his body survives, (because) he does not look upon it as himself nor as belonging to himself. Therefore that Sage is really bodiless.

Being embodied or bodiless is due to the attachment or non-attachment to it. In ignorance there is the sense of 'I am the body' or of 'this body is mine', that is, the body is either 'I' or 'mine'. When this attachment ceases, bondage is at an end. This is an intricate point, which will become clearer as we proceed. This survival of the body of the sage is very important, because without it he cannot fulfil his mission for the uplift of his disciples.

'Is that State desirable' is a question that is asked. The answer to it is now given.

21. यन्निर्मनस्कं पदमेवमुक्तं सुखं तदात्यन्तिकमन्तहीनम् ।
सुखं समावृत्य मनः स्वयं हि सदैव दुःखं विवृणोति जन्तोः ॥

yannirmanaskam padamevamuktam sukham tadātyantikamantahīnam |
sukham samāvṛtya manaḥ svayam hi sadaiva duḥkham vivṛṇoti jantoḥ ||

The Mind-free state stated above is itself complete and endless happiness, since it is the mind itself that covers up (overpowers) the (natural) happiness (of the Real Self) and unfolds suffering for every creature.

The desire for happiness, says Bhagavan Sri Ramana Maharshi, is natural, but it is not to be had in its perfection in the world, where the mind is dominant, but only in the Mind-free state. It should be noted that happiness, which is natural to the Real Self, is not to be confounded with pleasure, which belongs to the world-order, along with its opposite, namely suffering. True Happiness is just Peace.

The qualifications of the aspirant to the Supreme State are next stated.

22. ऋजुः शुचिः सत्यवचा अमानी धीरो विरक्तश्च गुरौ सुभक्तः ।
शमादिषट्केन युतो मुमुक्षुः स्थितिं परां तामचिराल्लभेत ॥

ṛjuḥ śuciḥ satyavacā amānī dhīro viraktaśca gurau subhaktaḥ |
samādiṣaṭkena yuto mumukṣuḥ sthitiṁ parāṁ tāmacirāllabheta ||

The lover of deliverance who is straightforward, pure, truthful, unassuming, valiant, profoundly devoted to the Guru and endowed with six perfections, viz., serenity of mind and the rest, will attain that supreme state without delay.

The unqualified one will be hindered in his efforts to attain that state by the defects of character which are the opposites of those specified here. The qualified one will succeed in reaching that state soon and with great ease. Defects arise from the ego, while the qualifications arise by the weakening of the ego.

The term 'valiant' used in the foregoing verse is next explained.

23. धीरक्षणं यद्विदधाति साधुर्निगृह्य वृत्तीर्निजमार्गणाय ।
तदेव धीरत्वमिहोपदिष्टं नापेक्ष्यतेऽन्या खलु धीरताऽत्र ॥

dhīrakṣaṇaṁ yadvidadhāti sādhurnigṛhya vṛttīrnijamārgaṇāya |
tadeva dhīratvamihopadiṣṭaṁ nāpekṣyate'nyā khalu dhīratā'tra ||

The 'valour' enjoined here is just the concentration of the mind which the aspirant (sadhaka) achieves by restraining its vagaries for pursuing the quest of the Self, since no other valour is needed here.

The word 'dhira' in Sanskrit consists of the two letters 'dhi' and 'ra'. The former means the series of thoughts that arise and pass through the mind. The latter is taken as a symbol for 'raksha' (rakshanam), meaning control, so as to achieve mental quietude, necessary for pursuing the quest of the Self.

Devotion to the Guru is another qualification needing to be clarified. In the first place, there is the question as to, what sort of person should be taken as the Guru. This question is first answered.

24. भजेत् प्रबुद्धं हि गुरुं मुमुक्षुः स्वाज्ञाननिद्रोत्थितमस्तमोहम् ।
कथं नु मर्त्यः स्वयमप्रबुद्धः प्रबोधयेदन्यनरानबुद्धान् ॥

bhajet prabuddhaṁ hi guruṁ mumukṣuḥ svājñānanidrotthitamastamoham |
kathaṁ nu martyaḥ svayamaprabuddhaḥ prabodhayedanyanarānabuddhān ||

The aspirant to deliverance must resort to a sage as his Guru, that is, one who has awakened from the sleep of ignorance of the Self and is therefore free from delusion. How can one, who has not awakened from sleep, awaken others who are of the same case?

This will be self-evident. Here there is a pun on the word 'Prabuddha', which has two meanings: it means 'a sage;' it also means one who has awakened. Awakening implies sleep from which one has to wake up; here the sleep of ignorance of the Self, in which the dream of worldly living goes on, is taken as sleep. This description of 'samsara' as a dream in the sleep of ignorance occurs in the ancient lore. The nature of the devotion to the Guru is next explained.

25.　ईशादभेदेन कृतैव बुद्धे गुरौ सुभक्तिर्गदिताऽत्र साधोः ।
　　निर्मोहितामेत्यचिरात् तयैव बुद्धः परस्मान्नहि कश्चिदन्यः ॥

īśādabhedena kṛtaiva buddhe gurau subhaktirgaditā'tra sādhoḥ |
nirrmohitāmetyacirāt tayaiva buddhaḥ parasmānnahi kaścidanyaḥ ||

Only that devotion to the Guru is good, which is rendered to a Sage-Guru, regarding him as identical with God. Only by such devotion does one attain freedom from delusion. Truly the Sage is not other than God.

The Sage who is accepted as one's Guru must not be regarded as just a human being, a person, but as an incarnation of God Himself, because that is the truth of the Sage, and because, if the Guru be so regarded, the goal will be reached soon. This point will be explained in detail later.

The sixfold endowment mentioned in verse 22 is next enumerated.

26.　शमो दमश्चोपरतिस्तितिक्षा श्रद्धा गुरोर्वाचि समाहितत्वम् ।
　　विधीयते षट्कमिदं मुमुक्षोः स्थिरं भवेद्येन मनो गवेषे ॥

śamo damaścoparatistitikṣā śraddhā gurorvāci samāhitatvam |
vidhīyate ṣaṭkamidaṁ mumukṣoḥ sthiraṁ bhavedyena mano gaveṣe ||

Mental calm, sense-control, withdrawal from worldly pursuits, fortitude, faith in the words of Guru, steadiness in Sadhana — these six are prescribed for the aspirant, whereby his mind will remain firm in the quest.

These will come and ripen if the aspirant persists in efforts to make the Quest. Faith, of course, must be present from the very beginning. Faith should be understood as adherence to conclusions arrived at rationally, not blindly.

All items of this endowment, especially the first two, depend upon the practice of abstemiousness in eating, a discipline which is usually neglected. Bhagavan Sri Ramana has said that eating the minimum of wholesome food — food of sattvika quality — is *necessary* for the sadhaka. The policy of living to eat was expressly condemned by him in a Tamil verse, of which the following is a rendering in Sanskrit, in which the stomach is represented as accusing the eater, the soul, as a violator of the law of fairness to the digestive organs:-

विश्रान्तिं जठरस्य मे न वितरस्येकां च नाडीमहो
नानश्नन् दिवसे च तिष्ठसि कदाप्येकामहो नाडिकाम् ।

नो जानासि मदीयदुःखमतुलं हे दुर्विनीत त्वया
साकं जीवनमत्र देहनिलये मे दुर्घटं संप्रति ॥

viśrāntiṁ jaṭharasya me na vitarasyekāṁ ca nāḍīmaho
nānaśnan divase ca tiṣṭhasi kadāpyekāmaho nāḍikām |

no jānāsi madīyaduḥkhamatulaṁ he durvinīta tvayā
sākaṁ jīvanamatra dehanilaye me durghaṭaṁ samprati ||

"Thou dost not allow me, your stomach, rest for even one half hour; nor dost thou refrain from eating for even half an hour at a time; thou dost not care to take note of the suffering thou inflictest on me, which is beyond bearing. (Understand) Oh! Unrighteous man, it will be hereafter impossible for me to live with you in this body."

Eating just enough for health is the means of maintaining vital economy, as much for the spiritual life as for the worldly. Health of mind is greatly dependent upon health of the body as a whole and especially of the nervous system. It must be noted that in the West gluttony is listed as the worst of the seven deadly sins. Self-control would be easy for him who eats righteously, not for him who is wanting in fairness to the stomach. A contented and cheerful mind should be maintained all the time, and this will be possible only by respecting the divinely ordained laws of health, of which right way of eating is by no means the least important.

The truth of the Natural State to be won by the pursuit of suitable Sadhana is then indicated, not directly, but indirectly, as follows: The next verse, which is introductory, explains that no direct description of the State is possible.

27. निजस्वरूपानुभवैकवेद्यं तन्नेति नेतीत्युदितं पदं हि ।
वाचाऽप्यनुक्तं मनसाऽमतं च मौनोपदिष्टं गुरुणाऽऽदिमेन ॥

nijasvarūpānubhavaikavedyaṁ tanneti netītyuditaṁ padaṁ hi |
vācā'pyanuktaṁ manasā'mataṁ ca maunopadiṣṭaṁ guruṇā"dimena ||

That State is knowable only by actual experience of the Truth of the Real Self. It is indicated (in the sacred lore) only by negations. 'Not so, not so'. It is not described by speech nor thought of by the mind. (Even) The Primal Guru (Dakshinamurty) taught It only by Silence.

The Primal Guru was God Himself as Dakshinamurty, who taught the four sages, Sanaka and the rest, by Silence alone. The Real Self, Bhagavan Sri Ramana has repeatedly said, is the eternal subject, who cannot be objectified, being the Self of him that seeks to objectify Him.

This Supreme State is therefore indirectly taught by contrasting It with the three states of life, that are experienced in the life of the world, while subject to ignorance.

28.   अतीत्य यज्जागरमुख्यभावांस्तन्निष्प्रपञ्चं भवति प्रशान्तम् ।
      अतस्तुरीयं पदमव्ययं तदित्येष माण्डूक्यनिरूपितार्थः ॥

atītya yajjāgaramukhyabhāvāṁstanniṣprapañcaṁ bhavati praśāntam |
atasturīyaṁ padamavyayaṁ tadityeṣa māṇḍūkyanirūpitārthaḥ ||

Since that State is changeless, worldless and calm, beyond the states of waking and the rest, it is called the Fourth State. Such is the teaching of the Mandukya Upanishad.

This is the shortest of all the chief Upanishads; but in it is given the essence of all of them. Life in the world is a continous cycle, consisting of three distinct states, viz., waking, dream and deep sleep.

These three states are a vicious circle, because all three are sustained by an underlying common cause, the nature of which is next explained.

29.   तिस्रो ह्यवस्थाः प्रभवन्ति जाग्रत् स्वप्नः सुषुप्तिश्च समस्तजन्तोः ।
      आधारभूता त्रितयस्य चास्य स्वाज्ञानरूपास्ति सुषुप्तिरन्या ॥

tisro hyavasthāḥ prabhavanti jāgrat svapnaḥ suṣuptiśca samastajantoḥ |
ādhārabhūtā tritayasya cāsya svājñānarūpā'sti suṣuptiranyā ||

For every creature there are three states, waking, dream and deep sleep; and sustaining these three there is another sleep, the sleep of ignorance.

This ignorance of the Self is the common factor in all the three, without which the vicious circle of the three states would come to an end. This means that for one that has transcended Ignorance, the three states do not exist. This basic sleep explains another fact, which will be stated later.

30. अस्मिन्नवस्थात्रितये समस्तमन्तर्भवत्येव हि विश्वमेतत् ।
अस्मादवस्थात्रितयात् परस्तादलौकिकं ह्यस्ति तुरीयसत्यम् ॥

asminnavasthātritaye samastamantarbhavatyeva hi viśvametat |
asmādavasthātritayāt parastādalaukikaṁ hyasti turīyasatyam ||

The whole of this world is contained within this trinity of states. The Reality of the Fourth State, which is worldless, transcends these three states.

Hence it is, there is no peace in the realm of ignorance. Peace prevails only in the transcendental state, which is the True State of the Self.

Among the three states, there is a distinction which is next stated.

31. अस्वप्ननिद्रेति सुषुप्तिरुक्ता सस्वप्ननिद्रेत्युभयं तदन्यत् ।
अनिद्रमस्वप्नकमस्तविश्वं पदं तुरीयं हि विमुक्तिधाम ॥

asvapnanidreti suṣuptiruktā sasvapnanidretyubhayaṁ tadanyat |
anidramasvapnakamastaviśvaṁ padaṁ turīyaṁ hi vimuktidhāma ||

Deep sleep is just dreamless sleep; the other two are sleep with dream. The Fourth State, being without sleep and without dream, is the Abode of Deliverance.

Thus it is stated that socalled waking is really a state of dream, because of the underlying sleep of ignorance. This will be elaborated later, when the question of the reality of the world is discussed.

The Fourth State is in perfect contrast with the other three, being sleepless, dreamless and therefore worldless. Therefore It is the Abode of Freedom. Freedom connot be had in any of the three states. This is one of the fundamentals of the transcendental metaphysics as taught by the sages.

32.   सन्धौ सुषुप्तेरथ जागरस्य चिद्रूपिणी निर्मनना स्थितिर्या ।
सा सुस्थिरा चेद् भविता कथञ्चित् सैवोच्यते मुक्तिरिति प्रबुद्धैः ॥

sandhau suṣupteratha jāgarasya cidrūpiṇī nirmananā sthitiryā |
sā susthirā ced bhavitā kathañcit saivocyate muktiriti prabuddhaiḥ ||

If that mind-free consciousness, which is at the meeting point of deep sleep and waking, somehow becomes continuous, then the State that then dawns is declared by the sages to be the State of Deliverance.

Consciousness without thoughts called Pure Consciousness, transcends time and hence it persists as the substratum even when the three states prevail. At the minute point of time when one of these two states gives place to the other, the consciousness is without thought. If this transitional state be sufficiently prolonged, then deliverance dawns, say the sages. In the Yoga Vasishta there is the following verse.

निद्रादौ जागरस्यान्ते यो भाव उपजायते ।
तं भावं भावयन् साक्षादक्षयानन्दमश्नुते ॥

nidrādau jāgarasyānte yo bhāva upajāyate |
taṁ bhāvaṁ bhāvayan sākṣādakṣayānandamaśnute ||

"If one meditates keenly on the state that prevails at the end of waking and just before sleep, he attains unending happiness".

The world-appearance, therefore, is just a dream — often assuming the quality of a nightmare — arising in the sleep, namely the Ignorance of the Real Self. This is next stated.

33. अज्ञाननिद्रापरिभूतभावाः पश्यन्ति दुस्स्वप्नमिमं प्रपञ्चम् ।
परिभ्रमन्ति त्रितयेऽत्र जीवा यावन्न निद्रेयमपैति बोधात् ॥

ajñānanidrāparibhūtabhāvāḥ paśyanti dussvapnamimaṁ prapañcam |
paribhramanti tritaye'tra jīvā yāvanna nidreyamapaiti bodhāt ||

Those that are overwhelmed by this Sleep of Ignorance are the seers of this bad dream, the world. And so long as this ignorance ceases not by the Right Awareness of the Real Self, the souls have to wander in this maze of the three states.

The only way to escape from this bad dream is to become fully aware of the Real Self, the dweller in the Supreme State, as He may be called for the present.

Thus it happens that all creatures — both men and the so-called inferior creatures — are really asleep all the time,

alternately dreaming and sleeping dreamlessly all the time.
Deep, dreamless sleep is just like an oasis in a desert route.

34. निद्रालुरेवं सकलोऽपि जन्तुर्न कोऽपि जागर्ति हि जीवलोके ।
     तीर्णास्तिसृभ्योऽज्ञतया विमुक्तो बुद्धस्तु जागर्ति तुरीयनिष्ठः ॥

nidrālurevaṁ sakalo'pi janturna ko'pi jāgarti hi jīvaloke |
tīrṇastisṛbhyo'jñatayā vimukto buddhastu jāgarti turīyaniṣṭhaḥ ||

Thus every creature is asleep; none in this world
of souls is awake. Only the Sage, who, being firmly
established in the Fourth State, has transcended the
three states and is free from Ignorance, is awake.

Being awake here means being aware of the Real Self
as He really is. Because of this awakening He is no more
troubled by the dream called the world.
This uniqueness of the Sage is explained in the next
two verses.

35. जागर्ति बुद्धो निजसत्यभावे समेत्य निष्ठां तमसा विहीने ।
     निद्राति च स्वप्नमये प्रपञ्चे स्वाज्ञानमूढैः परिदृश्यमाने ॥

jāgarti buddho nijasatyabhāve sametya niṣṭhāṁ tamasā vihīne |
nidrāti ca svapnamaye prapañce svājñānamūḍhaiḥ paridṛśyamāne ||

The Sage is wide-awake, having become
established in the True State of the Self which is
free from the darkness of ignorance; in respect of
the dream-world that is being seen by those
drowsy with the ignorance of the Self, he is asleep.

36. तन्नक्तमुक्तं विदुषो हि विश्वं नक्तं तथाऽऽत्माऽविदुषो जनस्य ।
    निष्ठामतस्तां सहजां तुरीयां जाग्रत्सुषुप्तिं निगदन्ति बुद्धाः ॥

tannaktamuktaṁ viduṣo hi viśvaṁ naktaṁ tathā"tmā'viduṣo janasya |
niṣṭhāmatastāṁ sahajāṁ turīyāṁ jāgratsuṣuptiṁ nigadanti buddhāḥ ||

Hence it is said that this world is as night to the Sage, whereas to the ignorant the Real Self is as night. For this reason that natural State, the Fourth State is described by the sages as a state of waking sleep.

This distinction between the Sage and the ignorant finds a place in the following verse of the Gita:

या निशा सर्वभूतानां तस्यां जागर्ति संयमी ।
यस्यां जाग्रति भूतानि सा निशा पश्यतो मुनेः ॥

yā niśā sarvabhūtānāṁ tasyāṁ jāgarti saṁyamī |
yasyāṁ jāgrati bhūtāni sā niśā paśyato muneḥ ||

"The Sage is awake in what is night to all the creatures. That in which the creatures are awake is night to the sage, though he is awake in fact".

This implies that from the standpoint of the Sage, the world is unreal. This verse suggests a question, how the sage, whose body is still alive, can carry on his mission as a teacher of the Supreme Wisdom. The solution to this riddle lies in the fact that the natural state of a sage does not interfere with the sage's work as a teacher; that activity goes on in a mysterious way, which is explained to the extent possible in a later context.

From all this it might appear that sagehood is something anomalous. What is anomalous is the worldly outlook, which is blind to the Real and attentive to the unreal dream, the world-appearance. The worldly ones are just like intoxicated or mad people. It is the Sage who is both sober and sane.

Upto now the Supreme State of the Sage has been called the Fourth State. But this name is only a concession to novices, as is shown presently.

37. सज्जाग्रदादित्रयमस्ति येषां तेषां तुरीयाभिधया तदुक्तम् ।
सत् तुर्यमेवासदिदं त्रयं यत् तुर्याभिधा तस्य भवत्यसाधु ॥

sajjāgradāditrayamasti yeṣāṁ teṣāṁ turīyābhidhayā taduktam ǀ
sat turyamevāsadidaṁ trayaṁ yat turyābhidhā tasya bhavatyasādhu ǁ

For those to whom the three Sates, waking and the rest, are real, that (Supreme) State is mentioned as the Fourth State. But since that so-called Fourth State alone is real, and these three are unreal, the term 'Fourth State' is not rightly applicable to it.

The Supreme State is therefore just the Transcendental State. As compared to It, the three worldly states cannot be considered as real. Their seeming reality is no more authentic than the reality that is ascribed to a dream while it lasts. This point will be further elaborated later.

The cause of the difference between the three States and the Supreme State is next explained.

38. स्वप्नेऽपि जाग्रत्यपि चेष्टमानं मनः प्रपञ्चं सृजति स्वयं हि ।
गत्वा सुषुप्तौ बत बीजभावं भूयः प्रबोधे सृजति प्रपञ्चम् ॥

svapne'pi jāgratyapi ceṣṭamānaṁ manaḥ prapañcam sṛjati svayaṁ hi |
gatvā suṣuptau bata bījabhāvaṁ bhūyaḥ prabodhe sṛjati prapañcam ||

In dream and waking the mind being active,
itself creates the world. In deep sleep it goes into
seed form and on awaking again creates the world.

In deep sleep the mind is not completely lost, but only
goes into a latent state, out of which it can emerge and
become active again as before. This is the reason for the
continuance of bondage. Thus these three states form a
vicious circle, which can be broken only by finally
extinguishing the mind, so that it cannot revive on waking.

To this end the mind-free state must be attained in the
waking state itself, the other two states being useless for this
purpose.

39. मनोऽन्ततो नश्यति नैव यावद् भवेदवस्थात्रितयं हि तावत् ।
मनोविनाशाद्धि तुरीयनिष्ठा यत्रान्ततः शाम्यति विश्वमेतत् ॥

mano'ntato naśyati naiva yāvad bhavedavasthātritayaṁ hi tāvat |
manovināśāddhi turīyaniṣṭhā yatrāntataḥ śāmyati viśvametat ||39||

Unless and until the mind becomes utterly
extinct, these three states will continue to prevail.
When the mind becomes extinguished the
Supreme State is won, wherein this world once
for all ceases to appear.

During the prevalence of the Ignorance, the three states conceal the Supreme State; the latter cannot be experienced, because of these. To be able to experience that state the mind must be destroyed, so that the world creation will also cease. To this end, the Quest must be taken up and pursued till mind-free state is established.

This is often styled the State of Knowledge. But this description is misleading for the reason stated presently.

40. ज्ञानाभिधा यद्यपि साऽऽत्मनिष्ठा ज्ञात्रादिकेन त्रितयेन हीना ।
तत्किं विजानात्युत केन को वा ज्ञानाभिधा स्वात्मतयैव निष्ठा ॥

jñānābhidhā yadyapi sā"tmaniṣṭhā jñātrādikena tritayena hīnā |
tatkiṁ vijānātyuta kena ko vā jñānābhidhā svātmatayaiva niṣṭhā ||

Though that state of being the Real Self is called the State of Knowledge, it is one in which there is none of the three, the knower, the object, and the act of knowing. That being the case, what does one know there, by what means, and who is here to know? It must be understood that knowledge is just a name for the State of Being the Self.

That State is different from anything else, because it is a state of Non-duality (Advaita). There is no object to be known; not is there a knower, the soul, and hence there is no knowing. So 'Knowledge' or 'Awareness' is just an arbitrary name for this state. This will be explained later.

41. आत्मैव यस्मिन्नभवत् समस्तं जानाति तस्मिन् बत केन किं नु ।
इत्यात्मनः केवलतैव तुर्ये संदर्शिताऽस्ति श्रुतिशीर्षवाचा ॥

ātmaiva yasminnabhavat samastaṁ jānāti tasmin bata kena kiṁ nu |
ityātmanaḥ kevalataiva turye sandarśitā'sti śrutiśīrṣavācā ||

The Upanishadic text which says: 'Where the Self is all there is, then how and what does one know there.' makes it clear that in the Supreme State the Real Self is alone, (as the One without a second).

A possible misconception is next pointed and the true State clearly explained.

42. स्थानं च तद्वानिति नास्ति तस्मिन् भेदः पदे कश्चन वास्तवो यत् ।
आत्माऽद्वितीयः परिपूर्ण एकः स्थानं स्वयं स्वस्य हि सन् स एकः ॥

sthānaṁ ca tadvāniti nāsti tasmin bhedaḥ pade kaścana vāstavo yat |
ātmā'dvitīyaḥ paripūrṇa ekaḥ sthānaṁ svayaṁ svasya hi san sa ekaḥ ||

Since in that State there is not, in reality, even the difference of place and occupant thereof, the Self being the One without a second, the All-inclusive Reality, therefore He, the Supreme Being, is His own Place.

This is an echo of the Upanishadic passage,

स्वे महिम्नि प्रतिष्ठितः । अथवा न महिम्नि ॥

sve mahimni pratiṣṭhitaḥ | athavā na mahimni ||

"He abides in His own greatness, or rather not even in that greatness", given to Narada by Guru Sanatkumara. This means that the Real Self is not in space.

Who then is the Advaiti?

43.   द्वैतं समस्तं खलु नीतमन्तं बुद्धेन तुर्ये स्थितिमेत्य सत्ये ।
        अद्वैतनिष्ठाऽधिगताऽस्ति तेनेत्यद्वैतिनं तेन तमेव विद्यात् ॥

dvaitaṁ samastaṁ khalu nītamantaṁ buddhena turye sthitimetya satye |
advaitaniṣṭhā'dhigatā'sti tenetyadvaitinaṁ tena tameva vidyāt ||

Since the Sage has put an end to all duality by attaining the Supreme, Real State, he has attained the Advaitic State. Hence He alone should be regarded as an Advaiti.

This is important, as Bhagavan has warned us against thinking of Advaita as a doctrine just like the doctrines of the sectarians. It being the Mind-free State, there is no room in it for doctrines. This is further explained as follows.

44.   अनात्मनि स्वात्मतया प्रतीत्या प्रतीयते द्वैतमिदं हि सद्वत् ।
        एवंविधाज्ञानविमुक्तभावमद्वैतनिष्ठां निगदन्ति बुद्धाः ॥

anātmani svātmatayā pratītyā pratīyate dvaitamidaṁ hi sadvat |
evaṁvidhājñānavimuktabhāvamadvaitaniṣṭhāṁ nigadanti buddhāḥ ||

Duality comes to be taken as real because of taking something not the Self to be the Self. The sages tell us that the state of being free from this Ignorance is itself the Advaitic state.

This means that so long as this ignorance endures, the Advaitic State is not attained.

45. अद्वैतमेवं न मतं यथाऽन्यन्नास्ति प्रचारो मनसो हि तत्र ।
अद्वैतमुक्तं निजसत्यभावे निष्ठैव चिन्तारहिताऽस्तलोका ॥

advaitamevaṁ na mataṁ yathā'nyannāsti pracāro manaso hi tatra |
advaitamuktaṁ nijasatyabhāve niṣṭhaiva cintārahitā'stalokā ||

Thus Advaita is not a dogma like those of other religions; also because the mind does not function in It. True Advaita is declared to be just the state of Being in one's own real nature (as the Real Self), free from thoughts and free from the world.

It must be remembered that the world can never be without the mind.

For this reason a merely theoretical — intellectual — belief in advaita is of no value whatever.

46. शास्त्रोदितार्थाधिगमेन यस्तु बुद्ध्वाऽद्वयत्वं मतवद्धियैव ।
तुष्यत्यनेनैव विनाऽनुभूतिं नाद्वैतनिष्ठाऽधिगताऽस्ति तेन ॥

śāstroditārthādhigamena yastu buddhvā'dvayatvaṁ matavaddhiyaiva |
tuṣyatyanenaiva vinā'nubhūtiṁ nādvaitaniṣṭhā'dhigatā'sti tena ||

On the other hand the Advaitic state has NOT been attained by one who, knowing the substance of the sacred lore as a doctrine by his intellect alone, is satisfied with it without striving to win actual experience of the real Self.

This is explained in detail as follows:-

47. न तेन दृश्यं प्रविलापितं हि स्वचित्स्वरूपे परमार्थसत्ये ।
शास्त्रार्थबोधात् समवैति यः स्वं न तस्य देहात्ममतिर्विनष्टा ॥

na tena dṛśyaṁ pravilāpitaṁ hi svacitsvarūpe paramārthasatye |
śāstrārthabodhāt samavaiti yaḥ svaṁ na tasya dehātmamatirvinaṣṭā ||

Such a one has not dissolved the world-appearance by remaining in the true state of the Self as the Supreme Reality. He that knows the Self by understanding the substance of the books has not got rid of his false notion that the body is the Self!

Identification of the body as the Self is the primary Ignorance, and theoretical knowledge has not the least effect on that ignorance. It survives. It ceases only by the attainment of the true state of the Self.

48. पश्वादिकेभ्योऽप्यविशेष एव तस्योच्यते शंकरदेशिकेन ।
पशुत्वमेतद् गदितं हि बुद्धैर्वपुर्मितं यत् स्वमवैति जन्तुः ॥

paśvādikebhyo'pyaviśeṣa eva tasyocyate śaṅkaradeśikena |
paśutvametad gaditaṁ hi buddhairvapurmitaṁ yat svamavaiti jantuḥ ||

It has been stated by Guru Sankara that such a one is really not different from the brutes. Brute-hood is defined by sages as that by which one regards the Self as limited to the body.

49. न व्येत्यतः शास्त्रविदो नरस्य जगत् स्वतः सत्यमिति प्रतीतिः ।
तया प्रतीत्या सततं विमूढः परिभ्रमत्येव भवे यथाऽन्ये ॥

na vyetyataḥ śāstravido narasya jagat svataḥ satyamiti pratītiḥ |
tayā pratītyā satataṁ vimūḍhaḥ paribhramatyeva bhave yathā'nye ||

Hence for him that just knows the sacred lore, the belief that the world is real as such (in its own sight), does not cease. Deluded by this false belief he ever wanders helplessly in samsara like all the rest.

50. वाग्यन्त्रतुल्योऽयमुदीर्यते च बुद्ध्वाऽपि शास्त्रार्थमशान्तचेताः ।
अपण्डितादप्यवरोऽयमुक्तो मदादिदोषैः परिभूतभावः ॥

vāgyantratulyo'yamudīryate ca buddhvā'pi śāstrārthamaśāntacetāḥ |
apaṇḍitādapyavaro'yamukto madādidoṣaiḥ paribhūtabhāvaḥ ||

It is said (by Sri Bhagavan) that the knower of the sacred lore whose mind has not subsided in Peace (of the Supreme State) is just like a gramophone. It is also said (by Sri Bhagavan) that he is even worse off than the man without learning, because unlike the latter, he is overwhelmed by moods of pride and so on.

In the Supplement to the Forty Verses on Reality Bhagavan has said thus:

"A sincere and wide awake aspirant may even bewail the barrenness of the result of his theoretical knowledge saying: 'Oh! The illiterate ones are better off than I am!' Such lamentations abound in the writings of the great saint Tayumanar".

Indeed, as shown below, this theoretical conviction is only belief, not knowledge.

51. बोधं परोक्षं तमिमं वदन्ति परोक्ष आत्मा तु न कर्हिंचित् स्यात्।
नित्यापरोक्षस्य परोक्षबोधो बोधो यथार्थो भविता कथं नु ॥

bodhaṁ parokṣaṁ tamimaṁ vadanti parokṣa ātmā tu na karhicit syāt |
nityāparokṣasya parokṣabodho bodho yathārtho bhavitā kathaṁ nu ||

This theoretical knowledge is styled inferential knowledge (as of a thing absent). But the Self is never absent. How can inferential knowledge of one that is ever present be true Knowledge?

Logicians distinguish knowledge as either direct or inferential, the former pertaining to objects perceived by the senses, and latter to objects not so pereceived but only inferred. But for the reason stated in this verse, there can be only Direct Experiential Knowledge of the Self, and hence the Self is never the subject-matter of inference. Descartes' famous proposition — 'I think, therefore I am' — is unphilosophical for this reason. The Self shines by his own light of consciousness, and not by any other light.

Also knowledge by sense-perception is not really direct, that is, immediate but only through a medium, a sense-organ. The Self, being Consciousness, needs no medium.

52. देहोऽहमस्मीत्यनुभूतिरूपो भवत्यबोधः खलु बन्धहेतुः।
बोधोऽहमस्मीति विनाऽनुभूतिं कथं व्रजेन्नाशमबोध एषः

deho'hamasmītyanubhūtirūpo bhavatyabodhaḥ khalu bandhahetuḥ |
bodho'hamasmīti vinā'nubhūtiṁ kathaṁ vrajennāśamabodha eṣaḥ ||

The Ignorance causing bondage is just the experience (though mistaken) of the form 'I am the body'. How can such ignorance come to an end, except by the Awareness, 'I am the Pure Consciousness'?

Illusory experience can cease only by illusion-free experience. That is the reason why learned men still remain in ignorance and bondage.

53. धिया धृतोऽयं हि परोक्षबोधो न धीप्रचारोऽस्ति तु सत्स्वरूपे।
दैत्यं यथा पुण्यजनं वदन्ति वदन्त्यबोधं बत बोधनाम्ना ॥

dhiyā dhṛto'yaṁ hi parokṣabodho na dhīpracāro'sti tu satsvarūpe |
daityaṁ yathā puṇyajanaṁ vadanti vadantyabodhaṁ bata bodhanāmnā ||

This theoretical knowledge is only intellectual. But the intellect has no access to the Real Self. Just as evil spirits are (ironically) styled as 'good people', so this Ignorance is styled 'Knowledge'.

In Sanskrit literature the term 'good people' is used ironically to designate evil spirits, the *asuras* or *rakshasas*.

54. यदाऽर्कतप्तो मृगतृष्णिकायां स्नात्वा नरस्तापविमुक्तिमेति।
अन्नं पचेच्चित्रगताग्निना वा परोक्षबोधेन तदाऽस्तु मुक्तिः ॥

yadā'rkatapto mṛgatṛṣṇikāyāṁ snātvā narastāpavimuktimeti ।
annaṁ paceccitragatāgninā vā parokṣabodhena tadā'stu muktiḥ ॥

When a man scorched by the sun becomes cooled by bathing in a mirage, or when one succeeds in cooking food on a painting of fire, then one may attain deliverance by theoretical knowledge.

Thus emphatically the notion that theoretical knowledge is Knowledge, is denounced.

55. तत्स्वानुभूत्या रहितोऽद्वयत्वं वाचा वदन् द्वैतिसमान एव ।
न गच्छतो वाङ्मनसे हि तुर्यं तत्र स्थितस्यास्ति मतं न किञ्चित् ॥

tatsvānubhūtyā rahito'dvayatvaṁ vācā vadan dvaitisamāna eva ।
na gacchato vāṅmanase hi turyaṁ tatra sthitasyāsti mataṁ na kiñcit ॥

Therefore one that talks Advaita without actual experience of that Truth is just the same as a Dvaiti. Neither speech nor mind has any access of the Supreme State. He that abides in that State has no doctrine whatever.

Doctrines, more or less true, are helps to the aspirant. They do not survive in the state of Deliverance (Illumination). The Sage does not 'know' the Self, because He IS the Self. This equation of him that has only theoretical knowledge with the Dvaiti is justified as follows:

56. अद्वैतिनः स्वान् गणयन्त आहुर्जगन्मृषा दुःखमयं जडं च ।
अतोऽन्यथैवेत्यपरे वदन्ति फले तु सर्वेऽपि समा भवन्ति ॥

advaitinaḥ svān gaṇayanta āhurjaganmṛṣā duḥkhamayaṁ jaḍaṁ ca |
ato'nyathaivetyapare vadanti phale tu sarve'pi samā bhavanti ||

Those that think of themselves as Advaitis say (from intellectual conviction alone) that the world is unreal, miserable and inert (unconscious). Others (professing Dvaitism) say otherwise. But in the result all are alike.

That is all are in bondage and suffer the evils of samsara. They all act as if the world were real.

57. विश्वं परो जीव इति त्रिरूपं विभाति सत्यं परमेकमेव ।
    ज्ञानं भवेन्नैव तु वाद एष ज्ञानं त्वहङ्कारविनाश एव ॥

viśvaṁ paro jīva iti trirūpaṁ vibhāti satyaṁ paramekameva |
jñānaṁ bhavennaiva tu vāda eṣa jñānaṁ tvahaṅkāravināśa eva ||

It is only the One Supreme Reality that appears as the three, namely the world, God and the Soul. But asserting this (as a doctrine) is not Right Awareness. Right Awareness is just the death of the ego.

We have seen before that Right Awareness — which is Experience, in the Supreme State of the Real Self as Pure Consciousness — is mind-free. Now we learn that it is also egoless. The natural state is therefore also called the egoless state.

The next three verses deal with the problem of controversies, which abound so long as the ignorance is not transcended.

58. निजस्वरूपानुभवे विनेच्छां मताग्रहेण प्रवदन्ति वादान् ।
अस्तीति नास्तीत्यपि रूप्यरूपीत्येकं द्विधा नोभयथेत्यनन्तान् ॥

nijasvarūpānubhave vinecchāṁ matāgraheṇa pravadanti vādān |
astīti nāstītyapi rūpyarūpītyekaṁ dvidhā nobhayathetyanantān ||

Indifferent to the actual experience of the Real Self, the sectarians affirm their dogmas with fanatical vehemence, saying 'There is a Reality', 'There is none', 'It has a form', 'It is formless', 'It is One', 'It is twofold', 'It is neither'.

This is the substance of verse 34 of the *Ulladu Narpadu* (Book of Forty Verses on Reality). All the main creeds are here briefly enumerated; among these even the advaitic doctrine is mentioned, to show that mere adherence to a doctrine, even though it is true, is useless. The last creed, 'It is neither', seems to be an intermediate creed between the advaitic and dvaitic, which is to the effect that the soul is different from God and yet part of God. These creeds are possible because of the continuing ignorance, with indifference to the Quest of the Real Self.

The disputants resort to logic in order to establish their own creeds as the true ones. But logic is inconclusive; this is stated in the following verse.

59. भवत्यनन्ताः खलु तर्कवादाः क्वचित्प्रतिष्ठां न हि याति तर्कः ।
अलौकिकोऽसौ खलु तुर्यनिष्ठा ज्ञेया कथं तर्काधिया भवेत् सा ॥

bhavatyanantāḥ khalu tarkavādāḥ kvacitpratiṣṭhāṁ na hi yāti tarkaḥ |
alaukiko'sau khalu turyaniṣṭhā jñeyā kathaṁ tarkadhiyā bhavet sā ||

There is no end to logical discussions, for logic does not come to rest anywhere. The

Supreme transcends the world. How can it become known by the logical mind?

The truth of the Supreme State is not within the scope of intellectual speculation. The sole authority on its nature and means of attainment is the actual experience of It by a sage. Logic can proceed only on the facts given by worldly experience, which is tainted because its parent is the primary ignorance. Until one attains that state by the same experience, one has to rely on the authority of a competent guru.

The attitude of the sage to the diverse creeds is next stated.

60.　मतं न किञ्चिद्विदुषोऽस्ति यस्मात् सज्जेत वादेषु कदाऽपि नासौ ।
सर्वं मतं सम्मतमेव तस्य मतिं न कस्याप्युत चालयेत् सः ॥

mataṁ na kiñcidviduṣo'sti yasmāt sajjeta vādeṣu kadā'pi nāsau ǀ
sarvaṁ mataṁ sammatameva tasya matiṁ na kasyāpyuta cālayet saḥ ǁ

Since the sage has no creed of his own, he never engages in (useless) discussions. All creeds are approved of by him. He does not (seek to) unsettle the faith of anyone.

All creeds are like paths leading to the same goal. So the sage does not seek to impose any faith on anybody, but helps everyone to follow the path which he chooses for himself.

It is the sadhana that is of value, not the beliefs; this is next explained.

61. द्वेषं विनाऽन्येषु मतेषु तस्माद्विहाय वादानपि शान्तचेताः ।
     यतेत साधुः स्वमतोक्तरीत्या मोक्षेच्छया साधनतत्परः सन् ॥

dveṣaṁ vinā'nyeṣu mateṣu tasmādvihāya vādānapi śāntacetāḥ |
yateta sādhuḥ svamatoktarītyā mokṣecchayā sādhanatatparaḥ san ||

Therefore, the aspirant should, with a mind at peace, cease from hatred of other faiths and from all disputation and engage in sadhana as taught by his own faith, intent on winning Deliverance.

The narrow mind, which causes one to assume that his own religion is alone true and all others are false, is a defect of character which must be given up, if one is to reach the egoless state, for all religions alike are inferior to that state. The beliefs inculcated are of no value except as inspiring zeal for the practice of the prescribed sadhana.

That earnest aspirant, says Bhagavan Sri Ramana Maharshi, does not need to come to any definite conclusion on the most vexed question, which concerns the reality or the illusory nature of the world, because the main thing is to know the truth of oneself, and the first step towards that knowledge is just to cease thinking of the world altogether as an obstacle to his quest. This is set forth in the next verse.

62. द्वैताद्वयत्वे भवतो मते द्वे सत्यं च मिथ्या वदतां प्रपञ्चम् ।
     वादावुभौ चापि विहाय शक्यो लब्धुं स्वरूपानुभवो मुमुक्षोः ॥

dvaitādvayatve bhavato mate dve satyaṁ ca mithyā vadatāṁ prapañcam |
vādāvubhau cāpi vihāya śakyo labdhuṁ svarūpānubhavo mumukṣoḥ ||

There are the two creeds held respectively by those who say the world is real and those who say it is unreal. The earnest aspirant for Deliverance can win experience of the Truth of the Self without taking up a definite stand on this question.

That this seemingly important question can be bye-passed by one who is intent on becoming free is next explained.

63.　अदुःखमिश्रं सुखमन्तहीनं वाञ्छन्ति सर्वे खलु जन्तवोऽपि ।
　　सुखं स्वभावो हि समस्तजन्तोस्तादृक्सुखं क्वेति हि
　　चिन्तनीयम् ॥

aduḥkhamiśraṁ sukhamantahīnaṁ vāñchanti sarve khalu jantavo'pi |
sukhaṁ svabhāvo hi samastajantostādṛksukhaṁ kveti hi cintanīyam ||

All creatures alike want perfect happiness, which is unmixed with suffering and will last forever. (This is not wrong, because) Happiness is the real nature of all creatures. So one should inquire where such happiness can be had.

That happiness is the very nature of the Self is the great discovery made by all the sages. In the Bhrigu Valli of the Taittiriya Upanishad it is said that as a result of this Quest of the Truth he realised this Truth, that the Supreme Reality, the Self, is Bliss. He also knew at the same time that Bliss is the source of all living creatures, their support during life and the goal they have to come back to in the end. Bhagavan Sri Ramana Maharshi also used to say in answer to the question how to become free: *"Go back to the Source, out of which you came forth"*.

Where then is that perfect Happiness?

64. कस्मिन् पदे तत् सुखमस्त्यनन्तं लभ्यं च तत् केन च साधनेन ।
     द्वयं तदेतद् भगवान् मुमुक्षोरत्यन्तवैराग्यवतो ब्रवीति ॥

kasmin pade tat sukhamastyanantaṁ labhyaṁ ca tat kena ca sādhanena |
dvayaṁ tadetad bhagavān mumukṣoratyantavairāgyavato bravīti ||

To the seeker of Deliverance who has perfect
non-attachment, Bhagavan Sri Ramana Maharshi
tells in what state that Happiness dwells and by
what means it can be won.

65. प्रिया सुषुप्तिर्हि समस्तजन्तोः प्रियत्वहेतुः सुखरूपताऽस्याः ।
     सुखाय तस्यां विषया न सन्ति किं मूलकं स्यान्नु सुखं सुषुप्तेः ॥

priyā suṣuptirhi samastajantoḥ priyatvahetuḥ sukharūpatā'syāḥ |
sukhāya tasyāṁ viṣayā na santi kiṁ mūlakaṁ syānnu sukhaṁ suṣupteḥ ||

The State of deep sleep is dear to all
creatures, and it is dear because it is happy. But
in that state there are no objects of enjoyment!
What can be the source of this sleep-happiness?

It is supposed by all people that happiness consists of
series of pleasures which come by the contact of external
objects through the senses. But deep, dreamless sleep is a
state of happiness, though there are no objects of enjoyment
therein. Everyone describes his sleep-experience thus: *"I slept
happily, but I knew nothing then'*. So this poses a question, rarely
asked, *'What is the cause or source of this happiness?'* That this
question needs to be posed and an answer obtained we learn
for the first time from the Guru Sage. Only He can give us
the answer, which is set forth in the next three verses.

66. सुषुप्तितुर्ये भवतः समाने द्वयोर्मनो नास्ति हि नापि विश्वं ।
आत्मा द्वयोरस्ति तु नित्यसत्यः स एव मूलं ह्युभयोः सुखस्य ॥

suṣuptiturye bhavataḥ samāne dvayormano nāsti hi nāpi viśvaṁ |
ātmā dvayorasti tu nityasatyaḥ sa eva mūlaṁ hyubhayoḥ sukhasya ||

Deep sleep and the Supreme State are similar; in both the mind and the world are absent. But in both, there is the eternal Reality, the Real Self, and therefore it follows that He is the cause of the Happiness of both the states.

Human intelligence cannot give this answer, but when this fact is revealed by the Guru, it is at once seen to be true. That the Self does not cease to exist, but is present in deep sleep as in the other states, is undeniable, because, as Bhagavan Sri Ramana has pointed out, excepting the highly sophisticated but purblind scientists, no one is able to say that he did not exist in sleep; this will be dealt with in detail later. So we learn that the Real Self of the Supreme State is the source of sleep-happiness.

It is next revealed that this happiness of the Self is infinite, whereas the happiness of sleep is nothing as compared to It.

67. अनित्यमल्पं च सुखं सुषुप्तौ मनोऽस्ति तस्यां खलु बीजभावे ।
तुर्ये प्रपूर्णं सुखमस्त्यनन्तमानन्दसंज्ञं श्रुतिषु प्रसिद्धम् ॥

anityamalpaṁ ca sukhaṁ suṣuptau mano'sti tasyāṁ khalu bījabhāve |
turye prapūrṇaṁ sukhamastyanantamānandasañjñaṁ śrutiṣu prasiddham ||

The happiness of sleep is fitful and meagre, because the mind survives there in seed-form. In the Supreme State there is infinite bliss, known as 'Ananda' in the Vedantic lore.

The happiness of the Mind-free state is perfect. That of sleep is not to be compared to It. To distinguish It from the pleasures of worldly life, it is named Ananda in the Upanishads.

It is next shown that even worldly enjoyment, though seemingly coming by the contact of objects, really has its source in this Happiness-Nature of the Self.

68.　तस्यैव मात्रां खलु जीवलोके लब्ध्वा रमन्तेऽखिलजन्तवोऽपि ।
　　न स्याद्यदीदं तु सुखस्य मूलं लोके क्षणार्धं बत को नु जीवेत् ॥

tasyaiva mātrāṁ khalu jīvaloke labdhvā ramante'khilajantavo'pi |
na syādyadīdaṁ tu sukhasya mūlaṁ loke kṣaṇārdhaṁ bata ko nu jīvet ||

Only by receiving a minute fraction of that Supreme Happiness do all the creatures enjoy life in this abode of the souls. If this source of Happiness were not present, who will care to live in this world for even half a moment?

This is what is revealed in the *Ananda Valli* of the *Taittriya Upanishad*, and all the sages have confirmed this fact.

What when is the conclusion? Bhagavan-Guru Ramana gives the answer.

69.　प्रेष्ठः समस्तस्य ततस्तुरीये विराजमानः सुखरूपकः स्वः ।
　　प्रेष्ठा च तस्मादखिलस्य जन्तोर्निष्ठा तुरीयैव न काचिदन्या ॥

preṣṭhaḥ samastasya tatasturīye virājamānaḥ sukharūpakaḥ svaḥ ǀ
preṣṭhā ca tasmādakhilasya jantorniṣṭhā turīyaiva na kācidanyā ǀǀ

Hence it follows that to all alike is the dearest of all things, the Real Self that shines in the Supreme State as Pure Bliss. Therefore to all creatures alike, the most beloved of all is the Supreme State, and nothing else.

Since it is the happiness of deep sleep that all people love, not the state itself, and since that happiness has it source in the Real Self of the egoless state, it would be right to conclude that what they really love is that Self, and the state in which His true nature is included, though only unknowingly. This is exactly what the Sage Yajnavalkya told his wise wife, Maireyi, in this passage: *"Not for the sake of the husband is the husband dear, but for the sake of the Self is the husband dear; nor for the sake of the wife is the wife dear, but for the sake of the Self is the wife dear"* and so on to the end of the passage: *"Not for the sake of anything is that thing dear, but for the sake of the Self is anything dear."* It is due to Ignorance that the love that we bear to the Self is mistakenly interpreted as love for something or other. So the problem of finding real Happiness and escaping from suffering is solved only by becoming aware of the Self as He really is; the teaching is clinched by the next passage which concludes with the declaration that the Self is all that there is.

If this teaching is accepted, then what is the use of the inquiry about the reality or unreality of the world?

70. तुर्यं पदं नित्यसुखस्य धामेत्येवं प्रबुद्धाद्धिदितेऽथ साधोः ।
इतो विरक्तस्य तुरीयलिप्सोजगद्गतिश्चारण फलं किमस्ति ॥

turyaṁ padaṁ nityasukhasya dhāmetyevaṁ prabuddhādvidite'tha sādhoḥ |
ito viraktasya turīyalipsorjagadvicāreṇa phalaṁ kimasti ||

For the aspirant who has thus learned from the Sage-Guru that the Supreme State is the Home of eternal Happiness and who is therefore indifferent to this world and intent on winning that State, what is the use of an inquiry concerning the world?

This is explained next.

71.   सन् वाऽन्यथा वा भवतु प्रपञ्चो लब्धव्यमत्रास्ति किमस्य साधोः ।
सत् तुर्यमद्वैतमुतान्यथा वाऽप्यास्तां तदेवेप्सितमस्य नान्यत् ॥

san vā'nyathā vā bhavatu prapañco labdhavyamatrāsti kimasya sādhoḥ |
sat turyamadvaitamutānyathā vā'pyāstāṁ tadevepsitamasya nānyat ||

Let the world be real or otherwise. What is there in it for the aspirant to strive for? And let the Reality in the Supreme State be non-dual or otherwise. It is That alone that he wants to win, naught else.

The two questions, one concerning the reality of the world, the other concerning the Non-Duality of the Real Self, are really one. Both questions become superfluous for one that has resolved to strive for that State.

There is also another reason for this:-

72.   किमद्वयं सत् किमु नेति बोद्धुं शक्ये हि तुर्ये स्थितिमेत्य सत्ये ।
शक्नोति कस्तत्त्वमदो निबोद्धुं भ्राम्यन्नवस्थात्रितये विमुग्धः ॥

kimadvayaṁ sat kimu neti boddhuṁ śakye hi turye sthitimetya satye |
śaknoti kastattvamado niboddhuṁ bhrāmyannavasthātritaye vimugdhaḥ ||

Only by becoming firmly established in the Real Self of that Supreme State can one know definitely whether that Reality is non-dual or not. How can anyone become aware of that Truth while still wandering confusedly in the three States?

Bhagavan Sri Ramana gives the following analogy to impress this fact.

73.   क्षेपो हि लोम्नां निकरस्य युक्तः क्षुरापनीतस्य विना परीक्षाम् ।
तुच्छस्य तद्वज्जगतोऽस्य दानं चर्चां विना युज्यत एव साधोः ॥

kṣepo hi lomnāṁ nikarasya yuktaḥ kṣurāpanītasya vinā parīkṣām |
tucchasya tadvajjagato'sya dānaṁ carcāṁ vinā yujyata eva sādhoḥ ||

Just as it is proper to throw away the heap of shorn hair without scrutiny, so it is right for the aspirant to turn away from the world, which (for him) is of no value, without inquiry concerning it.

74.   हेयं प्रपञ्चं स विहाय तूर्णमन्तर्मुखत्वेन यतेत सिद्धयै ।
अन्तर्मुखत्वेन हि साधनं स्याद् विश्वं तदर्थं ननु हेयमेव ॥

heyaṁ prapañcaṁ sa vihāya tūrṇamantarmukhatvena yateta siddhyai |
antarmukhatvena hi sādhanaṁ syād viśvaṁ tadarthaṁ nanu heyameva ||

The aspirant will naturally turn away from the world at once and with his mind turned inwards, will strive for the goal. It is by turning the mind away from the world that the quest is made, and for that reason the world is certainly to be renounced.

The quest taught by the Master implies turning away from the world, because the mind has to be turned inwards, towards the Self, because He dwells *within*. But this has been said for the fully ripe aspirant who is not attached to the world. For those who are not yet ripe for the quest, this inquiry is not useless as will be seen presently.

75.   परं तु वैराग्यबलेन हीना जगत् स्वतः सत्यमिति प्रतीत्या ।
न साधनेऽन्तर्मुखतां भजन्ते तेषामपेक्ष्यो हि विचार एषः ॥

param tu vairāgyabalena hīnā jagat svataḥ satyamiti pratītyā |
na sādhane'ntarmukhatāṁ bhajante teṣāmapekṣyo hi vicāra eṣaḥ ||

But those who have not the needed strength of non-attachment, believing, as they do, that the world is real in its own right, cannot turn the mind inwards for the quest; so, for them, this inquiry is surely needful.

76.   एते विचारेण गुरूक्तरीत्या जगन्न सत्यं स्वत इत्यवेत्य ।
तथैव बुद्ध्याऽप्यनुसंदधाना अन्तर्मुखत्वं शनकैर्भजेयुः ॥

ete vicāreṇa gurūktarītyā jaganna satyaṁ svata ityavetya |
tathaiva buddhyā'pyanusandadhānā antarmukhatvaṁ śanakairbhajeyuḥ ||

These, by making the inquiry on the lines indicated by the Master, would become convinced that the world is not real in its own right, and then by reflecting on this truth, will become able, by degrees, to turn their minds inwards.

This knowledge is therefore not a mere luxury of speculative philosophy, but is of practical value as shown here. The necessity for guidance by the Master in making this inquest on the world is next explained.

77. या लौकिकेनानुभवेन चर्चां स्वबुद्धिशक्त्याऽपि वृथैव सा स्यात्।
बुद्धं श्रयित्वैव गुरुं तु कुर्यात् तद्दिष्टरीत्यैव जगद्विचारम्॥

yā laukikenānubhavena carcā svabuddhiśaktyā'pi vṛthaiva sā syāt |
buddhaṁ śrayitvaiva guruṁ tu kuryāt taddiṣṭarītyaiva jagadvicāram ||

An inquiry conducted on the basis of worldly experience (alone), by relying on one's own (unaided) intelligence, is vain. One should resort to a Guru who is a Sage and make this inquest on the world only as guided by Him.

No inquiry can be made in a vacuum, but only on the basis of reliable evidence. Speculative philosophers, as in the West, proceed on the false assumption that worldly experience, the offspring of the primary Ignorance, is good enough to be used as evidence for coming to a conclusion on a Truth that transcends the world. Also they believe that their intelligence is equal to the task of making a dispassionate inquiry. The knowledge derived from worldly experience is ignorance. Hence this is no evidence; if relied upon, it will lead to wrong conclusions. The reason is next given briefly.

78. अज्ञानमूलोऽनुभवो हि सर्वः सांसारिकः स्वप्नसमोऽज्ञपुंसाम् ।
     मृषैव सर्वोऽयमतो मुमुक्षोर्न हि प्रमाणं सदसद्विवेके ॥

ajñānamūlo'nubhavo hi sarvaḥ sāṁsārikaḥ svapnasamo'jñapuṁsām |
mṛṣaiva sarvo'yamato mumukṣorna hi pramāṇaṁ sadasadviveke ||

Since all worldly experience is rooted in the Ignorance, dream-like, taking place in worldliness, pertaining to men ignorant (of the Real Self), it is false, and is therefore no evidence for the seeker of Deliverance in (this) discrimination between the real and the unreal.

It has been explained that the three states of life, waking, dream and sleep, take place in the profound Sleep of Ignorance and hence even waking experience is dreamlike. And this inquiry involves disentangling the Real from the unreal. Worldly experience is at best suspect; its reality is itself in question, as it is inseparable from the world. It must not therefore be assumed to be valid evidence. What then is valid evidence?

79. बुद्धानुभूतिर्हि परं प्रमाणं साधोस्तुरीयस्य पदस्य लिप्सोः ।
     स एव तत्त्वं जगतोऽप्यवैति बोधात् तुरीयस्य सतः परस्य ॥

buddhānubhūtirhi paraṁ pramāṇaṁ sādhosturīyasya padasya lipsoḥ |
sa eva tattvaṁ jagato'pyavaiti bodhāt turīyasya sataḥ parasya ||

For the aspirant who seeks to win the Supreme State transcending their relativity (of the three states), the supreme evidence is the Experience of the Sage. He alone knows also the truth about the world, because of His awareness of the Reality in that state.

This will become intelligible as we proceed.

80. निजानुभूतिं च वदन् स बुद्धः संदर्शयिष्यत्यमलाश्च युक्तीः ।
प्रश्नाननन्तांस्तु बुधो न कुर्यात् साधोर्न शङ्कास्पदमाप्तवाक्यम् ॥

nijānubhūtiṁ ca vadan sa buddhaḥ sandarśayiṣyatyamalāśca yuktīḥ |
praśnānanantāṁstu budho na kuryāt sādhorna śaṅkāspadamāptavākyam ||

The Sage not only testifies to his own experience, but also furnishes flawless reasons (drawn from our own worldly experience). But the disciple, if wise, will not go on posing questions without end; for the word of the saviour is not to be doubted by the aspirant.

The Sage's own experience is for us a conclusive evidence. He is the compassionate one, the saviour who has assumed human form for redeeming those that have begun to feel the illusory nature of wordly life. So one must as a rule accept what He says without cavil. At some stage the series of questions must come to an end and the way to the verification of the Truth by one's own experience must be entered upon. On the other hand, as the Gita says: संशयात्मा विनश्यति (saṁśayātmā vinaśyati), "The inveterate doubter verily loses the goal of life."

81. न संशयानां भविता विरामो यावन्न तुर्ये स्थितिमेति बोधात् ।
अन्तोऽस्ति तत्रैव हि संशयानामात्यन्तिकः संशयितुर्विनाशात् ॥

na saṁśayānāṁ bhavitā virāmo yāvanna turye sthitimeti bodhāt |
anto'sti tatraiva hi saṁśayānāmātyantikaḥ saṁśayiturvināśāt ||

There will be no end to doubt until one gets established in the Supreme State. Only in that State is there an end of all doubts, due to the extinction of the doubter, (the ego).

Here is a reference to the Upanishadic text:-

भिद्यते हृदयग्रन्थिः छिद्यन्ते सर्वसंशयाः।
क्षीयन्ते चास्य कर्माणि तस्मिन् दृष्टे परावरे ॥

bhidyate hṛdayagranthiḥ chidyante sarvasaṁśayāḥ |
kṣīyante cāsya karmāṇi tasmin dṛṣṭe parāvare ||

"When the One that is the Truth of the high and the low is experienced, then the heart-knot is cut, all doubts are dispelled, and all his actions are liquidated". Doubts we are here told, arise in the ego-ridden mind, not in the egoless state.

What then must the aspirant do?

82. तर्कोऽप्रतिष्ठो हि ततो मुमुक्षुः सद्योऽन्ततस्तर्कमतिं विहाय।
श्रद्धां समालम्ब्य गुरोर्वचस्सु तद्दिष्टमार्गेण यतेत सिद्धये ॥

tarko'pratiṣṭho hi tato mumukṣuḥ sadyo'ntatastarkamatiṁ vihāya |
śraddhāṁ samālambya gurorvacassu taddiṣṭamārgeṇa yateta siddhyai ||

Since there is no finality in reason, the aspirant should at once give up reliance on reason, and with faith in the Master's teaching, must strive for winning the goal on the lines taught by Him.

83. उदेति शङ्का यदि कस्य सेति पृच्छन् स्वतत्त्वस्य गवेषणेन ।
लभेत निष्ठां यदि तुर्यभावे शङ्का च तद्वानुभयं च नश्येत् ॥

udeti śaṅkā yadi kasya seti pṛcchan svatattvasya gaveṣaṇena |
labheta niṣṭhāṁ yadi turyabhāve śaṅkā ca tadvānubhayaṁ ca naśyet ||

If a doubt arises he should ask himself: 'Who is it that doubts thus'; if by thus seeking, he attains the Supreme State, then both doubt and doubter will cease to be.

The question 'Who is it that has this doubt' is the means prescribed by Bhagavan Sri Ramana to turn the mind away from the doubt to the doubter, the ego; the answer to this question will be 'I'; from this the question will arise, 'Who am I?' which is the quest. In the same way any extraneous thought that intrudes, distracting the mind from the quest, can be used as a means of returning to the quest. If thus the quest be pursued and persisted in, the ego, the doubter, becomes extinct, and then no more doubts will arise, because then the Mind-free State is attained.

Now we come to the question, 'Is the world real?' Bhagavan's teaching on this point is given in the next seven verses.

84. बुद्धो गुरुर्वक्ति जगन्मृषात्वं सहेतुकं स्वानुभवानुरूपम् ।
सत्योपदेशं तमिमं मुमुक्षुः सच्छ्रद्धयाऽऽलम्ब्य यतेत सिद्ध्यै ॥

buddho gururvakti jaganmṛṣātvaṁ sahetukaṁ svānubhavānurūpam |
satyopadeśaṁ tamimam mumukṣuḥ sacchraddhayā"lambya yateta siddhyai ||

The guru who is a Sage teaches the unreality of the world in accordance with his own experience, giving reasons supporting it. The disciple who aspires to become Free should accept this teaching with perfect faith and (with its help) strive for his goal.

85. जीवेश्वरौ विश्वमिति त्रिरूपं जगत् समस्तं च तुरीयसत्ये ।
अध्यस्तमेवात्मनि मानसेनेत्यज्ञानकार्यं बत सर्वमेतत् ॥

jīveśvarau viśvamiti trirūpaṁ jagat samastaṁ ca turīyasatye |
adhyastamevātmani mānasenetyajñānakāryaṁ bata sarvametat ||

The Universe, comprising these three, namely the soul, god and the world of visible objects, is superimposed by the mind on the Real Self, which is the Sole Reality of the Supreme State; hence all this is just an outcome of Ignorance.

The mind is the creator of the universe; Ignorance is the primal cause of the mind; hence it is said that this Ignorance is the cause of the universe.

86. सत्येवमज्ञानमिदं यदा तु स्वज्ञानभासा भजते विनाशम् ।
कार्यं तदीयं च सहैव नश्येत् तमो यथाऽर्कप्रभया प्रभाते ॥

satyevamajñānamidaṁ yadā tu svajñānabhāsā bhajate vināśam |
kāryaṁ tadīyaṁ ca sahaiva naśyet tamo yathā'rkaprabhayā prabhāte ||

That being so, when this Ignorance is annihilated by the light of the Awareness of that Self, then along with it, the outcome of it, (namely this world), will cease to appear, like darkness before the sunlight at sunrise.

This will become more and more intelligible as we proceed. The above are the actual facts of the Guru's own experience. The conclusion that follows for the disciple is next stated.

87. भातीदमज्ञानतमोविलासे न भाति सुज्ञानमहाप्रकाशे ।
सच्चेदिदं भाति कुतो न तुर्ये सत्यात्मनश्चित्प्रभया प्रदीप्ते ॥

bhātīdamajñānatamovilāse na bhāti sujñānamahāprakāse |
saccedidaṁ bhāti kuto na turye satyātmanaścitprabhayā pradīpte ||

This universe (we thus see) shines in the dense darkness of the Ignorance, but does not shine in the Great Splendour of the Light of Self-awareness. If this universe were real, why does it not shine in the Supreme State, lighted as It is by the Conscious-Effulgent Light of the Real Self?

An axiomatic distinction between the Real and unreal which is implicit in the Vedantic metaphysic is next enunciated.

88. शिष्येत यत्स्वानुभवे तुरीये सत्यं तदेवान्यदसत्यमेव ।
सत्यत्वमिथ्यात्वविभाग एष बुद्धोपदेशैर्भवति स्फुटो नः ॥

śiṣyeta yatsvānubhave turīye satyaṁ tadevānyadasatyameva |
satyatvamithyātvavibhāga eṣa buddhopadeśairbhavati sphuṭo naḥ ||

That alone is real which survives in the experience of the Real Self in the Supreme State; all else is only unreal. This is the distinction between the Real and the unreal, revealed to us by the teachings of all the sages.

By this test the world is shown to be unreal, next:

89. यतोऽज्ञतायामनुभूयमानं तस्मादसद् द्वैतमिदं निरुक्तम् ।
अज्ञाननाशादनुभूयमाना सत्या भवत्यद्वयताऽऽत्मनस्तु ॥

yato'jñatāyāmanubhūyamānaṁ tasmādasad dvaitamidaṁ niruktam |
ajñānanāśādanubhūyamānā satyā bhavatyadvayatā''tmanastu ||

Since the multiplicity is experienced only in the state of Ignorance, it is declared to be unreal. On the other hand, because the Unity (non-difference) of the Self is experienced on the liquidation of Ignorance, that Unity is real.

It may be questioned how, if the Ignorance be total darkness, anything can be experienced in this state. The explanation is that this Ignorance is not like perfect darkness, but like a greatly diminished light. As in dim light a rope is not unseen, but wrongly, as a snake, so, in Ignorance, the Real, the Self, is not unseen, but seen as the world.

The reality is only that which survives in the Supreme State.

90. पदे परस्मिन् भुवने विनष्टे यच्चिन्मयः स्वो लसति स्वभासा ।
शान्तः स एवाद्वय एककः सन्नित्यस्मदाचार्यनिरूपितार्थः ॥

pade parasmin bhuvane vinaṣṭe yaccinmayaḥ svo lasati svabhāsā |
śāntaḥ sa evādvaya ekakaḥ sannityasmadācāryanirūpitārthaḥ ||

That peaceful Self, who shines by the light of
His own nature as pure Consciousness in the
Supreme State where the world is lost, is the sole
Reality; such is the teaching of our holy Guru.

Here it is shown that the state is one of Peace because
there is no duality there; this is what we learn from all the
Upanishads.

This teaching is further confirmed by the analogy of
the dream-world.

91. स्वप्नः प्रबोधे निधनं प्रयातीत्यतो हि मिथ्येत्यवगम्यतेऽसौ ।
जाग्रत्प्रपञ्चोऽपि तथाऽऽत्मभावे विनश्यतीत्यस्य मृषात्वसिद्धिः ॥

svapnaḥ prabodhe nidhanaṃ prayātītyato hi mithyetyavagamyate'sau |
jāgratprapañco'pi tathā''tmabhāve vinaśyatītyasya mṛṣātvasiddhiḥ ||

As the dream world is known to be unreal
for the reason that it vanishes upon waking, so
this waking world also, is proved to be unreal by
its vanishing in the light of the Real Self.

Those who seek to discredit this teaching, it is next
pointed out, are those who do not ardently aspire to the
Supreme State.

92. पराङ्मुखास्तुर्यपदस्य लाभाद् वादांस्तु मुग्धाः प्रवदन्त्यनन्तान् ।
तज्जन्यशङ्काः शमयन्ति बुद्धा मुह्येद्यथा तैर्न मुमुक्षुलोकः ॥

parāṅmukhāsturyapadasya lābhād vādāṁstu mugdhāḥ pravadantyanantān |
tajjanyaśaṅkāḥ śamayanti buddhā muhyedyathā tairna mumukṣulokaḥ ||

But ignorant men, who are averse to winning
the Supreme State, put forth an endless series of
arguments, (trying to refute these teachings). The
sages clear the doubts generated by these
arguments so that earnest aspirants may not be
deluded by them.

The teaching is addressed, not to all men, but only to
those who aspire to win the Supreme State, because they
alone are qualified to receive it.

93. आत्मा शरीरं स्वयमेव येषां सोऽयं शरीरी भविता च येषाम् ।
नोक्तं हि तान् प्रत्यनृतत्वमस्य तेषां भवेद्विश्वमिदं सदेव ॥

ātmā śarīraṁ svayameva yeṣāṁ so'yaṁ śarīrī bhavitā ca yeṣām |
noktaṁ hi tān pratyanṛtatvamasya teṣāṁ bhavedviśvamidaṁ sadeva ||

This teaching of the unreality of the world is
not addressed to those who look upon the body
itself as the Self, or consider the Self to be the
owner of the body. For these people the world is
real, not unreal.

The teaching has to be adapted to the person to be
taught. The same teaching is not good for all. Here it is
shown that he who knew that the Self is not the body, but is

the owner of it, or the dweller therein, is for this purpose in the same category as one that believes the body itself to be the Self.

Why is it that the world is real to these persons?

94. जीवेश्वरौ विश्वमिति त्रयस्य मिथ्यात्वमुक्तं ह्यविभक्तमेव ।
त्रिष्वेककं सत्यमवैति यस्तु द्वयं तदन्यच्च सदेव तस्मै ॥

jīveśvarau viśvamiti trayasya mithyātvamuktaṁ hyavibhaktameva |
triṣvekakaṁ satyamavaiti yastu dvayaṁ tadanyacca sadeva tasmai ||

The teaching, that the trinity of the soul, God and the world is unreal, is indivisible. (So) For one that is convinced that one of these is real, the other two also are real.

That is, the teaching must either be accepted as a whole or rejected wholly. There is no option to split it up and accept it partially, rejecting a part of it.

95. मुमुक्षुपुंसामुपदिश्यते तु समानमेव त्रितयं मृषेति ।
ग्राह्यं तथैवेह यथोपदिष्टं विमुक्तिमिच्छद्भिरबोधनाशात् ॥

mumukṣupuṁsāmupadiśyate tu samānameva tritayaṁ mṛṣeti |
grāhyaṁ tathaiveha yathopadiṣṭaṁ vimuktimicchadbhirabodhanāśāt ||

To those that seek Deliverance the teaching is that all these three are equally unreal. This teaching must therefore be accepted exactly as taught by those who are earnest to win Deliverance by the extinction of the Ignorance.

For different aspirants there are different paths prescribed. This particular teaching is addressed only to those who believe that Deliverance must come by Right Awareness.

An analogy is next given to explain the indivisibility of the teaching.

96.	ग्राह्यः समग्रोऽप्युपदेश एष त्याज्योऽथवा बुद्धिमता समग्रम् ।
	कः कुक्कुटीं कल्पयितुं समर्थः पाकाय चार्धं प्रसवाय चार्धम् ॥

grāhyaḥ samagro'pyupadeśa eṣa tyājyo'thavā buddhimatā samagram |
kaḥ kukkuṭīṃ kalpayituṃ samarthaḥ pākāya cārdhaṃ prasavāya cārdham ||

One that is wise would either accept the teaching as a whole, or reject the whole of it. Who can make use of half of a hen for cooking, reserving the other half for laying eggs?

A hen must be killed and cooked for food, as a whole or the whole hen must be allowed to live for laying eggs. The same indivisibility is characteristic of this teaching.

Now we come to a discussion of the objections of those who assert the perfect reality of the world.

On what evidence do they base their belief?

97.	कुतो नु विश्वं सदिति प्रतीतमितीदमादौ परिशीलनीयम् ।
	प्रपञ्चसत्ताप्रतिपादनस्य भारोऽस्ति तद्वक्तृशिरस्थ एव ॥

kuto nu viśvaṃ saditi pratītamitīdamādau pariśīlanīyam |
prapañcasattāpratipādanasya bhāro'sti tadvaktṛśirastha eva ||

To begin with, it needs to be considered why the world is taken as real; for the burden of proving the reality of the world lies on him that asserts it, (not on those who simply deny it.)

98. यद्वीक्ष्यते विश्वमतोऽज्ञलोकः सदेव विश्वं मनुते हि सर्वः ।
नैतत् प्रमाणं व्यभिचारदोषान्मरीचिकारज्जुभुजङ्गमादौ ॥

yadvīkṣyate viśvamato'jñalokaḥ sadeva viśvaṁ manute hi sarvaḥ |
naitat pramāṇaṁ vyabhicāradoṣānmarīcikārajjubhujaṅgamādau ||

Everyone that is ignorant (of the Real Self) thinks the world is real because it is seen. This is no proof, because it proves too much, as the same reason would prove the reality of the mirage, the rope-snake, etc.

Usually the knowledge that arises from seeing is mixed up with imagination, or a false impression of what is seen. Hence this reason is inconclusive.

The question arises; 'What does the seeing of the world prove?'

99. यथा प्रतीतं भुवनं सदेवेत्येतन्न सिद्धं भवतीक्षणेन ।
किमप्यधिष्ठानसदस्ति यस्मिन्निदं विभातीत्यनुमेयमत्र ॥

yathā pratītaṁ bhuvanaṁ sadevetyetanna siddhaṁ bhavatīkṣaṇena |
kimapyadhiṣṭhānasadasti yasminnidaṁ vibhātītyanumeyamatra ||

The fact of being seen is no conclusive proof that the world exists exactly as imagined (by the seer). From the seeing it is proper to infer only that there is a Substratum in which the world appears.

Bhagavan Sri Ramana in the third verse, the first after the two benedictory verses, of the *Ulladu Narpadu* says: "Because we see the world, therefore it is indisputable that there exists a first cause (substratum or basic reality), which has the power to appear as many," and then in the same verse He proceeds to reveal, in the light of his own experience, that the substratum is only the Real Self, on whom is superimposed the four elements of the world-appearance, the pictures of names and forms, the seeing individual soul, the screen and the light. The seeing subject and the spectacle form the appearance imposed on the substratum; the lighted screen is the substratum. Here the analogy of the cinema-show is suggested. The pictures, wherein the seer is included, come and go, but the lighted screen exists unaffected throughout. The power by which the appearance is superimposed on the substratum is known as Maya.

By calling the world an effect of Maya all that is meant is that *things* are not what they seem to those that have not known the Real Self as He really is. This view is corroborated by recent science.

100.　यद्यद्यथा भाति न तत् तथेति वैज्ञानिकैरेव निरूपितं हि ।
द्रव्यं सुनीरन्ध्रमिव प्रतीतं चाकाशकल्पं गदितं यतस्तैः ॥

yadyadyathā bhāti na tat tatheti vaijñānikaireva nirūpitaṁ hi |
dravyaṁ sunīrandhramiva pratītaṁ cākāśakalpaṁ gaditaṁ yatastaiḥ ||

Even the scientists have proved that things are not exactly as they appear (to the seer); for they say that the solid-seeming objects are really little more than empty space.

Atomic physics now tell us that the *atom* is not a solid particle, but consists of a closed space in which electrons are rotating around a nucleus, composed of protons and neutrons, etc; the electrons rotate at different distances from the nucleus; the whole atom thus resembles a solar system. That things are not what they seem is thus indisputable. On the other hand there is no proof that things *are* what they seem to be. There is, in fact, an antithesis between appearance and reality. It is this that is called Maya, which is the illusion by which the reality appears as the world, the spectacle, which resembles a cinema-show. Due to this illusion there is ignorance (*Avidya*) which works through the mind, wrongly identifying the body as the Self. For this reason the truth about the world is a profound mystery, which transcends the human intellect, but is no mystery to the Sage, who alone is competent to tell us the truth as it really is, as the next verse points out.

101. जानात्यधिष्ठानसदस्य यस्तु तुरीयभावे समुपेत्य निष्ठाम्।
बुद्धः स एव प्रभवेद्धि वक्तुं किमस्य तत्त्वं भवतीति नान्यः ॥

janātyadhiṣṭhānasadasya yastu turīyabhāve samupetya niṣṭhām |
buddhaḥ sa eva prabhaveddhi vaktuṁ kimasya tattvaṁ bhavatīti nānyaḥ ||

Only the Sage, who knows the substratum of the world-appearance, the Reality, by His being firmly established in the Supreme State, is competent to reveal the truth of the world.

By his unawareness of that Truth, the common man, being a victim of his ignorance, cannot know the truth about the world.

102.   बहिर्मुखत्वे सति को नु विद्याद् यथावदात्मानमुत प्रपञ्चम् ।
अन्तर्मुखत्वेन तु बोधदृष्ट्या जानाति तत्त्वं ह्युभयोश्च बुद्धः ॥

bahirmukhatve sati ko nu vidyād yathāvadātmānamuta prapañcam |
antarmukhatvena tu bodhadṛṣṭyā jānāti tattvaṃ hyubhayośca buddhaḥ ||

When his vision is focussed on the outside,
who can know the Truth, whether of the Real Self
or of the world? But by the eye of right-Awareness,
due to the mind being turned inwards, the Sage
knows the Truth of both.

It is with the knowledge of this uniqueness of the Sage
that the disciple has to approach him and listen to his teachings.

103.   कथं नु मां ज्ञास्यसि तत्त्वतस्त्वं ज्ञातुं स्वमात्मानमुतासमर्थः ।
इत्यज्ञमर्त्यं हसति प्रपञ्च इत्येवमूचे भगवान् गुरुर्नः ॥

kathaṃ nu māṃ jñāsyasi tattvatastvaṃ jñātuṃ svamātmānamutāsamarthaḥ |
ityajñamartyaṃ hasati prapañca ityevamūce bhagavān gururnaḥ ||

Bhagavan Sri Ramana, our Guru, has said:
"The world laughs at the ignorant man, saying,
'How can'st thou know me aright, being unable
to know Thyself aright?'

By this it is meant that the disciple must be humble,
knowing the limitations of his own intelligence. Without this
humility he would not be a true disciple.

The next verse is an introduction to the detailed
exposition by Bhagavan Sri Ramana of the truth concerning
the world.

104. आविद्यकत्वाज्जगदीक्षणस्य वादं निराधारमिमं प्रदर्श्य ।
जगन्मृषात्वं प्रकटीकरोति स्फुटं गुरुर्नो भगवान् प्रबुद्धः ॥

āvidyakatvājjagadīkṣaṇasya vādaṁ nirādhāramimaṁ pradarśya |
jaganmṛṣātvaṁ prakaṭīkaroti sphuṭaṁ gururno bhagavān prabuddhaḥ ||

Bhagavan Sri Ramana, our Guru, being a Sage, expounds the unreality of the world by showing that the perception of the world takes place in the Ignorance, and that therefore the objector's argument, that the world is real because he sees it, does not avail to prove his contention.

The ignorant man's vision of the world is vitiated by the fact of his ignorance of his own Real Self. This point has been repeatedly urged by Bhagavan Sri Ramana. To know the world aright, one must first know Oneself aright.

The verses that follow show how the seeing of the world is affected and falsified by the primary ignorance.

105. शरीरमेवात्मतयाऽवगम्य तत् सत्यमेवेत्यपि निश्चयेन ।
प्रत्येति सत्यं सकलं हि रूपं सर्वोऽपि जन्तुः परिदृश्यमानम् ॥

śarīramevātmatayā'vagamya tat satyamevetyapi niścayena |
pratyeti satyaṁ sakalaṁ hi rūpaṁ sarvo'pi jantuḥ paridṛśyamānam ||

Every creature first identifies his own Self with the body, and thereby concludes that the body is real; then he comes to believe that all forms that are seen are also real.

Whatever is seen is a form. The initial question is therefore whether forms are real. Every seer comes to the conclusion that all forms are real. But the first step in the process of coming to this conclusion is a mistaken impression, that the body is the Self; philosophy begins with the knowledge that the body is not the Self, and that really the Self is formless, so that whatever is seen is for that very reason not the Self. The Self being indubitably real, that reality is ascribed to the body. So a part of the world is mistakenly concluded to be real. This mistake vitiates the whole process, by which the world is accepted as real. This and the succeeding verses are a commentary on the 4th verse of the *Ulladu Narpadu*.

106. रूपाणि सर्वाणि मृषैव तस्मान्न तानि सत्यानि हि बुद्धपुंसः।
यदस्ति सत्यं तदरूपमेव न रूपि किञ्चित् परमार्थदृष्टचा ॥

rūpāṇi sarvāṇi mṛṣaiva tasmānna tāni satyāni hi buddhapuṁsaḥ |
yadasti satyaṁ tadarūpameva na rūpi kiñcit paramārthadṛṣṭyā ||

Therefore all forms are unreal; to the Sage they are not real; what really exists is formless; in Right-Awareness nothing has form.

This is further explained as follows:

107. दृष्ट्यैकया पश्यति रूपिणं स्वं सरूपकं विश्वमुताज्ञमर्त्यः।
सा दृष्टिरज्ञानमयीति हेतोः प्रमाणहीनैव हि विश्वसत्ता ॥

dṛṣṭyaikayā paśyati rūpiṇaṁ svaṁ sarūpakaṁ viśvamutājñamartyaḥ |
sā dṛṣṭirajñānamayīti hetoḥ pramāṇahīnaiva hi viśvasattā ||

By a single act of vision the ignorant man sees both himself and the world as forms. Since this seeing is illusory, there is no evidence to prove that the world is real.

108. वपुःप्रपञ्चाविति दृश्यमेकं वीक्षाऽप्यवीक्षाऽप्युभयोः सहैव ।
विनाऽऽत्मनो रूपमिदं शरीरं किं न्वीक्षते कश्चन विश्वमेतत् ॥

vapuḥprapañcāviti dṛśyamekaṁ vīkṣā'pyavīkṣā'pyubhayoḥ sahaiva |
vinā"tmano rūpamidaṁ śarīraṁ kiṁ nvīkṣate kaścana viśvametat ||

One's own body and the world are one indivisible spectacle; either they are both seen together, or they are both not seen. Does any one see this world without at the same time seeing the body, which is the form ascribed to the Self?

The fact, that neither the body, nor the world, is seen apart from the other, is something we have never noticed before. We come to know of it for the first time only when the fact is pointed out by Bhagavan Sri Ramana. Since the Self is really formless, the whole spectacle is suspect, since it is indivisible.

It may be objected that we see the dream-world without a body. The answer to this follows.

109. स्वाप्नं प्रपञ्चं वपुषा विहीनाः पश्याम इत्येवमुदीर्यते चेत् ।
तिसृष्ववस्थास्वपि चास्ति देहः कदाऽप्यदेही न भवेद्धि जीवः ॥

svāpnaṁ prapañcam vapuṣā vihīnāḥ paśyāma ityevamudīryate cet |
tisṛṣvavasthāsvapi cāsti dehaḥ kadā'pyadehī na bhaveddhi jīvaḥ ||

If it be said that we see the dream-world without bodies, the answer is that that there is a body for the soul in all the three states; the soul is never bodiless.

Here it is the *soul* that is spoken of, not the Self; the two are not the same in Bhagavan Sri Ramana's teachings, as will be seen in due course. This and the succeeding verses give the meaning of the 5th verse of the *Ulladu Narpadu*.

110.   देहास्त्रयः सन्ति हि सर्वजन्तोः स्थूलोऽपि सूक्ष्मोऽपि च कारणात्मा ।
मनोमयः सूक्ष्म उदीयते चाप्युक्तस्त्यविद्यैव च कारणाख्यः ॥

dehāstrayaḥ santi hi sarvajantoḥ sthūlo'pi sūkṣmo'pi ca kāraṇātmā |
manomayaḥ sūkṣma udīryate cāpyuktastyavidyaiva ca kāraṇākhyaḥ ||

Every creature has three bodies, a gross one, subtle one and a causal one; the mind is the subtle body, and the Ignorance itself is called the causal body.

111.   उक्तं शरीरत्रितयं यदेतत् तत् पञ्चकोशात्मकमुच्यते च ।
मध्यं त्रयं सूक्ष्मशरीरमुक्तं कोशोऽन्तिमः कारणदेह उक्तः ॥

uktaṁ śarīratritayaṁ yadetat tat pañcakośātmakamucyate ca |
madhyaṁ trayaṁ sūkṣmaśarīramuktaṁ kośo'ntimaḥ kāraṇadeha uktaḥ ||

The three bodies mentioned here are also enumerated as five sheaths. The middle three sheaths are the (same as the) subtle body, and the last sheath is stated to be the causal body.

The gross body is identified with the first of the five sheaths called the food-sheath (*annamaya kosa*), being the product of food. This being obvious, is not stated in the verse.

112.	यावन्न बोधात् त्रितयं विनश्येत् स्याद् देहवानेव हि जीवनामा ।
	तुरीयभावे ह्यशरीरताऽस्ति सहैव यस्मिंस्त्रितयं विनश्येत् ॥

yāvanna bodhāt tritayaṁ vinaśyet syād dehavāneva hi jīvanāmā |
turīyabhāve hyaśarīratā'sti sahaiva yasmiṁstritayaṁ vinaśyet ||

So long as the three bodies remain undissolved by the light of right Awareness, the soul will be embodied. Only in the Supreme State, wherein all the three are together lost, will there by bodilessness.

113.	स्वाविद्यया कल्पयतेऽन्यदेहं स्वप्ने मनोऽन्यद् भुवनं स्वयं हि ।
	स्वाप्नेन देहेन सहैव सुप्तः स्वाप्नं जगत् पश्यति न त्वरूपः ॥

svāvidyayā kalpayate'nyadehaṁ svapne mano'nyad bhuvanaṁ svayaṁ hi |
svāpnena dehena sahaiva suptaḥ svāpnaṁ jagat paśyati na tvarūpaḥ ||

The mind by its own force of ignorance, itself creates another gross body, and also another dream world, and the sleeper sees this dream-world along with this dream-body, not disembodied.

Thus the objection is got over.

114.   देहं च विश्वं च समीक्षते हि नेत्रेण देहावयवेन सर्वः ।
       कथं प्रमाणं भवितेयमीक्षा विश्वस्य सत्यत्वविचारणेऽस्मिन् ॥

deham ca viśvam ca samīkṣate hi netreṇa dehāvayavena sarvaḥ |
katham pramāṇam bhaviteyamīkṣā viśvasya satyatvavicāraṇe'smin ||

Everyone sees both his own body and the world by the eye, which is a part of that very body. How can this seeing be admissible as evidence in this inquiry about the reality of the world?

The body being a part of the world, its reality also is in question, and cannot be assumed without proof. But it is so assumed when the eye is appealed to as a witness to the truth of the world. The question of the reality of forms is now further pursued.

115.   दृक् स्याद्यथा तादृशमेव दृश्यं दृगाश्रयोऽयं खलु दृश्यभावः ।
       दृक् चेत् सरूपाऽस्ति तथैव दृश्यं दृक् चेदरूपाऽस्ति न रूपवीक्षा ॥

dṛk syādyathā tādṛśameva dṛśyam dṛgāśrayo'yam khalu dṛśyabhāvaḥ |
dṛk cet sarūpā'sti tathaiva dṛśyam dṛk cedarūpā'sti na rūpavīkṣā ||

As is the eye, so is the spectacle, since the nature of the spectacle depends upon that of the seeing eye. If that eye be a form so will be the spectacle. But if the eye be the formless Self, there will be no seeing of forms at all.

This is a law of Nature that Bhagavan Sri Ramana reveals for the first time. Seeing with the eye of flesh, which is a form, one sees forms. Seeing with the eye of Right

Awarenss, as the Self, forms are not seen, says Bhagavan Sri Ramana, and this proves that forms are unreal, for the purpose of this philosophy.

The subject is further elucidated.

116.	भात्यज्ञतायां खलु सर्वजन्तोः प्रपञ्च आत्मा द्वितयं सरूपम् ।
	अज्ञाननाशे द्वयमप्यरूपमनन्त आत्मैव हि दृक् तदानीम् ॥

bhātyajñatāyaṁ khalu sarvajantoḥ prapañca ātmā dvitayaṁ sarūpam |
ajñānanāśe dvayamapyarūpamananta ātmaiva hi dṛk tadānīm ||

In the state of Ignorance both the world and the Self are seen as forms. But on the extinction of the ignorance both are (found to be) formless, because in the Supreme State the Infinite Self is the eye.

In the true state which is the Supreme State, the Self is Alone, and is described as Infinite, and therefore Formless, and there are no objects to be seen, nor is there any real seeing. Hence forms are unreal. If they were real, they would survive in that state.

117.	ज्ञानेक्षया ह्यात्मनि रूपहीने यात्येकतां विश्वमिदं सजीवम् ।
	द्रष्टाऽपि दृश्यं भवतो न यस्यां तां ज्ञानवीक्षां निगदन्ति बुद्धाः ॥

jñānekṣayā hyātmani rūpahīne yātyekatāṁ viśvamidaṁ sajīvam |
draṣṭā'pi dṛśyaṁ bhavato na yasyāṁ tāṁ jñānavīkṣāṁ nigadanti buddhāḥ ||

By the Vision of Right Awareness the world, with the soul, merges into the formless Real Self.

The Sages call it the Vision of Right Awareness,
wherein there is neither seer nor spectacle.

118.   चिद्रूप आत्मैव हि निष्प्रपञ्च एकः पदे स्वे परिशिष्ट आस्ते ।
       जन्मादिषड्भावविकारहीनः स एव तस्माद् गदितः स्वतः सन् ॥

cidrūpa ātmaiva hi niṣprapañca ekaḥ pade sve pariśiṣṭa āste |
janmādiṣaḍbhāvavikārahīnaḥ sa eva tasmād gaditaḥ svataḥ san ||

In that natural state (of the Self) there
survives only the Self, who is consciousness,
worldless, alone, and without the six modes of
change, namely birth, etc; and hence He alone is
real in his own right.

The world is *not* real in its own right; it has only a
borrowed reality as will become clear later on.

119.   अनन्तदृङ्नाम निगद्यतेऽसौ परः स आत्मा परिपूर्ण एकः ।
       न तस्य दृक्त्वं तु यथार्थतोऽस्ति सत्यात्मनो
       दृश्यविवर्जितत्वात् ॥

anantadṛṅnāma nigadyate'sau paraḥ sa ātmā paripūrṇa ekaḥ |
na tasya dṛktvaṃ tu yathārthato'sti satyātmano dṛśyavivarjitatvāt ||

That Supreme Being, the Self, who is perfect
as the sole Reality, is styled the Infinite Eye: but
because for that Self in His true state, there are
no objects to be seen, therefore He is not an eye
(really).

120. अचित्स्वरूपत्वनिवारणाय कृतो दृगित्यत्र पदप्रयोगः ।
ज्ञानस्वरूपत्वमुताद्वयत्वं तस्यैवमुक्ते भगवत्तमेन ॥

acitsvarūpatvanivāraṇāya kṛto dṛgityatra padaprayogaḥ |
jñānasvarūpatvamutādvayatvaṁ tasyaivamukte bhagavattamena ||

The term 'Eye' has been used in this context by the most holy one viz., Bhagavan Sri Ramana Maharshi, only to ward off the misconception that he is non-consciousness, (inert). Thus the most Holy One has conveyed the meaning that that Self is Consciousness and the Sole Reality.

121 अरूपिणः स्वस्य सरूपतां हि मत्वेक्षते विश्वमिदं सरूपम् ।
अविद्ययाऽध्यस्तमिदं समस्तं ह्यात्मन्यरूपे परसत्यनन्ते ॥

arūpiṇaḥ svasya sarūpatāṁ hi matvekṣate viśvamidaṁ sarūpam |
avidyayā'dhyastamidaṁ samastaṁ hyātmanyarūpe parasatyanante ||

It is only by conceiving the formless Self as a form that one sees this world as consisting of forms. All this is really a superimposition on the formless, infinite Reality, the Self, through Ignorance.

122. अनामकेऽरूपिणि चित्स्वरूपे तस्मिन्नविद्यापरिकल्पितानि ।
नामानि रूपाणि विभान्ति सद्वत् स्वं रूपिणं पश्यत एव पुंसः ॥

anāmake'rūpiṇi citsvarūpe tasminnavidyāparikalpitāni |
nāmāni rūpāṇi vibhānti sadvat svaṁ rūpiṇaṁ paśyata eva puṁsaḥ ||

It is only to him that sees himself as having a form, that the names and forms – which have been fabricated by Ignorance and superimposed on the Nameless Formless Self, who is Consciousness – appear as real.

123.   आविद्यकत्वं जगदीक्षणस्य विस्पष्टमेवं गुरुणोपदिष्टम् ।
एवं निरस्ता जगतोऽस्य सत्ता दिष्टाऽऽत्मनः केवलताऽपि सत्या ॥

āvidyakatvaṁ jagadīkṣaṇasya vispaṣṭamevaṁ guruṇopadiṣṭam |
evaṁ nirastā jagato'sya sattā diṣṭā''tmanaḥ kevalatā'pi satyā ||

Thus it has been made plain by the Master that the seeing of the world is an effect of the primary ignorance, and thus the claim that the world is real has been refuted by him. Also it has been shown by him that the aloneness of the real Self in the true state is real.

124.   स्थिरीकरोत्यर्थमिमं गुरुर्नो मनोमयत्वं जगतो निरूप्य ।
ततो मृषात्वं मनसोऽहमश्च मूलाज्ञताया अपि चोपदिश्य ॥

sthirīkarotyarthamimaṁ gururno manomayatvaṁ jagato nirūpya |
tato mṛṣātvaṁ manaso'hamaśca mūlājñatāyā api copadiśya ||

Our Master confirms this teaching first by showing that the world is mental, (inseparable from the mind); then by proving the unreality of the mind and the ego; and finally by teaching that even the primary Ignorance is non-existent.

A detailed exposition of the brief teaching given above is given in the 6th and succeeding verses of the Text, in which the conclusion is led up to by a series of steps as shown in this verse.

The next verse shows that the world does not exist apart from the mind, and is therefore mental.

125. शब्दादिका ये विषयास्त एव रूपं हि विश्वस्य न किञ्चिदन्यत् ।
प्रतीतयस्ते मनसो हि सर्वे तद्विश्वमेतन्मन एव नान्यत् ॥

śabdādikā ye viṣayāsta eva rūpaṃ hi viśvasya na kiñcidanyat |
pratītayaste manaso hi sarve tadviśvametanmana eva nānyat ||

The world is a totality of the five kinds of sensations, namely sounds and the rest and nothing else. All these are only mental impressions and hence the world is nothing but the mind.

126. यद्यस्ति विश्वं मनसो विभिन्नमभानमेतस्य कुतः सुषुप्तौ ।
चिद्रूप आत्मास्ति हि तत्र सत्यो यदीयभासा मनसो मनस्त्वम् ॥

yadyasti viśvaṃ manaso vibhinnamabhānametasya kutaḥ suṣuptau |
cidrūpa ātmā'sti hi tatra satyo yadīyabhāsā manaso manastvam ||

If the world were other than the mind, why does it not appear in deep sleep? Therein is the Real Self, who is consciousness and by whose consciousness-Light, the mind is mind!

The second half of the verse is an answer to the contention, which may be raised by the other school of thought, that the non-seeing of the world in deep sleep is no argument, because it is due to the absence, in that state, of the mind and the senses of perception. The mind is not conscious by its own nature, its consciousness being derived by association with the Real Self. Since that Self survives in deep sleep, the objection is vain. This reasoning finds a place in Bhagavan Sri Sankaracharya's Viveka Chudamani:

यदि सत्यं भवेद्विश्वं सुषुप्तावुपलभ्यताम् ।
यन्नोपलभ्यते किञ्चिदतोऽसत् स्वप्नवन्मृषा ॥

yadi satyaṁ bhavedviśvaṁ suṣuptāvupalabhyatām |
yannopalabhyate kiñcidato'sat svapnavanmṛṣā ||

"If the world be real, why then, let it be seen in deep sleep! Since it is not at all seen in it, it is unreal, like a dream".

127. यदा मनश्चेष्टितमस्ति पुंसां तदैव विश्वं खलु भाति तेषाम् ।
मनोमयं विश्वमिदं हि तस्मात् स्वप्ने यथा जागरिते तथैव ॥

yadā manaśceṣṭitamasti puṁsāṁ tadaiva viśvaṁ khalu bhāti teṣām |
manomayaṁ viśvamidaṁ hi tasmāt svapne yathā jāgarite tathaiva ||

Only then does the world appear to men, when their minds are functioning. Therefore the world is mental, in waking, as it is in dream.

This parallel between the waking and the dream states is elaborated in the next verse.

128. यथैव जाग्रज्जगदेवमेव स्वाप्नं स्वकाले प्रतिभाति सद्वत् ।
जाग्रत्प्रपञ्चो व्यवहारयोग्यो यद्वत् तथा स्वाप्न उत स्वकाले ॥

yathaiva jāgrajjagadevameva svāpnaṁ svakāle pratibhāti sadvat |
jāgratprapañco vyavahārayogyo yadvat tathā svāpna uta svakāle ||

Just like the waking world, the dream-world seems real during the dream. Also, just like the waking world, the dream-world, in its own time, is serviceable (for the purposes of life).

The conclusion is stated in the following verse.

129.　स्वाप्नं यथा दृश्यमभिन्नमेव चित्ताद् भवेत् स्वप्नदृशो नरस्य ।
दृश्यं तथा जाग्रति वीक्षकस्य चित्ताद् भवेत् सर्वमभिन्नमेव ॥

svāpnaṁ yathā dṛśyamabhinnameva cittād bhavet svapnadṛśo narasya |
dṛśyaṁ tathā jāgrati vīkṣakasya cittād bhavet sarvamabhinnameva ||

Just as the dream-world is not other than the mind of the dreamer, so the world of things, seen in waking, is not other than the mind of the seer.

Objections to this conclusion are then noticed.

130.　मनोमयत्वे जगतः सुसिद्धे सिद्धं मृषात्वं भवतीति भीताः ।
बहिःस्थितत्वं जगतोऽज्ञमर्त्या अनेकधा साधयितुं यतन्ते ॥

manomayatve jagataḥ susiddhe siddham mṛṣātvam bhavatīti bhītāḥ |
bahiḥsthitatvaṁ jagato'jñamartyā anekadhā sādhayituṁ yatante ||

Fearing that if it be concluded that the world is mental, then its unreality will be an inescapable conclusion, ignorant (sectarians) seek to prove in a variety of ways that the world exists outside (as an independent reality).

That these disputants have no *locus standi* in this discussion is first shown.

131. जगन्मृषात्वं गदितं तु बुद्धैः स्वान्वेषणात् तुर्यपदस्य लिप्सोः ।
नान्यान् प्रतीदं ह्युपदिष्टमस्ति ततो वृथैवेह तदीयवादाः ॥

jaganmṛṣātvaṁ gaditaṁ tu buddhaiḥ svānveṣaṇāt turyapadasya lipsoḥ |
nānyān pratīdaṁ hyupadiṣṭamasti tato vṛthaiveha tadīyavādāḥ ||

The truth that the world is unreal is taught by the sages only to him who aspires to attain the highest state by the quest of the Self. It is not addressed to others and hence the contentions of these objections are wholly in vain.

The uniqueness of the Vedanta is that no one is coerced by threats of hell or otherwise to accept its highly elusive teachings, but is given out only to those whose minds are ripe and have become receptive to these metaphysical truths. Indeed the Vedanta advises ordinary people **not** to dabble in Vedantic studies. The Vedanta makes a distinction between those who are qualified to receive its Advaitic Teaching and those who are not so qualified. This is called the *Adhikara Vada*.

The difficulty in accepting the Vedantic stand-point is next pointed out.

132. स्वाप्नस्य विश्वस्य मृषात्मकत्वं
स्वप्ने न शक्नोति हि कोऽपि बोद्धुम् ।
तथैव जाग्रद्भुवनं मृषेति शक्नोति बोद्धुं नहि जाग्रदस्मिन् ॥

svāpnasya viśvasya mṛṣātmakatvaṃ svapne na śaknoti hi ko'pi boddhum |
tathaiva jāgradbhuvanaṃ mṛṣeti śaknoti boddhuṃ nahi jāgare'smin ||

No one is able to know the unreality of the dream-world during the dream itself. In the same way no one is able to know the unreality of the waking world while he is in the waking state.

The Primary Ignorance dominates the ego-mind at all times, while dreaming or in the waking state, and this is the cause of the inability of most men even to entertain the thought that the waking world may not be real. The disciple is in a better position, because of his faith in the competence of his Guru, who has experience of the egoless state to tell him the truth of the world and of the worldless egoless State.

The flaw in the contentions of these disputants is next indicated.

133. न दोषहीनं भवति प्रमाणं बहिःस्थितत्वे जगतोऽस्य किंचित् ।
साध्यं स्वपक्षं बत सिद्धवत्तु कृत्वैव वादांस्त इमे वदन्ति ॥

na doṣahīnaṃ bhavati pramāṇaṃ bahiḥsthitatve jagato'sya kiñcit |
sādhyaṃ svapakṣaṃ bata siddhavattu kṛtvaiva vādāṃsta ime vadanti ||

There is no flawless evidence tending to prove that the world exists outside (apart from the mind of its seer). But these partisans assume the truth of their contention, which is required to be proved, and then concoct arguments for their case.

The arguments put forward by these disputants, if carefully scrutinised, are found to be based on a subtle process of "begging the question" as they call it in logic.

One such argument is stated and discussed in the following verses.

134. अन्तर्हि शब्दादिकबोधजन्म बहिस्तु तत्कारणमस्ति विश्वम् ।
इत्युच्यते चेत् वद सन् कथं स्यादन्तर्बहिश्चेति विभाग एषः ॥

antarhi śabdādikabodhajanma bahistu tatkāraṇamasti viśvam |
ityucyate cet vada san kathaṁ syādantarrbahiśceti vibhāga eṣaḥ ||

If it be said that the sense-impressions of sounds and the rest arise inside the mind, while their cause, the world, lies outside, how is this division of inside and outside to be accepted as real?

This argument is not a proof, but a mere assertion. Its inadequacy is seen in that it assumes the reality of the distinction between inside and outside, which is an outcome of the assumption that the body is the Self, and in that assumption the body is assumed to be real, without offering any proof of its reality and we have seen that as the body is a part of the world, whose reality is in dispute, this assumption is improper.

135. लोकेऽनुभूतः सकलो विभागो देहाश्रयेणैव हि भाति सद्वत् ।
देहस्य सत्तां प्रति न प्रमाणं पृथक् किमप्यस्ति समर्पितं तैः ॥

loke'nubhūtaḥ sakalo vibhāgo dehāśrayeṇaiva hi bhāti sadvat |
dehasya sattāṁ prati na pramāṇaṁ pṛthak kimapyasti samarpitaṁ taiḥ ||

All the divisions experienced in the worldly life appear as real only in relation to the body. No separate proof is offered by them to prove the reality of the body!

Another argument is noticed next.

136. अल्पं मनो विश्वमिदं विशालं स्यादन्तरेतन्मनसः कथं नु ।
इत्येष वादोऽप्युत मुग्धतैव विशालमुक्तं मन एव बुद्धैः ॥

alpaṁ mano viśvamidaṁ viśālaṁ syādantaretanmanasaḥ kathaṁ nu |
ityeṣa vādo'pyuta mugdhataiva viśālamuktaṁ mana eva buddhaiḥ ||

The argument, 'The mind is small and the world is vast. How can it be within the mind?' is also mistaken. It has been taught by the Sages that it is the mind that is vast (not the world).

137. आकाशातश्चापि बृहन्मनो हि तस्मिन् हि खादीनि भवन्ति पञ्च ।
चिन्निश्चला ब्रह्म चला मनश्चेत्येवं मनो ब्रह्ममयं निरुक्तम् ॥

ākāśataścāpi bṛhanmano hi tasmin hi khādīni bhavanti pañca |
cinniścalā brahma calā manaścetyevaṁ mano brahmamayaṁ niruktam ||

The mind is vaster than even the sky, and in it are the five materials of creation, the outer space (sky) and the rest. Consciousness, in its motionless state is Brahman; the same when moving is mind; thus it has been made clear (by Bhagavan Sri Ramana) that the mind is of the nature of the Brahman.

Bhagavan Sri Ramana and the vedantas recognize three skies, namely the outer sky, the mind-sky and the sky of Pure Consciousness. This last is styled as a sky, because it contains the mind-sky, which in its turn contains the outer sky and all the worlds.

The fact that the world ceases to appear in deep sleep — wherein the exposition of the mental nature of the world is based – is sought to be countered by the following contention.

138.   सुप्तौ तवासीत् किमिदं न वेति शङ्कास्ति चेत् पृच्छ नरानसुप्तान् ।
आसीदविच्छिन्नतयैव विश्वमित्येव तेषामवगच्छ वाचा ॥

suptau tavāsīt kimidaṁ na veti śaṅkāsti cet pṛccha narānasuptān |
āsīdavicchinnatayaiva viśvamityeva teṣāmavagaccha vācā ||

"If you doubt whether or not the world existed during your sleep, then ask those that did not sleep (during the time you slept), and know from their words that the world existed continuously (without a break)."

This is considered by the Dvaitis to be an unanswerable argument. But Bhagavan Sri Ramana himself, when this argument was stated as a difficulty to be overcome, showed that this also is a case of 'begging the question', as will be shown next.

139.   एवं स्वपक्षं बत सिद्धवत्तु कृत्वैव वादोऽयमुदीर्यतेऽज्ञैः ।
अन्तर्भवन्त्येव हि तेऽप्यसुप्ता नराः प्रपञ्चेऽत्र विचार्यमाणे ॥

evaṁ svapakṣaṁ bata siddhavattu kṛtvaiva vādo'yamudīryate'jñaiḥ |
antarbhavantyeva hi te'pyasuptā narāḥ prapañce'tra vicāryamāṇe ||

This argument is put forward by the Ignorant, only by taking as proved the truth of their main contention; for the men, that slept not, are part and parcel of the world under inquiry.

What Bhagavan Sri Ramana said on this point is next given.

140.   वीक्षामहे तान् मनुजानसुप्तान् वयं प्रबुध्यैव हि नैव सुप्तौ ।
        असुप्तपुंसां न हि सत्यतायाः किञ्चित् प्रमाणं पृथगस्ति दत्तम् ॥

vīkṣāmahe tān manujānasuptān vayaṁ prabudhyaiva hi naiva suptau |
asuptapuṁsāṁ na hi satyatāyāḥ kiñcit pramāṇaṁ pṛthagasti dattam ||

We see these men, that slept not, only after we awake, not in our sleep! (and) no separate proof is offered to prove the reality of these men that did not sleep.

The reason for not accepting the common view of the reality of the world was that it is not seen during deep sleep. That same objection holds good in respect of these men who did not sleep when we slept, and hence this argument of the Dualists fails utterly. It would be a valid argument, suggests Bhagavan Sri Ramana, if we saw them during our dreamless sleep, which of course is impossible.

These men too have no valid argument for believing the world to be real, as is shown next.

141.   ते चाप्यसुप्ता मनसैव विश्वं जानन्ति नो तेन विना कदाऽपि ।
        सर्वस्य तन्मानसमेव विश्वं स्वप्ने यथा जागरितेऽपि तद्वत् ॥

te cāpyasuptā manasaiva viśvaṁ jānanti no tena vinā kadā'pi |
sarvasya tanmānasameva viśvaṁ svapne yathā jāgarite'pi tadvat ||

Even those that remained awake (while we slept) know the world only by the mind and never otherwise. Hence for all alike, the world is only mental, in waking, as in dream.

Another argument is stated and refuted next.

142. भात्येकरूपं हि जगद् बहूनामित्युच्यते चास्य बहिःस्थितत्वम्‌।
      न वीक्षकाणां बहुता यथार्थेत्युक्त्यैष वादो गुरुणा निरस्तः ॥

bhātyekarūpaṁ hi jagad bahūnāmityucyate cāsya bahiḥsthitatvam |
na vīkṣakāṇām bahutā yathārthetyuktyaiṣa vādo guruṇā nirastaḥ ||

The objectivity of the world is also asserted on the ground that it appears the same to diverse seers. But the Master refutes the argument by asserting that the diversity of observers is unreal.

This diversity of souls is part of the world-illusion, and is hence no more real than the rest of it. The truth on this point is expounded by Bhagavan Sri Ramana in the next verse.

143. अनेकतैषा मनसा कृतैव स्वप्ने यथा जागरितेऽप्यबोधात्‌।
      नानेकता भाति हि वीक्षकाणां सुषुप्तिभावे मनसा विहीने ॥

anekataiṣā manasā kṛtaiva svapne yathā jāgarite'pyabodhāt |
nānekatā bhāti hi vīkṣakāṇām suṣuptibhāve manasā vihīne ||

As in dream, so in waking, this diversity (of souls) is only a mental creation, since in deep sleep, which is mind-free, this diversity does not appear.

144. मनः प्रपञ्चं सृजति स्वयं हि स्वप्ने यथा जागरिते तथैव ।
स्वसृष्टमेवेति मनो न वेत्ति स्वप्ने यथा जागरितेऽपि तद्वत् ॥

manaḥ prapañcam sṛjati svayam hi svapne yathā jāgarite tathaiva |
svasṛṣṭameveti mano na vetti svapne yathā jāgarite'pi tadvat ||

The mind itself creates the world in waking, as it does in dream. But the mind does not know that this is its own creation, in waking, as in dream.

145. यथेप्सितं स्रष्टुमशक्तमेव मनोऽवशं सत् सृजति प्रपञ्चम् ।
अतो हि विश्वं सदिति प्रतीत्या भ्रान्तं भृशं संसरति स्वयं च ॥

yathepsitam sraṣṭumaśaktameva mano'vaśam sat sṛjati prapañcam |
ato hi viśvam saditi pratītyā bhrāntam bhṛśam samsarati svayam ca ||

The mind creates the world subject to a superior power (Avidya-Maya) and therefore is unable to create it to its own liking. The mind, believing the world to be real, is deluded and suffers the woes of samsara.

That the mind has this anomalous power as well as weakness is shown next.

146. मनोरथे नाटकवीक्षणे च तथा कथासंश्रवणेऽपि चित्तम् ।
प्रत्येति सत्यं सकलं स्वसृष्टमेष स्वभावो मनसो हि नित्यः ॥

manorathe nāṭakavīkṣaṇe ca tathā kathāsaṁśravaṇe'pi cittam |
pratyeti satyaṁ sakalaṁ svasṛṣṭameṣa svabhāvo manaso hi nityaḥ ||

This is the very nature of the mind, that it takes as real all that it creates, as is seen in day-dreaming, witnessing dramas, or listening to stories.

These instances, taken from our waking experience itself, prove this self-torturing quality of the mind, which is worse in dreams.

The conclusion is then stated.

147. दृष्टेर्न सृष्टिः पृथगस्ति काचिद् दृष्टिश्च सृष्टिर्द्वयमेकमेव ।
दृष्टेर्विरामो निधनं हि नान्यन्नश्येद्धि विश्वं विजतत्त्वबोधात् ॥

dṛṣṭerna sṛṣṭiḥ pṛthagasti kācid dṛṣṭiśca sṛṣṭirdvayamekameva |
dṛṣṭervirāmo nidhanaṁ hi nānyannaśyeddhi viśvaṁ vijatattvabodhāt ||

Creation is not other than seeing; seeing and creating are one and the same process. Annihilation is only the cessation of seeing and nothing else; for the world comes to an end by the right awareness of Oneself.

The next step is the demonstration that the mind also is unreal. The next verse begins this exposition.

148. सिद्धे प्रपञ्चस्य मनोमयत्वे सचेन्मनः सन् भविता प्रपञ्चः ।
असन् प्रपञ्चोऽपि मनस्त्वसचेत् ततो विचार्या मनसोऽथ सत्ता ॥

siddhe prapañcasya manomayatve saccenmanaḥ san bhavitā prapañcaḥ |
asan prapañco'pi manastvasaccet tato vicāryā manaso'tha sattā ||

As it is settled that the world is mental, the
world will be real if the mind were real; but if the
mind is unreal, then the world also would be
unreal. Hence it becomes needful to inquire
whether the mind is real.

But there is a preliminary question to be taken up and
answered, namely as to the test or tests of reality to be applied.

149. कैर्लक्षणैः स्यात् सदसद्विवेक इत्यत्र पूर्वं परिशीलनीयम् ।
सल्लक्षणं लौकिकसम्मतं यत् तन्न प्रमाणं खलु सद्विचारे ॥

kairlakṣaṇaiḥ syāt sadasadviveka ityatra pūrvaṁ pariśīlanīyam |
sallakṣaṇaṁ laukikasammataṁ yat tanna pramāṇaṁ khalu sadvicāre ||

First it is needful to inquire by what tests one
can distinguish the real from the unreal, because,
in (this) inquiry as to what is real, the test of reality
that is approved of by the worldly ones is not valid.

150. कीरो यथा शाल्मलिभूरुहस्य लुब्धः फले वञ्चित एव याति ।
एवं स्वयं वञ्चयतः स्वमेव मतं प्रमाणं भविता कथं नु ॥

kīro yathā śālmalibhūruhasya lubdhaḥ phale vañcita eva yāti |
evaṁ svayaṁ vañcayataḥ svameva mataṁ pramāṇaṁ bhavitā kathaṁ nu ||

The parrot, who is wishful to eat the fruit of the silk-cotton tree, (at last) goes away disappointed. How can the beliefs of one, who thus deludes himself, be accepted as reasonable?

This conduct of the parrot, whether true or not, is proverbial. And man is in the same case. He expects to reap unalloyed happiness in the worldly life and is always disappointed, thus demonstrating his capacity for self-deception. Philosophers will not be philosophers if they accepted the credulous views of unthinking men.

Unless used under the guidance of a perfectly competent Guru, the worldly means of knowledge are certain to prove misleading. This truth is expressed in the next verse.

151. धीरिन्द्रियाण्यप्युत मानसं च भवन्त्यविद्यापरिचारकाणि ।
अतः प्रमाणानि हि लौकिकानि नैवोपकुर्वन्ति विचारणेऽस्मिन् ॥

dhīrindriyāṇyapyuta mānasaṁ ca bhavantyavidyāparicārakāṇi |
ataḥ pramāṇāni hi laukikāni naivopakurvanti vicāraṇe'smin ||

The intellect, the sense-organs, and the mind are servants of the primary Ignorance. Hence the worldly methods of seeking knowledge do not at all favour success in this inquiry.

The worldly means of knowledge, called *proofs*, are direct perception, inference, analogy, tradition and so on, as understood by logicians and philosophers. In Vedantic reasoning these are not to be relied upon, for the reason stated, namely that they are naturally the servants of the

Ignorance, having been created in order to protect and confirm that Ignorance.

152. सल्लक्षणं लौकिकसम्मतं यत् तदेतदाविद्यकमित्यसाधु ।
साधोः प्रमाणं गदितो हि बुद्धैः सत्यत्वमिथ्यात्वविभाग एव ॥

sallakṣaṇaṁ laukikasammataṁ yat tadetadāvidyakamityasādhu |
sādhoḥ pramāṇaṁ gadito hi buddhaiḥ satyatvamithyātvavibhāga eva ||

The characteristic of reality, that is considered good by the worldly, is unreliable because it is a child of the Ignorance. For the Sadhaka the reliable test for distinguishing Truth from falsehood is that which the Sages have stated.

That test is next set forth.

153. भासा स्वया यद्विलसत्यजस्रं विना विकारं च लयोदयाभ्याम् ।
तदेव सत्यं हि ततोऽन्यथा तु सर्वं मृषैवेति वदन्ति बुद्धाः ॥

bhāsā svayā yadvilasatyajasraṁ vinā vikāraṁ ca layodayābhyām |
tadeva satyaṁ hi tato'nyathā tu sarvaṁ mṛṣaiveti vadanti buddhāḥ ||

That which shines by its own light (of consciousness) without change, and without setting and rising, is alone Real. All that is not so is unreal. So say the Sages.

This is the test approved of in Vedantic metaphysics and is that which is used in the Upanishads.
The Bhagavad Gita is next referred to.

154. कदाऽप्यसत्यस्य भवेन्न सत्ता भवेदसत्ता न सतः कदाऽपि ।
इत्येवमूचे सदसद्विवेकं गीतासु कृष्णो भगवान् स्वयं हि ॥

kadā'pyasatyasya bhavenna sattā bhavedasattā na sataḥ kadā'pi |
ityevamūce sadasadvivekaṁ gītāsu kṛṣṇo bhagavān svayaṁ hi ||

'There is never any (real) existence for the unreal, neither is there any non-existence for the Real'. Thus Bhagavan Sri Krishna Himself stated the distinction between the real and the unreal.

Thus things that appear at certain times and disappear at other times are excluded from the category of the Real.

155. आद्यन्तयोर्भावविवर्जितं यन्मध्येऽपि तद् भावविहीनमेव ।
यद्देशकालप्रमितं विभाति तत्सत्यताधीर्बत मुग्धतैव ॥

ādyantayorbhāvavivarjitaṁ yanmadhye'pi tad bhāvavihīnameva |
yaddeśakālapramitaṁ vibhāti tatsatyatādhīrbata mugdhataiva ||

What had no existence in the beginning and will not exist after sometime is non-existent even in the intervening period (during which it seems to exist). The notion that anything which appears limited in space or time is real is ignorance.

156. सत्योपमानं गदितं सुवर्णं मिथ्योपमानानि विभूषणानि ।
सत्यं सुवर्णं रुचकान्यपेक्ष्य विनश्वरत्वाद्रुचकानि मिथ्या ॥

satyopamānaṁ gaditaṁ suvarṇam mithyopamānāni vibhūṣaṇāni |
satyaṁ suvarṇam rucakānyapekṣya vinaśvaratvādrucakāni mithyā ||

The analogy for the real is gold and for the unreal the analogies are jewels. Gold is real in comparison with jewels; the latter are unreal because they are perishable.

157. सुवर्णमासन् रुचकानि पूर्वं तदेव मध्येऽपि तदेव चान्ते ।
असन्ति सत्ये विलसन्ति सद्वत् स्वर्णे यथा सन्ति विभूषणानि ॥

suvarṇamāsan rucakāni pūrvaṁ tadeva madhye'pi tadeva cānte |
asanti satye vilasanti sadvat svarṇe yathā santi vibhūṣaṇāni ||

The jewels were gold before (being made), and they are gold even in the middle (when they appear as jewels) and also at the end, (when they are melted). (Thus) the Unrealities appear as real on a substratum of the Real, just as unreal jewels appear as real in a substratum of gold (which is comparatively real).

This is one of the analogies employed in the Chhandogya Upanishad to illustrate the Truth taught here, that the one Supreme Reality, which is the Real Self, is the substratum of the world appearance.

158. रीत्याऽनया विश्वमिदं मनश्च द्वयं च मिथ्यैव परीक्षमाणे ।
इत्येवमर्थो भगवत्तमेन दिष्टो यथा तत्क्रम उच्यतेऽत्र ॥

rītyā'nayā viśvamidaṁ manaśca dvayaṁ ca mithyaiva parīkṣamāṇe |
ityevamartho bhagavattamena diṣṭo yathā tatkrama ucyate'tra ||

If the two, the world and the mind, are scrutinised in this wise, they are found to be unreal. The process of this demonstration, as taught by the Most Holy One (Bhagavan Sri Ramana) is here set forth.

159.   भास्यं जगद् भासकमस्य चेतो लयोदयौ द्वे भजतः सहैव ।
       न भात्यविच्छिन्नतया द्वयं चेत्यतो द्वयं चापि मृषेति विद्यात् ॥

bhāsyaṁ jagad bhāsakamasya ceto layodayau dve bhajataḥ sahaiva |
na bhātyavicchinnatayā dvayaṁ cetyato dvayaṁ cāpi mṛṣeti vidyāt ||

The world which is caused to shine and the light, namely the mind, which caused the world to shine, arise and set together (as one); also this pair does not appear uninterruptedly; therefore the pair should be known to be unreal.

160.   भवेत् तु यद्यद् विरलप्रकाशं तत्तज्जडत्वेन परप्रकाश्यं ।
       जडस्य सर्वस्य च भासकं यत् स्वयम्प्रभं तद्धि चितिस्वभावम् ॥

bhavet tu yadyad viralaprakāśaṁ tattajjaḍatvena paraprakāśyam |
jaḍasya sarvasya ca bhāsakaṁ yat svayamprabhaṁ taddhi citisvabhāvam ||

Whatever shines intermittently is insentient and therefore shines by the light of another. That, by which all insentient things shine, is self-shining, being consciousness by Nature.

Here the light meant is not that of the sun, moon, or lamps, but the light of consciousness.

In the test of reality, two conditions were set out, namely continuous, uninterrupted shining and the capacity of being self-shining. The two are only one being inseparable. The first was shown to be fulfilled by the Supreme Reality alone. The second condition also is here shown to be fulfilled by It alone, so that It alone can be Vedantically real, and nothing else, neither the mind, nor the world.

161. स्वतत्त्वबोधादहमादिनाशे यच्छिष्यते शान्तपदे परस्मिन् ।
सत्यं तदन्यन्निखिलं मृषेति जानीमहेऽस्मद् गुरुदेववाग्भिः ॥

svatattvabodhādahamādināśe yacchiṣyate śāntapade parasmin |
satyaṁ tadanyannikhilaṁ mṛṣeti jānīmahe'smad gurudevavāgbhiḥ ||

We know by the words of our divine Guru that That alone is real, which survives in that state of Peace, which is the highest, on the destruction of the ego and the rest, consequent on the realization of one's own True Nature, and that all else is unreal.

Thus by the application of the Vedantic Test of Reality it has been shown that the inseparable pair, the mind and the world, is unreal, and that the Real self, which is the Brahman, is alone Real.

Now a doubt is raised, and is set at rest in the following verses:

162. मनोऽपि मिथ्या यदि शून्यतैव प्राप्ता सुषुप्तौ न हि किञ्चिदस्ति ।
ये वादमेवं समुदाहरन्ति स्वानेव तेऽज्ञा बत विस्मरन्ति ॥

mano'pi mithyā yadi śūnyataiva prāptā suṣuptau na hi kiñcidasti |
ye vādamevaṁ samudāharanti svāneva te'jñā bata vismaranti ||

"If even the mind be unreal, then it will follow that what remains is only a Void, since in deep sleep there is nothing at all." Those who raise this contention are committing the mistake of forgetting themselves!

163. शून्यत्वमेतद्विदितं कथं नु नैवास्य साक्षी यदि कश्चिदस्ति ।
नित्साक्षिका नैव हि शून्यतेयमतो न शून्यत्वमिदं यथार्थम् ॥

śūnyatvametadviditaṁ kathaṁ nu naivāsya sākṣī yadi kaścidasti |
nissākṣikā naiva hi śūnyateyamato na śūnyatvamidaṁ yathārtham ||

How can this 'void' be known at all, if there be no one to witness it? This 'void' is certainly not without a witness, and hence this void is not the final Reality.

164. शून्यत्ववादो भगवत्तमेन निस्संशयं ह्यस्ति निरस्त एवम् ।
नास्माकमत्रास्ति हि कापि शङ्का तुर्येऽस्ति शिष्टः खलु
सत्य आत्मा ॥

śūnyatvavādo bhagavattamena nissaṁśayaṁ hyasti nirasta evam |
nāsmākamatrāsti hi kā'pi śaṅkā turye'sti śiṣṭaḥ khalu satya ātmā ||

This doctrine of the 'void' has thus been clearly refuted by the most holy one; for us there is not the least doubt on this point, because (as shown by Him), there is the Real Self, the Sole Survivor in the Supreme State.

165. आत्मा स्वयञ्ज्योतिरहंस्वरूपो भाति स्वभासा हृदि सर्वजन्तोः ।
सर्वोऽप्यतः स्वं समवैति सन्तं नास्मीति को न्वस्ति वदन्नृलोके ॥

ātmā svayañjyotirahaṁsvarūpo bhāti svabhāsā hṛdi sarvajantoḥ |
sarvo'pyataḥ svaṁ samavaiti santaṁ nāsmīti ko nvasti vadannṛloke ||

In the heart of every living creature the self-shining Real Self shines by his own light (of consciousness) as 'I', and hence everyone knows himself as real. Who is there in the world of men, who says: 'I do not exist!'

Thus it is made clear that the Self is self-revealed. This means that knowledge of the Self is by Direct Experience and not by inference. But many philosophers seem to be unaware of this.

166. मन्ये ततोऽस्मीत्यनुभूयते तु वृत्त्या धियः कैश्चन नैजसत्ता ।
अमी गजं यान्तमुपेक्ष्य मन्दाः पदानि वीक्ष्य प्रतियन्ति पश्चात् ॥

manye tato'smītyanubhūyate tu vṛttyā dhiyaḥ kaiścana naijasattā |
amī gajaṁ yāntamupekṣya mandāḥ padāni vīkṣya pratiyanti paścāt ||

The existence of their own Self is inferred by some from mental functioning, by the reasoning: 'I think, therefore I am.' These men are like those dull-witted ones who ignore the elephant when it goes past and become convinced afterwards by looking at the foot-prints.*

---

* Here the reference is to the French Philosopher, Descartes.

167.   सर्वानुभूताऽस्ति हि नैजसत्ता सुषुप्तिभावे मनसा विहीने ।
सुखं मया सुप्तमिति ब्रुवाणः सुखस्मृतिं च प्रकटीकरोति ॥

sarvānubhūtā'sti hi naijasattā suṣuptibhāve manasā vihīne |
sukhaṁ mayā suptamiti bruvāṇaḥ sukhasmṛtiṁ ca prakaṭīkaroti ||

Indeed every one experiences his own existence during deep sleep, where the mind is absent. Also the sleeper manifests remembrance of the happiness (of sleep), saying 'I slept happily'.

168.   अन्यानुभूतस्मरणं कुतः स्यात् स्वेनानुभूतं हि सुखं सुषुप्तेः ।
अन्योऽहमन्यः पुरुषः सुषुप्तेः पूर्वं य आसीदिति को नु वक्ति ॥

anyānubhūtasmaraṇaṁ kutaḥ syāt svenānubhūtaṁ hi sukhaṁ suṣupteḥ |
anyo'hamanyaḥ puruṣaḥ suṣupteḥ pūrvaṁ ya āsīditi ko nu vakti ||

How can anyone remember the happiness experienced by someone else? The happiness of sleep was surely enjoyed by oneself. Does anyone say: "He that was before going to sleep is not the same person as myself?"

As Bhagavan Sri Ramana himself has pointed out, when Johnson goes to sleep, Benson does not awake, but only Johnson.

169.   लयोदयाभ्यां रहिते हि तस्मिन् मनः सविश्वं लयमेति सुप्तौ ।
उदेति तस्माच्च पुनः प्रबोधे शून्यत्ववादोऽयमतो मृषैव ॥

layodayābhyāṁ rahite hi tasmin manaḥ saviśvaṁ layameti suptau |
udeti tasmācca punaḥ prabodhe śūnyatvavādo'yamato mṛṣaiva ||

The mind, with the universe, merges in Him in deep sleep, and from Him it rises again (with the universe) on waking. Hence the creed of the void is untrue.

170. आधारसद्वस्तु विना कथं नु विश्वं मनश्चेत्युभयं च भायात्।
रज्जुं विना कोन्विह वीक्षतेऽहिं शुक्तिं विना पश्यति को नु
रौप्यम् ॥

ādhārasadvastu vinā kathaṁ nu viśvaṁ manaścetyubhayaṁ ca bhāyāt |
rajjuṁ vinā konviha vīkṣate'hiṁ śuktiṁ vinā paśyati ko nu raupyam ||

Without a supporting substratum, how can the two, the universe and the mind, appear at all? Is there anyone who sees the serpent without its basis, the rope, or one who sees silver without its basis, the oyster shell?

171. अस्तित्वभाने भुवनस्य यच्छदस्त्येव सत् किञ्चन चित्स्वरूपम्।
नो चेत् कथं धीरुदियान्मृषेदमस्तीति भातीत्यपि लौकिकानाम् ॥

astitvabhāne bhuvanasya yacchadastyeva sat kiñcana citsvarūpam |
no cet kathaṁ dhīrudiyānmṛṣedamastīti bhātītyapi laukikānām ||

Surely there does exist a Reality – Consciousness, which lends (an appearance of) existence and shining to the universe (including the mind). Else how can worldly people have the notion that this unreal universe exists and shines?

172. तद्भास्यमेव द्वितयं च यस्मात् स्वयम्प्रभं तच्चितिरूपमेव ।
      नात्मस्वरूपात् पृथगस्ति सत्यं स्वयम्प्रभं किञ्चन कुत्रचिद्वा ॥

tadbhāsyameva dvitayaṃ ca yasmāt svayamprabhaṃ taccitirūpameva |
nātmasvarūpāt pṛthagasti satyaṃ svayamprabhaṃ kiñcana kutracidvā ||

Because these two shine only by His Light, therefore that One is Self-shining Consciousness. Apart from (That) Self there is nothing else, anywhere, which is self-shining.

173. बोधोदये स्वात्मनि भासमाने नार्केन्दुनक्षत्रगणा विभान्ति ।
      तस्यैव भासा खलु भान्ति तानि बहिर्मुखस्याज्ञजनस्य लोके ॥

bodhodaye svātmani bhāsamāne nārkendunakṣatragaṇā vibhānti |
tasyaiva bhāsā khalu bhānti tāni bahirmukhasyājñajanasya loke ||

When the Real Self shines on the dawn of right awareness, neither the sun nor the moon nor the stars shine. By his light alone do these shine here for the ignorant one, whose mind is turned outwards.

174. चिता यया भाति जगत् समस्तं भासाऽपि यस्या मनसो मनस्त्वम् ।
      सैवात्मरूपं भवतीति हेतोरात्मास्तितायां न हि काऽपि शङ्का ॥

citā yayā bhāti jagat samastaṃ bhāsā'pi yasyā manaso manastvam |
saivātmarūpaṃ bhavatīti hetorātmāstitāyāṃ na hi kā'pi śaṅkā ||

There is not the least doubt about the existence of the Real Self, because that same (Pure) Consciousness, by which the whole world shines, and by whose Light the mind becomes mind, is the Self.

175.　अस्मीति बोधं न रुणद्ध्यविद्या बोधोऽहमस्मीति तु बोधमेव ।
　　　स्वं वेत्ति सन्तं खलु सर्व एव विहाय वैज्ञानिकवादमुग्धान् ॥

asmīti bodhaṁ na ruṇaddhyavidyā bodho'hamasmīti tu bodhameva |
svaṁ vetti santaṁ khalu sarva eva vihāya vaijñānikavādamugdhān ||

The Ignorance does not obstruct the awareness of 'I AM', but only the awareness of the fact 'I AM AWARENESS', since everyone – with the exception of those deluded by the scientific creed – knows of his own existence.

176.　नित्योऽव्ययः सन्ततभानकः स्वः
　　　सर्वास्ववस्थास्वपि सत्य आस्ते ।
　　　तस्मिन्नधिष्ठानसति ह्यशेषमारोपितं विश्वमिदं विभाति ॥

nityo'vyayaḥ santatabhānakaḥ svaḥ sarvāsvavasthāsvapi satya āste |
tasminnadhiṣṭhānasati hyaśeṣamāropitaṁ viśvamidaṁ vibhāti ||

The eternal, unchanging ever-shining Self persists continuously as the Real through all the varying states. Superimposed on Him, the Substratum, does the whole world shine.

177.　पूर्णस्य तस्यैव चिदात्मकस्य सत्यस्य सत्तामुपजीव्य सद्वत् ।
　　　समानसं विश्वमिदं विभाति स्वाविद्यया मोहितमानसानाम् ॥

pūrṇasya tasyaiva cidātmakasya satyasya sattāmupajīvya sadvat |
samānasaṁ viśvamidaṁ vibhāti svāvidyayā mohitamānasānām ||

It is by borrowing the reality of this Reality, which is Perfect Consciousness, that this world and the mind appear as real to all those whose minds are deluded, due to their ignorance of their own selves.

Bhagavan's own pronouncement is next quoted.

178.   ब्रह्मैककं सत् सकलस्य जन्तोः स्वयं सदैवाहमहन्तयाऽन्तः ।
भात्यात्मरूपेण हि नान्य आत्मेत्येषाऽस्ति वाणी
भगवत्तमस्य ॥

brahmaikakaṁ sat sakalasya jantoḥ svayaṁ sadaivāhamahantayā'ntaḥ |
bhātyātmarūpeṇa hi nānya ātmetyeṣā'sti vāṇī bhagavattamasya ||

Here is the utterance of the Most Holy One: 'The Brahman, which is only One, Itself shines inside (in the Heart) of all creatures as the Real Self in the form, 'I', 'I'; there is no other Self.'

179.   चैतन्यमस्मीति मदीयरूपमिति श्रुता मोससनामकेन ।
या देववाणी प्रथिताऽस्ति तस्या भावोऽयमेवेत्यपि सोऽयमूचे ॥

caitanyamasmīti madīyarūpamiti śrutā mosasanāmakena |
yā devavāṇī prathitā'sti tasyā bhāvo'yamevetyapi so'yamūce ||

He also said: This same is the meaning of the utterance of the famous Heavenly Voice which told Moses, "My real nature is just the Consciousness, "I AM'.

180.   विज्ञाय सत्यात्मतया तमेव ब्रह्मात्मकं तुर्यपदे लसन्तम् ।
लब्ध्वेव कामानखिलान् सहैव सदैव तृप्ता हि लसन्ति बुद्धाः ॥

vijñāya satyātmatayā tameva brahmātmakaṁ turyapade lasantam |
labdhveva kāmānakhilān sahaiva sadaiva tṛptā hi lasanti buddhāḥ ||

The sages, becoming aware of Him, who is
Brahman, shining in the Supreme State, as the
Real Self, are ever contented as if they had had
all their desires fulfilled simultaneously.

The perfect happiness in which the sages live is
inexplicable in any other way.

181.   सैषा विशुद्धा चितिरात्मरूपा स्वाज्ञस्य विश्वाकृतिका हि भाति ।
सत्यात्मनीत्थं विपरीतबुद्धिर्निजस्वरूपानवबोधमूला ॥

saiṣā viśuddhā citirātmarūpā svājñasya viśvākṛtikā hi bhāti |
satyātmanīttham viparītabuddhirnijasvarūpānavabodhamūlā ||

This Pure Consciousness, which is the Real
Self, appears to him that knows not Himself, as
the world. This misunderstanding of the true
nature of the Real Self is rooted in the ignorance
of one's own Self.

182.   आविद्यकं विश्वमिदं सदैव समावृणोत्येव हि तत्स्वरूपम् ।
धीरिन्द्रियाण्यप्युत मानसं च भवन्त्यविद्यापरिचारकाणि ॥

āvidyakaṁ viśvamidam sadaiva samāvṛṇotyeva hi tatsvarūpam |
dhīrindriyāṇyapyuta mānasaṁ ca bhavantyavidyāparicārakāṇi ||

This world, the outcome of the ignorance, of course conceals the Truth of That (Self); and the intellect, the senses and the mind are the servants of (that) ignorance.

183.   अतः प्रमाणानि हि लौकिकानि प्रत्यक्षमैतिह्यमुतानुमानम् ।
प्रतारणायैव भवन्ति जन्तोर्नैवोपकुर्वन्ति हि बोधलब्ध्यै ॥

ataḥ pramāṇāni hi laukikāni pratyakṣamaitihyamutānumānam |
pratāraṇāyaiva bhavanti jantornaivopakurvanti hi bodhalabdhyai ||

Hence it is that the worldly means of proof, namely direct perception, tradition and inference, serve only to deceive the creature; they do not at all subserve the attainment of Right Awareness.

184.   अतः किमाश्चर्यमिदं यदज्ञा मत्वा स्वतः सत्यमिमं प्रपञ्चम् ।
संसारिणं च प्रतियन्ति पूर्णं शिवं सदात्मानमसङ्गमेकम् ॥

ataḥ kimāścaryamidaṁ yadajñā matvā svataḥ satyamimaṁ prapañcam |
saṁsāriṇaṁ ca pratiyanti pūrṇaṁ śivaṁ sadātmānamasaṅgamekam ||

Hence where is the wonder that the Ignorant, thinking the world to be real in its own right, also become persuaded that the Real Self, the Ever-Blissful one who has no wants, unrelated and alone, is in bondage to worldliness.

185.   निरुक्तमेवं जगतो मृषात्वं नैकोपमानेन सुबोधमस्ति ।
अतः स्फुटीकर्तुमिदं मुमुक्षोस्तिस्रो गुरुवक्त्युपमाः क्रमेण ॥

niruktamevaṁ jagato mṛṣātvaṁ naikopamānena subodhamasti |
ataḥ sphuṭīkartumidaṁ mumukṣostisro gururvaktyupamāḥ krameṇa ||

The unreality of the world, which has thus been expounded, is not easy to understand by the aid of one single simile. Hence, to make this intelligible to the Sadhaka, the holy Guru gives three similes in succession.

186. भ्रमः प्रपञ्चस्य सदात्मरूपे रज्ज्वां यथाऽहेरिति दर्शितेऽर्थे।
उक्तोपमाया विषमत्वबुद्ध्या शिष्यस्य शङ्का समुदेति काचित्॥

bhramaḥ prapañcasya sadātmarūpe rajjvāṁ yathā'heriti darśite'rthe |
uktopamāyā viṣamatvabuddhyā śiṣyasya śaṅkā samudeti kācit ||

When it is explained that the illusory appearance of the world is like that of the serpent in the rope, a doubt occurs to the disciple, because he thinks that the simile is not in all forms.

187. सर्पभ्रमः शाम्यति रज्जुबोधान्नैवं जगद् भ्रान्तिरपैति साधोः।
श्रुत्याऽपि युक्त्या विदितेऽपि तत्त्वे पूर्वं यथा दृश्यत एव विश्वम्॥

sarpabhramaḥ śāmyati rajjubodhānnaivaṁ jagad bhrāntirapaiti sādhoḥ |
śrutyā'pi yuktyā vidite'pi tattve pūrvaṁ yathā dṛśyata eva viśvam ||

The illusory notion of the serpent ceases when the rope is known (to be the truth). Not so does the world-illusion cease for the aspirant. Even after the truth (the unreality of the world) is known by the help of Revelation and by arguments, still the world continues to appear (as real).

There is an explanation for this apparent anomaly, which is given next.

188.   जगद्भ्रमो नैति परोक्षबोधान्निरास्पदेयं खलु तेन शङ्का ।
तथाऽपि सन्देहनिवारणाय गुरुर्द्वितीयामुपमां ब्रवीति ॥

jagadbhramo naiti parokṣabodhānnirāspadeyaṁ khalu tena śaṅkā |
tathā'pi sandehanivāraṇāya gururdvitīyāmupamāṁ bravīti ||

The world-illusion does not come to an end by theoretical knowledge and hence there is no room for this doubt. Yet in order to remove this doubt the Guru gives a second simile.

189.   भूयोऽपि वीक्षा मृगतृष्णिकाया अस्त्येव तत्त्वे विदितेऽपि तस्याः ।
एवं निरस्तेऽपि च संशयेऽस्मिन्नुदेति भूयोऽपि च संशयोऽत्र ॥

bhūyo'pi vīkṣā mṛgatṛṣṇikāyā astyeva tattve vidite'pi tasyāḥ |
evaṁ niraste'pi ca saṁśaye'sminnudeti bhūyo'pi ca saṁśayo'tra ||

Even after the truth of it becomes known, there persists the vision of water in the mirage. But even when this doubt is cleared, another doubt arises (in its place).

190.   कार्योपयोगीनि हि जागतानि वस्तूनि नैवं तु मरीचिकाम्भः ।
अत्रोच्यते स्वप्रसमीक्षितानि कार्योपयोगीनि तथाऽपि मिथ्या ॥

kāryopayogīni hi jāgatāni vastūni naivaṁ tu marīcikāmbhaḥ |
atrocyate svapnasamīkṣitāni kāryopayogīni tathā'pi mithyā ||

It is objected: 'Worldly objects serve some useful purposes; but the water of the mirage is not so'. To this the reply is: 'Things seen in a dream are useful (in the dream), but all the same they are unreal.'

191.   कार्योपयोगीन्यपि तद्वदेव मिथ्यैव वस्तून्यपि जागतानि ।
स्वप्नो ह्ययं जागरिताभिधानः स्वाज्ञाननिद्रावशगस्य जन्तोः ॥

kāryopayogīnyapi tadvadeva mithyaiva vastūnyapi jāgatāni |
svapno hyayaṁ jāgaritābhidhānaḥ svājñānanidrāvaśagasya jantoḥ ||

In the same way the objects of the world, though useful (during their pendency), are unreal. This state, called waking, is really a dream seen by the creature who is a victim of the sleep which consists in the ignorance of the Real Self.

192.   निद्रेयमज्ञानमयी न यावद् व्यपैति साधोरपरोक्षबोधात् ।
स्वप्नोऽनुवर्तेत हि जागराख्यो यस्मिञ्जगत् सत्यवदेव भाति ॥

nidreyamajñānamayī na yāvad vyapaiti sādhoraparokṣabodhāt |
svapno'nuvarteta hi jāgarākhyo yasmiñjagat satyavadeva bhāti ||

So long as this sleep of ignorance does not cease by Direct Experience (of the Truth of the Self), this dream called waking, wherein the world appears as real, will continue.

The test of reality is again repeated in this context.

193. ज्ञेयं हि सत्यत्वमबाधितत्वं बाध्यत्वमेवात्र मृषात्वलिङ्गम् ।
      आत्मैव सन्नित्यमबाधितत्वान्मृषा जगद् बाध्यतयाऽऽत्मबोधे ॥

jñeyaṁ hi satyatvamabādhitatvaṁ bādhyatvamevātra mṛṣātvaliṅgam |
ātmaiva sannityamabādhitatvānmṛṣā jagad bādhyatayā"tmabodhe ||

It must be understood that reality is freedom
from being contradicted and unreality is being
subject to extinction. The Self alone is Real,
because He never ceases to be; the world is unreal
because it ceases to appear when there is the
Awareness of the Self.

The nature of the world's unreality is next further
clarified.

194. आत्मन्यधिष्ठानसति ह्यशेषमारोपितं विश्वमिदं विभाति ।
      अतो न विश्वं नरशृङ्गतुल्यं सत्यं स्वतो नेत्युपदिश्यते तु ॥

ātmanyadhiṣṭhānasati hyaśeṣamāropitaṁ viśvamidaṁ vibhāti |
ato na viśvaṁ naraśṛṅgatulyaṁ satyaṁ svato netyupadiśyate tu ||

The whole universe appears as a superimposition
on the Real Self, the Substratum, which is the Reality,
and hence it is not like a man's horn. But it is taught
that it is not real in its own right.

This distinction is important. There are two kinds of
unreality. The utterly unreal, which is never conceivable as

real, is one which has no substratum like a man's or hare's horn. The other kind is that which can and does appear as real like the rope snake. The world's unreality is of the latter kind. It is not real in its own right, since it owes its appearance as real to its substratum. This point will be dealt with later.

So far the question of the reality of the world as a whole has been discussed and the conclusion has been reached as stated above. Bhagavan Sri Ramana next deals with the same question in detail and thus confirms this conclusion.

195.　भेदैरनन्तैः प्रविभक्तमेव प्रतीयते विश्वमिदं हि सर्वम् ।
　　　भेदा इमे चापि भवन्ति मिथ्येत्यर्थं गुरुर्नो विशदीकरोति ॥

bhedairanantaiḥ pravibhaktameva pratīyate viśvamidaṁ hi sarvam |
bhedā ime cāpi bhavanti mithyetyarthaṁ gururno viśadīkaroti ||

This whole world appears divided into an endless variety of parts. Our Holy Guru makes it clear that all these parts also are unreal, (when taken separately).

196.　भेदं च जीवेश्वरयोस्तथाऽन्यान् प्रत्येति भेदान् मन एव सर्वान् ।
　　　भेदप्रतीतिर्मनसो हि धर्मो भावेऽमनस्के न हि सन्ति भेदाः ॥

bhedaṁ ca jīveśvarayostathā'nyān pratyeti bhedān mana eva sarvān |
bhedapratītirmanaso hi dharmo bhāve'manaske na hi santi bhedāḥ ||

It is the mind that knows the difference between the individual soul and God and all other differences. It is the nature of the mind to perceive differences. In the Mind-free state there are no differences.

Differences are perceived in waking and in dream, where the mind is present, not in deep sleep, nor in the Supreme State, because there the mind is absent, as shown already.

This appearance of difference is next traced to its root, which is stated.

197.   मनः प्रतीत्यात्मकमेव तस्मादज्ञानुभूतं बत भेदजातम् ।
सर्वप्रतीतेर्मनसस्तु मूलं भवत्यनात्मात्मभिदाप्रतीतिः ॥

manaḥ pratītyātmakameva tasmādajñānubhūtaṁ bata bhedajātam |
sarvapratītermanasastu mūlaṁ bhavatyanātmātmabhidāpratītiḥ ||

Hence the totality of all these differences, experienced by the unwise consists only in the mind's perception. All the mind's perceptions have their root in the perception of the difference between the self and the not-self.

198.   सैषा शरीरोऽहमिति प्रतीतिः संसारवृक्षस्य निदानभूता ।
प्रतीतिरेषा गदिताऽज्ञतैवेत्याविद्यका एव समस्तभेदाः ॥

saiṣā śarīro'hamiti pratītiḥ saṁsāravṛkṣasya nidānabhūtā |
pratītireṣā gaditā'jñataivetyāvidyakā eva samastabhedāḥ ||

This is the persuasion 'I am this body' which is the root-cause of the tree of samsara and since this persuasion is declared to be Ignorance, therefore all differences are the outcome of the Ignorance.

199. जीवाभिधानं मन एव भेदानविद्यया कल्पयतीक्षते च ।
सुषुप्तिभावेऽपि तुरीयभावे जीवेश्वराद्या न हि सन्ति भेदाः ॥

jīvābhidhānaṁ mana eva bhedānavidyayā kalpayatīkṣate ca |
suṣuptibhāve'pi turīyabhāve jīveśvarādyā na hi santi bhedāḥ ||

The mind which is named 'the soul' itself creates and perceives these differences through the Ignorance. This is so, because there are no differences in the state of deep sleep and in the Supreme State there are no differences, namely the difference between God and the soul and all the rest.

200. द्वन्द्वानि सर्वाण्यपि च त्रिपुट्यो भवन्त्यसत्यान्यत एव हेतोः ।
सत्यात्मभावे न हि सन्ति तानि न बाध्यते तुर्यपदस्थ एतैः ॥

dvandvāni sarvāṇyapi ca triputyo bhavantyasatyānyata eva hetoḥ |
satyātmabhāve na hi santi tāni na bādhyate turyapadastha etaiḥ ||

For this reason all the pairs and the triads are unreal. They are non-existent in the Natural State of the Self, and the one that dwells in that State, the Supreme State, is unaffected by them.

The pairs of opposites are exemplified in the next two verses.

201. अन्तर्बहिर्जन्ममृती समष्टिव्यष्टिर्जगत्सृष्टिलयौ तमो भाः ।
आत्माऽप्यनात्माऽप्युत बन्धमुक्ती ज्ञानाज्ञते जीव उतेश्वरश्च ॥

antarbahirjanmamṛtī samaṣṭirvyaṣṭirjagatsṛṣṭilayau tamo bhāḥ |
ātmā'pyanātmā'pyuta bandhamuktī jñānājñāte jīva uteśvaraśca ||

202. स्वेच्छा च दैवं च सुखं च दुःखं दोषा गुणाश्चाप्युत पुण्यपापे ।
इत्याद्यहङ्कारनिदानकत्वात् स्वप्नोपमं वक्ति गुरुः समस्तम् ॥

svecchā ca daivaṁ ca sukhaṁ ca duḥkhaṁ doṣā guṇāścāpyuta puṇyapāpe |
ityādyahaṅkāranidānakatvāt svapnopamaṁ vakti guruḥ samastam ||

The Master declares that all these and the like, because their root-cause is the ego sense, are (unreal) like dreams, namely the difference of inside and outside, birth and death, the totality and the units, the creation and dissolution of the world, darkness and light, the Self and the not-self, bondage and deliverance, knowledge and ignorance, the soul and God, free will and fate, pleasure and pain, bad and good qualities and merit and sin.

These are pairs of opposites, called *dvandvas*. The triads (*triputis*) are exemplified next.

203. ज्ञाताऽपि तज्ज्ञेयमनात्मसंज्ञं ज्ञानं तथा वैषयिकं तदीयम् ।
समस्तमेवं त्रिपुटिप्रकारं चाविद्यकं स्वप्नसमं निरुक्तम् ॥

jñātā'pi tajjñeyamanātmasañjñaṁ jñānaṁ tathā vaiṣayikaṁ tadīyam |
samastamevaṁ triputiprakāraṁ cāvidyakaṁ svapnasamaṁ niruktam ||

The knower, the objects of his knowledge, which are non-self, and his knowledge of objects, and all else that consists similarly of three factors, being the outcome of the Ignorance, are said to be unreal like dreams.

The world is found on scrutiny to consist of these pairs and triads. The first pair to be dealt with is that of the soul and God.

204. आत्मन्यविद्यापरिकल्पितौ द्वौ जीवेश्वराख्यौ भवतो न भिन्नौ ।
उपाधिसम्बन्धधिया भिदेयं प्रतीयते सत्यवदज्ञतायाम् ॥

ātmanyavidyāparikalpitau dvau jīveśvarākhyau bhavato na bhinnau |
upādhisambandhadhiyā bhideyaṁ pratīyate satyavadajñatāyām ||

The two, namely those named the soul and God, which are created and projected on the Real Self by the Ignorance, are not different from each other. This difference is perceived during the prevalence of the Ignorance, due to the identification with the form assumed, as if it were real.

Apart from the limitation imposed by the form, the two are not different. This is explained next.

205. ईशस्य माया गदिताऽस्त्युपाधिर्जीवस्य तूपाधिरबोध एव ।
मायाऽस्त्यधीना परमस्य तस्य जीवस्त्वविद्यापरतन्त्र एव ॥

īśasya māyā gaditā'styupādhirjīvasya tūpādhirabodha eva |
māyā'styadhīnā paramasya tasya jīvastvavidyāparatantra eva ||

*Maya is the body (or attribute) of God. Ignorance is that of the soul. Maya is subject to that Supreme One. But the soul is subject to the Ignorance.

206. मायाऽप्यविद्या गदिते तु शास्त्रे जीवेशयोर्भेदनिरूपणाय ।
मिथ्यैव भेदोऽयमबोधमूलस्तथाऽपि सत्यो व्यवहारदृष्ट्या ॥

māyā'pyavidyā gadite tu śāstre jīveśayorbhedanirūpaṇāya |
mithyaiva bhedo'yamabodhamūlastathā'pi satyo vyavahāradṛṣṭyā ||

Maya and the Ignorance are mentioned in the sacred lore in order to account for the difference between the soul and God. This difference, being rooted in the Ignorance, is unreal, but it is (regarded as) real from the stand-point of worldly activity.

This is the explanation of diversity, also called Duality. This will appear as real so long as the cause, the Ignorance, prevails.

207. द्वैतं भवेत् सत्यवदेव तावद् यावन्न जीवत्वमपैति बोधात् ।
अतो भवेत् सत्यवदेव पुंसां भेदो ह्ययं यद्वदिहान्यभेदाः ॥

dvaitaṁ bhavet satyavadeva tāvad yāvanna jīvatvamapaiti bodhāt |
ato bhavet satyavadeva puṁsāṁ bhedo hyayaṁ yadvadihānyabhedāḥ ||

---

* Maya is the illusory power veiling the Real Self and making the world-appearance possible.

Duality will continue to appear as real, so long as this quality of being a 'soul' does not cease by Right Awareness (of the Self). For this reason this difference will appear as real to men, just like all other differences here.

208. विश्वं परो जीव इति त्रयस्य मृषात्वमुक्तं ह्यविभक्तमेव ।
न कुक्कुटी कल्पयितुं हि शक्या पाकाय चार्धं प्रसवाय चार्धम् ॥

viśvaṁ paro jīva iti trayasya mṛṣātvamuktaṁ hyavibhaktameva |
na kukkuṭī kalpayituṁ hi śakyā pākāya cārdhaṁ prasavāya cārdham ||

The unreality of the three, namely the world, God and the soul, is taught as a single indivisible truth. It is not possible to use a hen, one half for cooking and the other half for laying eggs.

The analogy is to impress the truth taught here that the three mentioned are real or unreal as one whole, and not separately. So the teaching of their unreality cannot be accepted in regard to one and rejected as to the other two. This will become clear later.

209. स्वं देहिनं चाप्युत जीवभूतं यो मन्यतेऽज्ञातनिजस्वरूपः ।
आत्मैव तस्मै भजतीशभावं तमेव भक्त्या स भजेद्विमुक्त्यै ॥

svaṁ dehinaṁ cāpyuta jīvabhūtaṁ yo manyate'jñātanijasvarūpaḥ |
ātmaiva tasmai bhajatīśabhāvaṁ tameva bhaktyā sa bhajedvimuktyai ||

For him who regards himself as owner of or dweller in the body and as being a 'soul', the Real

Self Himself becomes God, and he should practise devotion to Him for the sake of Deliverance.

This need for devotion exists even for an Advaiti, believer in Non-Difference, as shown below.

210.   सत्यां विदित्वाऽद्वयतां धियैव लब्धुं स्वरूपानुभवं त्वशक्तः ।
कुर्यात् प्रयत्नं भवबन्धमुत्त्यै भक्त्या परस्मिन्नपि च प्रपत्त्या ॥

satyāṁ viditvā'dvayatāṁ dhiyaiva labdhuṁ svarūpānubhavaṁ tvaśaktaḥ ।
kuryāt prayatnam bhavabandhamuktyai bhaktyā parasminnapi ca prapattyā ॥

He that knows the Truth of non-difference by the intellect alone, but is unable to achieve experience of the True Nature of the Real Self, must strive to attain Deliverance by devotion and self-surrender to God.

There are two paths prescribed, because of difference of qualifications. This is next explained.

211.   धीरस्य पुंसो निजमार्गणं च भीरोः प्रपत्तिः पुरुषे परस्मिन् ।
द्वावेव मार्गौ गदितौ मुमुक्षोरन्तर्भवन्त्यत्र समस्तमार्गाः ॥

dhīrasya puṁso nijamārgaṇam ca bhīroḥ prapattiḥ puruṣe parasmin ।
dvāveva mārgau gaditau mumukṣorantarbhavantyatra samastamārgāḥ ॥

Only two Paths are laid down, for the aspirant to Deliverance, namely, for the Valiant, the quest of one's own Self, and for the fearful, self-surrender to God; and in these two all the paths are included.

A great many paths are known and followed; but all come under these two. The valiant one has been already described. The other is the one that is afraid of samsara, but is unable to take to the quest taught by Bhagavan Sri Ramana as being the *Direct Path*, in which all preconceived notions are dropped, as will be seen later. Self-surrender is the final step in the practice of devotion to God, which is the only other alternative to the Direct path.

212. अन्वेषयाहङ्कृतिमूलमन्तर्नाशाय तामर्पय वा परस्मै ।
मार्गो द्विधैवं भगवत्तमेन मुमुक्षुपुंसां रमणेन दिष्टः ॥

anveṣayāhaṅkṛtimūlamantarnāśāya tāmarpaya vā parasmai |
mārgo dvidhaivaṁ bhagavattamena mumukṣupuṁsāṁ ramaṇena diṣṭaḥ ||

This two-fold path has been taught by the Most Holy One, Ramana, thus: 'Either seek the Root of the Ego-sense (the I, rising in respect of the body) or surrender that Ego-sense to God for being destroyed (By His Grace)'.

The Advaiti who looks down upon Devotion as inferior is next censured.

213. अद्वैतिनं स्वं गणयन्नधीरो भक्तिं परस्मिन्नवरां च मत्वा ।
वृथैव जीवत्यभजन् य ईशं मुग्धः स मर्त्यो मलिनान्तरङ्गः ॥

advaitinaṁ svaṁ gaṇayannadhīro bhaktiṁ parasminnavarāṁ ca matvā |
vṛthaiva jīvatyabhajan ya īśaṁ mugdhaḥ sa martyo malināntaraṅgaḥ ||

That foolish man, who, considering himself as an Advaiti, but not being valiant enough (to take to the Quest as taught by the Bhagavan) and, looking upon devotion as inferior, lives in vain, without devotion to God, is a man with a tainted mind.

The devotee is next shown to be better off than the rest of men.

214. कूपे यथा रज्जुनिबद्धकुम्भो भक्तो भवेऽस्मिन् भविता तथैव ।
रज्जुं विना कूपनिमग्नकुम्भो यथा तथा भक्तिविहीनमर्त्यः ॥

kūpe yathā rajjunibaddhakumbho bhakto bhave'smin bhavitā tathaiva |
rajjuṁ vinā kūpanimagnakumbho yathā tathā bhaktivihīnamartyaḥ ||

In this samsara the devotee is like a pot let down into a well with a rope tied to it. The man without devotion is like a pot fallen into the well, without a rope being tied to it.

The meaning is that the devotee is destined to be rescued from Samsara by God's Grace, not so those that have no devotion.

The path of devotion is next dealt with.

215. य आसुरीं सम्पदमाश्रयन्ते न भक्तिरच्छा भविता हि तेषाम् ।
दैवीमतः सम्पदमाश्रितः सन् भक्तिं परस्मिन् विदधीत साधुः ॥

ya āsurīṁ sampadamāśrayante na bhaktiracchā bhavitā hi teṣām |
daivīmataḥ sampadamāśritaḥ san bhaktiṁ parasmin vidadhīta sādhuḥ ||

Those who are endowed with the diabolic temperament cannot have the right kind of devotion. Hence the good one should take hold of the Divine temperament for practising devotion to God.

216. लोकप्रसिद्धा परमस्य पुंसः कृपेति शक्तिर्भवति त्रिरूपा ।
       ईशस्वरूपा गुरुरूपिणी च सत्यात्मरूपा च तुरीयभावे ॥

lokaprasiddhā paramasya puṁsaḥ kṛpeti śaktirbhavati trirūpā |
īśasvarūpā gururūpiṇī ca satyātmarūpā ca turīyabhāve ||

The power of God, well-known in the world as Grace, has three forms, namely as God, the Supreme Being, as the Holy Guru and as the Real Self in the Supreme State.

These three are thus declared to be One. Devotion to God leads to the finding of the Guru who is God Himself. Devotion to the Guru leads upto the right Awareness of the Self, who is none other than God.

217. कृपा तु सेयं स्थितिरेव तस्य परस्य सत्यात्मतया हृदन्तः ।
       कृपा स्वरूपं हि परस्य तस्य कृपां विना नास्ति हि तस्य सत्ता ॥

kṛpā tu seyaṁ sthitireva tasya parasya satyātmatayā hṛdantaḥ |
kṛpā svarūpaṁ hi parasya tasya kṛpāṁ vinā nāsti hi tasya sattā ||

This Grace (of God) is just the fact that He Himself is present in the Heart as the Real Self. Grace is the very nature of that Supreme One, and without Grace He can have no existence.

218. सदैव जागर्ति कृपा परस्य कालो न कोऽप्यस्ति यदा न सा स्यात् ।
जीवत्यहन्ता तु नरस्य यावदपेक्षते सा पुरुषस्य यत्नम् ॥

sadaiva jāgarti kṛpā parasya kālo na ko'pyasti yadā na sā syāt |
jīvatyahantā tu narasya yāvadapekṣate sā puruṣasya yatnam ||

That Grace of God is ever wide awake; there is never a time when that Grace is absent. But so long as the man's ego-sense is alive, he needs effort on his part.

219. त्यजेन्न कश्चित् करुणा परस्य सर्वान् नयेत् सा हि विमुक्तिमेव ।
मुच्यन्त एके त्वचिरेण बन्धादन्ये तु कालेन चिरेण जीवाः ॥

tyajenna kañcit karuṇā parasya sarvān nayet sā hi vimuktimeva |
mucyanta eke tvacireṇa bandhādanye tu kālena cireṇa jīvāḥ ||

That Grace of God will not desert any one; she will (surely) lead all to Deliverance. Some will be delivered soon, others after a long time.

220. मन्येत भक्तः स्वयमेव भक्त्या परं भजामीति न तद्यथार्थम् ।
धावन्तमज्ञं भवकाननेऽस्मिन् परो हि गृह्णात्यनुधाव्य मुग्धम् ॥

manyeta bhaktaḥ svayameva bhaktyā paraṁ bhajāmīti na tadyathārtham |
dhāvantamajñaṁ bhavakānane'smin paro hi gṛhṇātyanudhāvya mugdham ||

The devotee may think, 'I am practising devotion to God by my own efforts'; but this is not true, because it is God who pursues the deluded soul, who is wandering blindly in this forest of Samsara, and takes hold of him (by His Grace).

It is next shown that God's Grace is immeasurable.

221. दयालुरेवं हि पुमान् परोऽसौ स्वमेव यद्यच्छति भक्तिभाजाम् ।
नाशोऽहमस्तत्कृपया हि साधुस्तस्मिन्नभेदेन लभेत निष्ठाम् ॥

dayālurevaṁ hi pumān paro'sau svameva yadyacchati bhaktibhājām |
nāśe'hamastatkṛpayā hi sādhustasminnabhedena labheta niṣṭhām ||

The extent of God's Grace is so much, that He gives Himself to devotees; for when by His Grace, the ego is destroyed, then the aspirant obtains the State of Non-difference from Him.

This is one of the sayings of Bhagavan Sri Ramana.

222. कान्ताचलोऽसौ हि विकृष्य जीवान् कृत्वाऽचलांस्तानपि भक्षयित्वा ।
स्वस्मिन् पदे नित्यसुखे परस्मिन् प्रेम्णा सदा रक्षति तुर्यभावे ॥

kāntācalo'sau hi vikṛṣya jīvān kṛtvā'calāṁstānapi bhakṣayitvā |
svasmin pade nityasukhe parasmin premṇā sadā rakṣati turyabhāve ||

God is that kind of magnetic mountain which draws the souls to Himself, makes them motionless and consumes them (like food) and ever after safeguards them in the Supreme State which is one of Endless Bliss, which is His own State.

This truth is set forth in the 10th and 11th verse of one of Bhagavan Sri Ramana's Hymns to Sri Arunachala, called the Arunachala Dasakam.

That all souls are destined to reach this Goal by Divine Grace is next described as expressed by Bhagavan Sri Ramana in His Arunachala Ashtakam.

223.　यथाऽर्णवोत्थाम्बुदवृष्टिजाता भूयोऽर्णवं याति नदी स्वयोनिम् ।
भ्रान्त्वा यथा खे सुचिरं च पक्षी विश्रान्तिमाप्नोत्यवनिं निवृत्य ॥

yathā'rṇavotthāmbudavṛṣṭijātā bhūyo'rṇavaṁ yāti nadī svayonim |
bhrāntvā yathā khe suciraṁ ca pakṣī viśrāntimāpnotyavaniṁ nivṛtya ||

224.　एवं परस्मादुदितोऽपि जीवो भ्रान्त्वा भवेऽस्मिन् सुचिरं कदाचित् ।
यथा प्रवृत्तो विनिवृत्य भूयः सङ्गच्छते तं पुरुषं स्वयोनिम् ॥

evaṁ parasmādudito'pi jīvo bhrāntvā bhave'smin suciraṁ kadācit |
yathā pravṛtto vinivṛtya bhūyaḥ saṅgacchate taṁ puruṣaṁ svayonim ||

As the river, born by the rains of the clouds rising from the sea, returns to its source, the sea, and as the bird, wandering a long time in the sky, obtains rest by returning to the (its home in) earth, so the soul, which has originated from the Supreme One, after wandering in this Samsara for immense period, returning in the reverse direction, rejoins that Supreme One, from whom he originated.

225.　भक्तिः परस्मिन् द्विविधोपदिष्टा चित्तस्य पुंसः परिपाकभेदात् ।
आदौ तु कीशार्भकरीतिभक्तिः पश्चाच्चमार्जारकिशोरभक्तिः ॥

bhaktiḥ parasmin dvividhopadiṣṭā cittasya puṁsaḥ paripākabhedāt |
ādau tu kīśārbhakarītibhaktiḥ paścāccamārjārakiśorabhaktiḥ ||

Devotion is taught as of two kinds, according to the degree of ripeness of the devotee; in the beginning it is devotion like that of the baby-monkey, and afterwards devotion like that of the kitten.

The baby-monkey keeps hold of its mother by its own effort, whereas the kitten makes no effort, but relies entirely on the mother-cat. The unripe devotee is like the former and the ripe one is like the latter; the former has his egoism rampant; the egoism of the latter is greatly subdued, and hence he is the recipient of more abundant grace, and reaches the goal much sooner.

226.　अभ्यस्य कीशार्भकभक्तिमेव भवेष्वनेकेषु कथञ्चिदन्ते ।
क्षीणेत्वहङ्कारबले नितान्तं भक्तिं बिडालार्भकवत् करोति ॥

abhyasya kīśārbhakabhaktimeva bhaveṣvanekeṣu kathañcidante |
kṣīṇetvahaṅkārabale nitāntaṁ bhaktiṁ biḍālārbhakavat karoti ||

After practising devotion like that of the baby monkey through a great many lives, in the end, when his egoism is greatly reduced, he practises devotion like the kitten.

227.　मार्जारडिम्भोपमभक्तिरेव प्रपत्तिरप्यात्मनिवेदनं च ।
सेयं विशुद्धा मनसः प्रसादात् कालेन बोधेन भवेत् समाना ॥

mārjāraḍimbhopamabhaktireva prapattirapyātmanivedanaṁ ca |
seyaṁ viśuddhā manasaḥ prasādāt kālena bodhena bhavet samānā ||

The devotion that is like the kitten is the same as taking refuge at the Feet of God and self-surrender to Him. This devotion, becoming further purified by the refinement of the mind, becomes equal to Right Awareness in course of time.

228. पुंसः परस्मै स्वनिवेदनं तु पुंसा भवेत् तेन कृतं यथार्थम् ।
जानाति यः स्वं निजमार्गणेनेत्युक्ताऽस्ति वाणी भगवत्तमेन ॥

puṁsaḥ parasmai svanivedanaṁ tu puṁsā bhavet tena kṛtaṁ yathārtham |
jānāti yaḥ svaṁ nijamārgaṇenetyuktā'sti vāṇī bhagavattamena ||

There is the saying of the Most Holy One that real surrender is what is made by him that knows the Truth of Himself by the Quest of that Self.

Self-surrender is real and effective to the extent of attenuation of the ego-sense. Hence, so long as the ego survives, self-surrender is imperfect and incomplete. It becomes complete and fruitful only when the ego dies once for all, never to revive.

229. पृथक्त्वमत्याऽप्यपृथक्त्वमत्याऽप्येवं च भक्तिर्गदिता द्विरूपा ।
असंस्कृतानां प्रथमोपदिष्टा सुसंस्कृतानामितरा प्रशस्ता ॥

pṛthaktvamatyā'pyapṛthaktvamatyā'pyevaṁ ca bhaktirgaditā dvirūpā |
asaṁskṛtānāṁ prathamopadiṣṭā susaṁskṛtānāmitarā praśastā ||

Devotion is of two kinds, also, as being with sense of separateness and with sense of non-difference. The former is prescribed for the unrefined; the latter is excellent for the well-refined ones.

The sense of difference detracts from the quality of devotion. He who is convinced that difference is not true is alone capable of real surrender of himself, and hence his devotion is superior. But the devotion with sense of difference is not to be despised, as is shown next.

230. तमात्मभूतं पृथगेव मत्वा रूपेऽपि नाम्नाऽपि च तं प्रपूज्य ।
बुद्धिप्रसादात् परमं च धाम कालेन यात्येव न तत्र शङ्का ॥

tamātmabhūtaṁ pṛthageva matvā rūpe'pi nāmnā'pi ca taṁ prapūjya |
buddhiprasādāt paramaṁ ca dhāma kālena yātyeva na tatra śaṅkā ||

If one, considering Him, who is only the Self, as other than oneself, worships Him in a form and by a name, then in course of time, through the clarification of his intellect, he surely reaches the Supreme State; there is no doubt about this.

Ascribing a form and a name to God is unavoidable for those who, being unable to take to the Direct Path, nevertheless want Deliverance and wish to worship God to win His Grace.

The ignorance and narrowness of those sectarians, such as the Jews and the Muslims, who condemn the use of images in Divine worship, was well exposed by Bhagavan Sri Ramana in a talk with some Muslims, which is reported in the *Maha Yoga* and in the *Talks with Sri Ramana Maharshi*, in three Volumes. The gist of Sri Bhagavan's reply to the Muslims was that one who thinks himself to be a form, a mortal body, being really formless and nameless — has no right to raise this question. During the state of Ignorance, it is permissible to a sincere devotee to regard God as having a form and a name, and to use images or symbols to facilitate worship. There is another saying of the Bhagavan Sri Ramana, which is given in the next verse.

231. नाम्नाऽपि रूपेण विहीनमीशं नाम्नाऽपि रूपे भजते नरश्चेत् ।
स नामरूपोद्भवबन्धमुक्तिं भजेदिति श्रीरमणोपदेशः ॥

nāmnā'pi rūpeṇa vihīnamīśaṁ nāmnā'pi rūpe bhajate naraścet |
sa nāmarūpodbhavabandhamuktiṁ bhajediti śrīramaṇopadeśaḥ ||

"If a man adores God, who is nameless and formless through names and in a form, he will be liberated from the bondage due to names and forms", such is the Teaching of Sri Ramana.

Also the following:-

232. यामेव निष्ठां लभते मुमुक्षुर्ध्यानादरूपस्य सतः परस्य ।
लभेत तामेव हि दैवसम्पद्युक्तः सरूपं तमुपास्य भक्त्या ॥

yāmeva niṣṭhāṁ labhate mumukṣurdhyānādarūpasya sataḥ parasya |
labheta tāmeva hi daivasampadyuktaḥ sarūpaṁ tamupāsya bhaktyā ||

The man, who meditates with devotion on God with a form, being endowed with the divine temperament, will attain that same state (of Deliverance), which one attains meditating on Him as formless.

The next verse shows that the devotee is free to ascribe to God, for his devotion, *any* Name or Form that appeals to himself as lovable.

233.　भजेत् तमेकं पुरुषं यथेष्टं केनापि नाम्ना क्वचनापि रूपे ।
　　परस्य रूपेषु न तारतम्यं वीक्षेत धीमान् परिशुद्धचेताः ॥

bhajet tamekaṁ puruṣaṁ yatheṣṭaṁ kenāpi nāmnā kvacanāpi rūpe |
parasya rūpeṣu na tāratamyaṁ vīkṣeta dhīmān pariśuddhacetāḥ ||

One may adore that One Being by any name and in any form as he likes. Among the forms of the Supreme One the wise one, whose mind is pure, will not see any superiority or inferiority.

Thus true catholicity is the distinguishing feature of the Teaching of the Vedantas. Catholicity consists not in claiming that all people should give up their own faiths and embrace one's own, but in recognising that all religions are paths to God. The *Advaitis* are expected to understand this.

Then the dictum of the great poet, Kalidasa, on this point, is quoted.

234.　एकैव मूर्तिर्बिभिदे त्रिधा सा सामान्यमेषां प्रथमावरत्वम् ।
　　एवं स्फुटं मूर्तिभिदामृषात्वमूचे कवीन्द्रः किल कालिदासः ॥

ekaiva mūrtirbibhide tridhā sā sāmānyameṣāṁ prathamāvaratvam |
evaṁ sphuṭaṁ mūrtibhidāmṛṣātvamūce kavīndraḥ kila kālidāsaḥ ||

"There is only One God-Form; (but) It became divided into three; and common to all the three is superiority and inferiority (by turns). Kalidasa, the

King of poets, has indeed stated clearly in this manner, the falseness of differences in form.

Among them there is no real superiority; nor inferiority. But superiority or inferiority is allowed to be ascribed to them by devotees, to suit their needs. They are all equally Forms of the Formless Brahman, the Real Self. These forms disappear when the Real Self is experienced as He really is.

Which, of all available forms, is the best, is the next question, which is answered next.

235. सर्वोत्तमं रूपममुष्य बुद्धः स्वस्मान्न यस्तं समवैति भिन्नम् ।
परात्मशक्तेः करुणाभिधाया रूपं द्वितीयं हि गुरुः प्रबुद्धः ॥

sarvottamaṁ rūpamamuṣya buddhaḥ svasmānna yastaṁ samavaiti bhinnam |
parātmaśakteḥ karuṇābhidhāyā rūpaṁ dvitīyaṁ hi guruḥ prabuddhaḥ ||

Of all the forms of God, the best is the Sage, who does not consider Him as other than the Self. Indeed the Sage, who is the Guru, is the second of the (three) forms of Divine Grace.

236. अहं स्वयं बुद्ध इति ब्रवीति गीतासु कृष्णो भगवान् स्वयं यत् ।
ईशादभिन्नं गणयेत् प्रबुद्धं शास्त्रोदितं तत्त्वममुष्य जानन् ॥

ahaṁ svayaṁ buddha iti bravīti gītāsu kṛṣṇo bhagavān svayaṁ yat |
īśādabhinnaṁ gaṇayet prabuddhaṁ śāstroditaṁ tattvamamuṣya jānan ||

Since Bhagavan Sri Krishna Himself says in the Gita: 'I Myself am the Sage', therefore knowing this truth of Him as stated in the sacred lore, one should regard the Sage as not different from God.

237.   अभ्यर्चयेदात्मविदं मुमुक्षुरित्यस्ति वाणी श्रुतिमस्तकेषु ।
मन्वीत चेद् भिन्नममुं परस्मात् सा धीर्मुमुक्षोः प्रतिहन्ति मार्गम् ॥

abhyarcayedātmavidaṁ mumukṣurityasti vāṇī śrutimastakeṣu |
manvīta ced bhinnamamuṁ parasmāt sā dhīrmumukṣoḥ pratihanti mārgam ||

(Also) there is the text of the Upanishads, that one who wants Deliverance must worship the Knower of the Self. If he thinks of Him (the Sage, who is the Guru) as other than God, that thought will obstruct his path.

One of the prominent defects of devotees who regard God as other than the Self is next noticed.

238.   देवं त्वनात्मानमुपासते ये ते सामरस्येन भवन्ति हीनाः ।
चिरेण कालेन मतिप्रसादादपैति केषाञ्चन दोष एषः ॥

devaṁ tvanātmānamupāsate ye te sāmarasyena bhavanti hīnāḥ |
cireṇa kālena matiprasādādapaiti keṣāñcana doṣa eṣaḥ ||

Those devotees who worship God as not the Self are wanting in Catholicity. In the case of a few of them this defect ceases by the clarification of the intellect after a long time.

Narrowness of mind is a serious defect, and till it is overcome, the aspirant will not reach his goal.

The next topic is 'God-Vision' on which some ignorance prevails.

239. यथा मतं स्वेन परस्य रूपं रूपं तदेवेक्षितुमीहतेऽसौ ।
कदाचिदीक्षेत च रूपमेवं वीक्षा त्वनित्येयमतो मृषैव ॥

yathā matam svena parasya rūpam rūpam tadevekṣitumīhate'sau |
kadācidīkṣeta ca rūpamevam vīkṣā tvanityeyamato mṛṣaiva ||

The devotee yearns to see the Form of God as conceived by Himself; sometimes he may even see that very form; but this vision is transitory and hence unreal.

The absurdity of this desire is now shown up.

240. स एव साक्षात् पुरुषः परः सन् स्वतः पृथक् तं गणयन्नबोधात् ।
भक्त्या तदीक्षां यतते च लब्धुमितोऽन्यदाश्चर्यतरं किमस्ति ॥

sa eva sākṣāt puruṣaḥ paraḥ san svataḥ pṛthak tam gaṇayannabodhāt |
bhaktyā tadīkṣām yatate ca labdhumito'nyadāścaryataram kimasti ||

Being himself that very Supreme Being, but regarding Him as other than the Self through Ignorance, he strives through devotion to obtain a Vision of Him! Is there anything more surprising than this?

Indeed this is topsy-turveydom!

241. रूपेक्षणं रूपविवर्जितस्य कथं भवेत् तस्य यथार्थवीक्षा ।
तस्यात्मनोऽनात्मवदीक्षणं च सत्येक्षणं तस्य भवेत् कथं नु ॥

rūpekṣaṇaṁ rūpavivarjitasya kathaṁ bhavet tasya yathārthavīkṣā |
tasyātmano'nātmavadīkṣaṇaṁ ca satyekṣaṇaṁ tasya bhavet kathaṁ nu ||

How can the seeing of a form of the Formless
One be a true vision? And how can the vision as
not-self, of Him that is the Self, be a true vision?

The Bhagavan unties this riddle with ease.

242. रूपं समस्तं च मनोमयं यदन्तर्भवेद् द्रष्टरि दृश्यरूपम् ।
द्रष्टुः स्वरूपं हि गवेषणीयं तदेव तत्त्वं हि परस्य पुंसः ॥

rūpaṁ samastaṁ ca manomayaṁ yadantarbhaved draṣṭari dṛśyarūpam |
draṣṭuḥ svarūpaṁ hi gaveṣaṇīyaṁ tadeva tattvaṁ hi parasya puṁsaḥ ||

All form is mental, and hence the form of the
spectacle is inside the spectator; it is the Truth of
the Seer that should be sought, since that is the
Truth of the Supreme Being:

The unreality of these visions is next declared.

243. द्रष्टुः स्वरूपं य उपेक्ष्य देवं स्वतोऽन्यवत् पश्यति भक्तियोगात् ।
स वीक्षते मानसरूपमेवेत्येषाऽस्ति वाणी भगवत्तमस्य ॥

draṣṭuḥ svarūpaṁ ya upekṣya devaṁ svato'nyavat paśyati bhaktiyogāt |
sa vīkṣate mānasarūpamevetyeṣā'sti vāṇī bhagavattamasya ||

'The man who, by the practice of devotion,
sees God as someone other than himself, sees only

a mental form' — such is the utterance of the Most Holy One (on this point).

What then is the Reality of God?

244. द्रष्टुः स्वरूपस्य गवेषणेन द्रष्टुर्विनाशात् परिशिष्यते यत् ।
तदेकमेव स्वयमात्मरूपं रूपं च सत्यं परमस्य पुंसः ॥

draṣṭuḥ svarūpasya gaveṣaṇena draṣṭurvināśāt pariśiṣyate yat |
tadekameva svayamātmarūpaṁ rūpaṁ ca satyaṁ paramasya puṁsaḥ ||

That which remains over on the annihilation of the (would-be) seer, by the Quest of (the Truth of) the seer, is itself the Truth of the Self and also the Truth of the Supreme Being.

Herein the Quest of the Self, the Direct Path taught by Bhagavan Sri Ramana, is referred to. It will be dealt with later. The real Vision is the same.

245. जीवाभिधं यत्र मनो निगीर्णं तेनान्नवद्याति तदात्मभावम् ।
सैवात्मवीक्षाऽपि परस्य वीक्षेत्येषा गुरोः श्रीरमणस्य वाणी ॥

jīvābhidhaṁ yatra mano nigīrṇaṁ tenānnavadyāti tadātmabhāvam |
saivātmavīkṣā'pi parasya vīkṣetyeṣā guroḥ śrīramaṇasya vāṇī ||

That State, in which the mind, called the soul, is swallowed up and has become One with Him, is itself both the True Vision of the Self, and the Right Vision of God, so says the Holy Guru, Sri Ramana.

The next question is about how to meditate on God.

246.　उपासनं स्वात्मतयैव तस्य श्रुतेर्वचोभिर्विहितं मुमुक्षोः ।
　　　मत्वा स्वतोऽन्यं तमुपासते ये श्रुतिः पशूंस्तान् बत वक्ति पुंसः ॥

upāsanaṁ svātmatayaiva tasya śrutervacobhirvihitaṁ mumukṣoḥ |
matvā svato'nyaṁ tamupāsate ye śrutiḥ paśūṁstān bata vakti puṁsaḥ ||

Revelation prescribes that the aspirant should meditate on Him as one's own Real Self. The Revelation styles as beasts, those who meditate on Him as not the Self.

247.　हित्वाऽऽत्मदेवं भजते स्वतोऽन्यं य एष
　　　हस्तस्थितकौस्तुभं सः ।
　　　अपास्य रत्नं विचिनोति किञ्चिदित्येवमूचे भगवान् वसिष्ठः ॥

hitvā"tmadevaṁ bhajate svato'nyaṁ ya eṣa hastasthitakaustubhaṁ saḥ |
apāsya ratnaṁ vicinoti kiñcidityevamūce bhagavān vasiṣṭhaḥ ||

Bhagavan Vasishta has said that he that worships God as not-Self, turning away from the Real God who is the Self, is like one that goes about seeking a precious stone, throwing away the gem named Kaustubha already in his hand!

This is a quotation from the Yoga Vasishtam. The same subject is dealt with from another point of view.

248.　वपुष्यहन्तैव हि पापमाद्यं निरूपितं यद् भगवत्तमेन ।
　　　पापादमुष्मादुदिता परस्य स्वतोऽन्यताधीरपि पापमेव ॥

vapuṣyahantaiva hi pāpamādyaṁ nirūpitaṁ yad bhagavattamena |
pāpādamuṣmāduditā parasya svato'nyatādhīrapi pāpameva ||

Since the Most Holy One has shown that the Original Sin (spoken of by Christians) is just the sense of 'I am the body', therefore the sense of separateness of God from oneself, which is the outcome of this Sin, is itself only sinful!

249.   पूर्णत्वमुक्तं श्रुतिभिः परस्य सत्यं भवत्यात्मतयैव तस्य ।
तत्पूर्णताया बत भङ्ग एव पृथक्त्वमत्या क्रियते हि मूढैः ॥

pūrṇatvamuktaṁ śrutibhiḥ parasya satyaṁ bhavatyātmatayaiva tasya |
tatpūrṇatāyā bata bhaṅga eva pṛthaktvamatyā kriyate hi mūḍhaiḥ ||

The completeness (All-ness) of the Supreme Being, asserted by Revelation, becomes true only by His being the Self. The deluded ones are just denying this completeness of His by their notion of His being separate from themselves!

250.   अभेदमत्या रचिता तु भक्तिस्तत्पूर्णताङ्गीकरणस्य रीतिः ।
सुभक्तिमेतामतिपावनीं च ब्रूते मुमुक्षोर्भगवान् गुरुर्नः ॥

abhedamatyā racitā tu bhaktistatpūrṇatāṅgīkaraṇasya rītiḥ |
subhaktimetāmatipāvanīṁ ca brūte mumukṣorbhagavān gururnaḥ ||

But devotion practised without sense of difference is the way of accepting this completeness of God, and Bhagavan Sri Ramana, our Guru, says that this Devotion is the most excellent and highly purifying to the aspirant for Deliverance.

Bhagavan Sri Ramana also shows that devotion with sense of difference does not lead to the goal.

251. प्रदीपमादाय तमोऽनुधावन् नरो यथा तद्वदुपासकोऽपि ।
पृथक्त्वयोपास्य परं न यातीत्येवं च दिष्टं भगवत्तमेन ॥

pradīpamādāya tamo'nudhāvan naro yathā tadvadupāsako'pi |
pṛthaktvayopāsya paraṁ na yātītyevaṁ ca diṣṭaṁ bhagavattamena ||

Also the Most Holy One has shown that, like the man that pursues darkness, light in hand, the devotee who meditates on God as separate does not reach God (so long as he has this false notion).

The light in the hand is the Real Self, and darkness is the non-existent separate God. This is said by Bhagavan Sri Ramana in the Arunachala Ashtakam.

The superior devotion, on the other hand, leads to the goal which is the Egoless State.

252. भिदामहन्तारचितां मृषेति बुद्ध्वा भजत्यात्मतया यदीशम् ।
अतो मुमुक्षोरनयैव भक्त्या सिद्ध्येदहन्तानिधनं जवेन ॥

bhidāmahantāracitāṁ mṛṣeti buddhvā bhajatyātmatayā yadīśam |
ato mumukṣoranayaiva bhaktyā siddhyedahantānidhanaṁ javena ||

Since the better devotee approaches God as the Self, knowing that the notion of difference due to the ego is false, therefore for this aspirant for Deliverance, the annihilation of the ego will be accomplished quickly.

Another point is this.

253. स्वतोऽन्यमीशं बत मन्यते यो मृषैव तेनात्मसमर्पणं हि ।
       मृषैव चोलेषु यथा विवाहे स्यान्नारिकेलस्य फलस्य दानम् ॥

svato'nyamīśaṁ bata manyate yo mṛṣaiva tenātmasamarpaṇaṁ hi |
mṛṣaiva coleṣu yathā vivāhe syānnārikelasya phalasya dānam ||

In the case of him who adores God as non-Self, the surrender of himself is a sham, just like the gift of a cocoanut (to a guest) is a sham in the Chola region.

The analogy given here is the custom of placing a cocoanut on a plate, just for form's sake, without intending to give it.

Another consequence of the sense of difference is next noted.

254. अनात्मतायां परमस्य पुंसः प्रेष्ठेतरत्वं बत तस्य सिद्धम् ।
       आत्मैव हि प्रेष्ठ इति प्रसिद्धः श्रुत्याऽनुभूत्याऽपि हि सर्वजन्तोः ॥

anātmatāyāṁ paramasya puṁsaḥ preṣṭhetaratvaṁ bata tasya siddham |
ātmaiva hi preṣṭha iti prasiddhaḥ śrutyā'nubhūtyā'pi hi sarvajantoḥ ||

When the Supreme Being is reduced to the status of a non-Self, then it results that He is not the Most Beloved of all. For, both according to Revelation and the common experience of all creatures, the Self is the Dearest of all!

The concluding verse of the Teaching in the Gita is a riddle. How the Bhagavan, our Master, solved this riddle is next shown.

255. परं प्रपद्येत विहाय धर्मानारोपितानात्मनि जीवताद्यान् ।
अवोचदेवं भगवान् गुरुर्नो गीतान्तिमश्लोकनिगूढमर्थम् ॥

param prapadyeta vihāya dharmānāropitānātmani jīvatādyān |
avocadevaṁ bhagavān gururno gītāntimaślokanigūḍhamartham ||

Bhagavan, our Guru, declared the secret of the correct meaning of the last verse of the Gita thus: 'One should make surrender of oneself to the Supreme One by giving up the attributes falsely ascribed to the Real Self, namely that he is a 'soul' and so on.

The word Dharma in that verse of the Gita must not be taken as meaning righteous action, but as meaning status or quality. Thus interpreted, the verse makes good sense, not otherwise.

This brings us to the topic of self-surrender, which is now explained.

256. पुंसे परस्मै स्वनिवेदनं यत् सा भक्तियोगस्य परा हि निष्ठा ।
क्षीणे त्वहङ्कारबले तदेतद् विशुद्धचित्तेन भवेत् तु साध्यम् ॥

puṁse parasmai svanivedanaṁ yat sā bhaktiyogasya parā hi niṣṭhā |
kṣīṇe tvahaṅkārabale tadetad viśuddhacittena bhavet tu sādhyam ||

What is called surrender of oneself to God is the final consummation of the practice of Devotion. This can be achieved by the purified mind when the might of the ego is greatly reduced.

257. लघ्वी यथा कान्तशिला महत्या विभिन्नकोट्याश्रयणात् तथैव ।
जीवोऽल्पको मस्तकपादयोगादैक्यं भजेत् तेन परेण पुंसा ॥

laghvī yathā kāntaśilā mahatyā vibhinnakoṭyāśrayaṇāt tathaiva |
jīvo'lpako mastakapādayogādaikyaṁ bhajet tena pareṇa puṁsā ||

Just as a small magnet becomes united to a big one by the juxtaposition of the opposite poles, so the finite soul becomes One with that Supreme Being by the conjunction of its head with his Feet.

This simile of the magnet serves to bring out the need of perfect humility of the devotee. If the ego is rampant there can be no self-surrender.

How the one that has surrendered himself to God must get through life until he attains perfect egolessness is next described.

258. इष्टं यथा ते भवतात् तथैव सर्वात्मनाऽहं त्वदधीन एव ।
एवं धिया तिष्ठति यः सदैव तेनार्पणं स्वस्य भवेद्यथार्थम् ॥

iṣṭaṁ yathā te bhavatāt tathaiva sarvātmanā'haṁ tvadadhīna eva |
evaṁ dhiyā tiṣṭhati yaḥ sadaiva tenārpaṇaṁ svasya bhavedyathārtham ||

The self-surrender is truly made by him who always has the feeling "Let all things happen according to Thy Will. In all respects, I am bound to you."

That is, after self-surrender he must resign himself to the Divine Will without any reservations.

259. भूभारवोढा स इति प्रपन्नस्तस्मिन् भरं न्यस्य भजेत्
प्रशान्तिम् ।
वहन् स्वयं गोपुरधारिबिम्बो यथा तथा स्यात्
परिहासपात्रम् ॥

bhūbhāravoḍhā sa iti prapannastasmin bharaṁ nyasya bhajet praśāntim |
vahan svayaṁ gopuradhāribimbo yathā tathā syāt parihāsapātram ||

He that has surrendered himself will be at peace, remembering that He (God) is the bearer of the world's burden. The one that bears the burden himself will be ridiculous, like the figure on the temple-tower appearing to bear the tower on its own shoulders.

260. याने यथा स्वीयभरं निवेश्य करोति यात्रामुपविश्य तत्र ।
एवं परस्मिन् स्वभरं निवेश्य समापयेत् स्वामिह लोकयात्राम् ॥

yāne yathā svīyabharaṁ niveśya karoti yātrāmupaviśya tatra |
evaṁ parasmin svabharaṁ niveśya samāpayet svāmiha lokayātrām ||

As one travelling in a carriage puts down his luggage in the carriage itself and completes his journey, so should he resign his own (samsaric) burden to God and complete his life in the world.

Those who take on themselves the task of reforming the world or of alleviating the sufferings of others, are next dealt with.

261. यथा निजां देहकुटुम्बचिन्तां त्यजेद्धरं न्यस्य बुधः परस्मिन् ।
त्यजेत्तथा लोकहितार्थचिन्तां तस्मिन् समस्तं च भरं निवेश्य ॥

yathā nijāṁ dehakuṭumbacintāṁ tyajedbharaṁ nyasya budhaḥ parasmin |
tyajettathā lokahitārthacintāṁ tasmin samastaṁ ca bharaṁ niveśya ||

The wise one should resign to God his cares concerning the good of the world, just as he resigns to Him his cares about his own body and family.

262. अनिष्टमिष्टं च सुखं च दुःखं कालोपनीतं सहमान एव ।
शोकं मुदं चाप्यभजन् सुभक्तः कालं नयेत् तत्परया धियैव ॥

aniṣṭamiṣṭaṁ ca sukhaṁ ca duḥkhaṁ kālopanītaṁ sahamāna eva |
śokaṁ mudaṁ cāpyabhajan subhaktaḥ kālaṁ nayet tatparayā dhiyaiva ||

The ripe devotee must pass his time, patiently enduring whatever happens to him, whether pleasant or otherwise, without yielding to sorrow or joy, with his heart absorbed in Him.

263. यदा निगीर्णा कृपया परस्य नश्येदहन्ता सहजात्मभावे ।
निवेदनं स्वस्य तदा परस्मै सत्यं च पूर्णं च भवेद्धि साधोः ॥

yadā nigīrṇā kṛpayā parasya naśyedahantā sahajātmabhāve |
nivedanaṁ svasya tadā parasmai satyaṁ ca pūrṇaṁ ca bhaveddhi sādhoḥ ||

When the ego dies in the natural state of the Self, being swallowed by Divine Grace, then the devotee's self-surrender becomes true and complete.

This has been said in the language of the intellect. But the actual truth of this consummation transcends the intellect and is hence not easy to convey in words. Indeed the notion of self-surrender is absorbed from the standpoint of the absolute Truth.

264. गणेशमूर्तेर्गुडनिर्मितस्य यथांऽशमादाय निवेदनं स्यात् ।
तथा परस्मै स्वनिवेदनं स्यात् स्वो नाम तस्मान्न हि कश्चिदन्यः ॥

gaṇeśamūrtergudanirmitasya yathā'ṁśamādāya nivedanaṁ syāt |
tathā parasmai svanivedanaṁ syāt svo nāma tasmānna hi kaścidanyaḥ ||

As would be the offering of a portion, taken from an image of Ganesa made of jaggery, so is the surrender of one's self to God, since there is no self apart from Him.

265. आत्मा स्वयं यत् परमः स एव निवेदनं केन कथं च कस्मै ।
येनाहमा भेदमवैति तस्मात् तन्नाश एवात्मनिवेदनं स्यात् ॥

ātmā svayaṁ yat paramaḥ sa eva nivedanaṁ kena kathaṁ ca kasmai |
yenāhamā bhedamavaiti tasmāt tannāśa evātmanivedanaṁ syāt ||

Since the Self is the Supreme Being Himself, by whom, how and to whom is the surrender to be made? True self-surrender is only the extinction of the ego, by which the sense of being different from Him arises.

266. पुंसे परस्मै यदि दित्ससि स्वमन्विष्य पूर्वं स्वमवेहि साक्षात् ।
एवं स्वदानं कृतमेव तस्मा इत्यस्ति वाणी भगवत्तमस्य ॥

puṁse parasmai yadi ditsasi svamanviṣya pūrvaṁ svamavehi sākṣāt |
evaṁ svadānaṁ kṛtameva tasmā ityasti vāṇī bhagavattamasya ||

If thou desirest to give thyself to God, then first seek out and know thy Self; thus will be accomplished the gift of oneself to God. So said the Most Holy One.

The truth about *namaskara* (prostration) is the same as self-surrender. This is explained next.

267. अहङ्कृतेरेव नितान्तहानं नमस्कृतेस्तत्त्वमुदीर्यते च ।
ज्ञानं प्रपत्तिश्च नमस्कृतिश्चेत्येतत् त्रयं तत्त्वत एकमेव ॥

ahaṅkṛtereva nitāntahānaṁ namaskṛtestattvamudīryate ca |
jñānaṁ prapattiśca namaskṛtiścetyetat trayaṁ tattvata ekameva ||

The truth of Namaskara also is only the perfect giving up of the ego-sense. Right Awareness, self-surrender and Namaskar, all these three are one and the same.

Thus it is shown that God does not become an object of vision. Neither does He become an object of knowledge. This is shown next.

268. यथा न वीक्षाविषयः परात्मा बोधस्य तद्वद्विषयो न सोऽयम् ।
अगोचरत्वान्मनसः परस्य विद्यान्मनस्तं ह्ययथावदेव ॥

yathā na vīkṣāviṣayaḥ parātmā bodhasya tadvadviṣayo na so'yam |
agocaratvānmanasaḥ parasya vidyānmanastaṁ hyayathāvadeva ||

As God does not become an object of vision, neither does He become an object of knowledge. Since He transcends the mind, the mind will know Him (if at all) only wrongly.

269. चिद्रूप आत्मैव हि सन् परो यन्नैवास्ति चित् काचन तद्विभिन्ना ।
ज्ञाता न तस्यास्ति हि कश्चिदन्यो ज्ञानस्य नासौ विषयो हि तस्मात् ॥

cidrūpa ātmaiva hi san paro yannaivāsti cit kācana tadvibhinnā |
jñātā na tasyāsti hi kaścidanyo jñānasya nāsau viṣayo hi tasmāt ||

Since the Real Self, who is Consciousness, is the same as God, and there is no consciousness apart from Him, (it follows that) there is no one to know Him, other than He, nor does He become an object of knowledge.

The Real Self is the eternal subject, and hence He can never become an object, says the Bhagavan Sri Ramana.

270. चैतन्यदीप्तिर्मनसो भवेद्या तस्या निदानं स हि सत्य आत्मा ।
अतो विभिन्नं भविता न तस्मात् किञ्चिन्मनोनामकमत्र सत्यम् ॥

caitanyadīptirmanaso bhavedyā tasyā nidānaṁ sa hi satya ātmā |
ato vibhinnaṁ bhavitā na tasmāt kiñcinmanonāmakamatra satyam ||

The Source of the light of consciousness there is
in the mind is just the Real Self, and hence there is no
such thing as mind apart from Him, as something real.

271.   चैतन्यमात्माकृतिकं हृदन्तर्भासा स्वया भास्करवद्विभाति ।
भासाऽऽत्मनस्तस्य शशाङ्कवत्तु जडं मनश्चेतनवद्विभाति ॥

caitanyamātmākṛtikaṁ hṛdantarbhāsā svayā bhāskaravadvibhāti |
bhāsā''tmanastasya śaśāṅkavattu jaḍaṁ manaścetanavadvibhāti ||

The Consciousness which is the Self, shines in
the heart by Its own Light (of consciousness) like
the Sun. By its light the mind — which by itself is
insentient — appears as sentient like the moon
(shining by the borrowed light of the sun).

272.   चितिस्वभावं न मनोऽस्ति यस्मात् ततो मनो याति लयं सुषुप्तौ ।
चितिस्वभावः खलु सत्य आत्मा न यात्यसौ तेन लयं कदाऽपि ॥

citisvabhāvaṁ na mano'sti yasmāt tato mano yāti layaṁ suṣuptau |
citisvabhāvaḥ khalu satya ātmā na yātyasau tena layaṁ kadā'pi ||

Since consciousness is not of the nature of
the mind, it goes into latency in deep sleep. (But)
the Real Self never goes into latency, because
consciousness is His very Nature.

But the mind has the power of veiling the Self.

273.   निमीलत्येव मनो हि नित्यं स्वप्नेऽपि जाग्रत्यपि तत्स्वरूपम् ।
लीनं सुषुप्तौ च मृतं तुरीये मनो विबुध्येत कथं तमेकम् ॥

nimīlayatyeva mano hi nityaṁ svapne'pi jāgratyapi tatsvarūpam |
līnaṁ suṣuptau ca mṛtaṁ turīye mano vibudhyeta kathaṁ tamekam ||

The mind always veils (for itself) the Real Nature of that Self, both in dream and in waking. Becoming latent in deep sleep and wholly extinguished in the Supreme State, how can it ever know Him, who is the Sole Reality?

What then is 'knowing God'?

274.　स्वमूलमन्विष्य मनः परस्मिन् यात्येकतां यत् सहजात्मभावे ।
स एव सत्यः परमस्य बोध इत्यस्ति वाणी भगवत्तमस्य ॥

svamūlamanviṣya manaḥ parasmin yātyekatāṁ yat sahajātmabhāve |
sa eva satyaḥ paramasya bodha ityasti vāṇī bhagavattamasya ||

There is the pronouncement of the Most Holy One, that the true knowing of God is simply the mind becoming one with Him in the Natural State by seeking the Source wherefrom it has come into being.

Thus the pair of God and the individual soul is resolved. The conclusion is the following:-

275.　भिन्नौ भवेतां न हि तत्त्वदृष्ट्या जीवेश्वरौ द्वाविति निश्चयेन ।
भक्त्याऽथवा स्वात्मगवेषयोगात् तस्मिन्नभेदेन लभेत निष्ठाम् ॥

bhinnau bhavetāṁ na hi tattvadṛṣṭyā jīveśvarau dvāviti niścayena |
bhaktyā'thavā svātmagaveṣayogāt tasminnabhedena labheta niṣṭhām ||

What one has to do is to obtain perfect poise in unity with the Supreme Being, whether by devotion or by the Quest of the Real Self, with the clear understanding that God and the soul are not distinct entities in reality.

The next pair to be discussed is that of Knowledge and Ignorance.

276.   ज्ञानाज्ञते भिन्नपदेऽज्ञते द्वे सांसारिके स्वाज्ञजनानुभूते ।
द्वाभ्यां विमुक्तो भवति प्रबुद्धो द्वन्द्वं मृषेदं खलु यद्वदन्यत् ॥

jñānājñate bhinnapade'jñate dve sāṁsārike svājñajanānubhūte |
dvābhyāṁ vimukto bhavati prabuddho dvandvaṁ mṛṣedaṁ khalu
yadvadanyat ||

There is a twofold ignorance experienced by those not aware of the Real Self, which are named as knowledge and ignorance. The Sage is delivered from both. This pair is unreal just like all else.

277.   उभेऽपि चैते भवतः सहैव नैकं विनाऽन्येन भवेत् कदाऽपि ।
स्वाज्ञानमूलं द्वयमित्यतश्चाप्यज्ञानमेव द्वितयं समानम् ॥

ubhe'pi caite bhavataḥ sahaiva naikaṁ vinā'nyena bhavet kadā'pi |
svājñānamūlaṁ dvayamityataścāpyajñānameva dvitayaṁ samānam ||

The two are inseparable; neither exists without the other; and because both arise from Ignorance of the Self, therefore both are equally ignorance.

Worldly knowledge and worldly ignorance, are both ignorance for the reason stated here. This is explained further.

278. ज्ञातृस्वरूपावगतिं विनैव ज्ञातुं स्वतोऽन्यद्यतते हि सर्वः ।
अज्ञानजं ज्ञानमिदं हि तस्मादज्ञानमेवेति गुरूपदेशः ॥

jñātṛsvarūpāvagatiṁ vinaiva jñātuṁ svato'nyadyatate hi sarvaḥ |
ajñānajaṁ jñānamidaṁ hi tasmādajñānameveti gurūpadeśaḥ ||

Since every one seeks to know what is not-self, being ignorant of his own Real Self, therefore this (relative) knowledge is an out-come of the Ignorance, and hence, says our Guru, it is only ignorance.

279. ज्ञाताऽहमस्मीत्युदियाद्य एष तदीयतत्त्वावगतिं विनैव ।
यद्यद्विजानाति धियेन्द्रियैर्वा तत्तद्विजानात्ययथावदेव ॥

jñātā'hamasmītyudiyādya eṣa tadīyatattvāvagatiṁ vinaiva |
yadyadvijānāti dhiyendriyairvā tattadvijānātyayathāvadeva ||

Whatever one knows by the intellect or the senses, without first knowing the Truth of the one that arises, saying 'I am the knower', all that he knows only wrongly.

280. अविद्यमानं बत विश्वमेतत् सद्वद्विजानाति हि बोधहीनः ।
अलौकिकं चापि निजं स्वरूपं जानाति लोके बत जीवभूतम् ॥

avidyamānaṁ bata viśvametat sadvadvijānāti hi bodhahīnaḥ |
alaukikaṁ cāpi nijaṁ svarūpaṁ jānāti loke bata jīvabhūtam ||

He that knows not the Self might consider the world, which is unreal, as real, and looks upon his own Real Self, which transcends the world, as an individual soul contained in the world.

281.	धीरिन्द्रियाण्यप्यपि मानसं च भवन्त्यविद्यापरिचारकाणि ।
अतः प्रमाणानि हि लौकिकानि सम्मोहनायैव भवन्ति जन्तोः ॥

dhīrindriyāṇyapyapi mānasaṁ ca bhavantyavidyāparicārakāni |
ataḥ pramāṇāni hi laukikāni sammohanāyaiva bhavanti jantoḥ ||

The intellect, the senses and the mind are only the servants of the primary Ignorance. Hence the worldly modes of proof serve only to delude the creature.

282.	ज्ञानाज्ञते द्वे भवतोऽनुभूते येनाहमा तस्य कुतो नु जन्म ।
इति स्वतत्त्वस्य गवेषणेन नष्टेऽहमाख्ये द्वितयं च नश्येत् ॥

jñānājñate dve bhavato'nubhūte yenāhamā tasya kuto nu janma |
iti svatattvasya gaveṣaṇena naṣṭe'hamākhye dvitayaṁ ca naśyet ||

If by the Quest, 'Whence arises the Ego, the experiencer of the two, knowledge and ignorance' the Ego dies, with it will be extinguished this pair (of knowledge and ignorance).

283.	ज्ञानं यथार्थं त्वहमो विनाशो निजस्वरूपे सहजा स्थितिर्हि ।
शिष्टे न तस्यां भवतोऽज्ञते द्वे सांसारिके द्वैतविवर्जितायाम् ॥

jñānaṁ yathārthaṁ tvahamo vināśo nijasvarūpe sahajā sthitirhi |
śiṣṭe na tasyāṁ bhavato'jñate dve sāṁsārike dvaitavivarjitāyām ||

Right Awareness is only dwelling in the Natural State of the Self, on the extinction of the Ego. In that State which is free from duality, these two ignorances, which belong to the worldly life, do not survive.

284. तां ज्ञाननिष्ठां निगदन्ति बुद्धा ज्ञानाज्ञते द्वे भवतो न यस्याम् ।
निष्ठा परा सा विदुषो हि यस्यां नास्ति स्वतोऽन्यच्चिदचित्स्वरूपम् ॥

tāṁ jñānaniṣṭhāṁ nigadanti buddhā jñānājñate dve bhavato na yasyām |
niṣṭhā parā sā viduṣo hi yasyāṁ nāsti svato'nyaccidacitsvarūpam ||

The sages (Buddhas) call that the State of Right Awareness, in which there is neither knowledge nor ignorance. That is the Highest State, wherein there is nothing other than the Self, whether sentient or insentient.

285. अपण्डितः पण्डित आत्मविच्च त्रयोऽपि चाज्ञा हि समानमेव ।
अज्ञस्तृतीयोऽपि यतो न तस्य स्वस्मात् पृथक्किञ्चन वेद्यमस्ति ॥

apaṇḍitaḥ paṇḍita ātmavicca trayo'pi cājñā hi samānameva |
ajñastṛtīyo'pi yato na tasya svasmāt pṛthakkiñcana vedyamasti ||

The illiterate, the literate and the 'Knower of the Self' are all three equally ignorant. The third one also is ignorant, because for him there is nothing knowable, other than the Self.

This was what Bhagavan Sri Ramana said. The first two are ignorant because they know not the self. The Sage is ignorant for different reasons which is here stated. He also said:

286. निष्ठां गतोऽसौ निजधाम्नि सत्ये वन्द्यः समस्तैर्मनुजैः सुरैश्च ।
पुंसः परस्मादपृथक्तयाऽसौ मुमुक्षुपुंसां भजनीय एव ॥

niṣṭhāṁ gato'sau nijadhāmni satye vandyaḥ samastairmanujaiḥ suraiśca |
puṁsaḥ parasmādapṛthaktayā'sau mumukṣupuṁsāṁ bhajanīya eva ||

That One, who has become established in his own Natural State, is adorable by all, whether men or angels. As he is not distinct from the Supreme Being, he is also fit to be adored (as God) by the seekers of Deliverance.

A doubt raised by some disciples is next answered.

287. अज्ञानमन्तं भजतां तुरीये नश्येत् कुतो ज्ञानमुतेति केचित् ।
पृच्छन्त्यबोधात्मकतामबुद्ध्वा ज्ञानाभिधस्यास्य हि लौकिकस्य ॥

ajñānamantaṁ bhajatāṁ turīye naśyet kuto jñānamuteti kecit |
pṛcchantyabodhātmakatāmabuddhvā jñānābhidhasyāsya hi laukikasya ||

Not knowing that this worldly knowledge is only ignorance, some ask: 'Let ignorance come to an end in the Supreme State, but why should knowledge also cease?'

288.　नैवास्ति बोध्यं न च कोऽपि बोद्धा न चास्ति बोधोऽपि तुरीयभावे ।
　　　द्वन्द्वानि यद्वन्न भवन्ति तुर्ये तथा त्रिपुट्योऽपि न तत्र सन्ति ॥

naivāsti bodhyaṁ na ca ko'pi boddhā na cāsti bodho'pi turīyabhāve |
dvandvāni yadvanna bhavanti turye tathā tripuṭyo'pi na tatra santi ||

In the Supreme state there is nothing to be known, neither a knower, nor knowledge (of objects). Just as pairs of opposites are absent in that State, so the triads are also absent.

289.　एकः स आत्मैव हि तुर्यभावे ज्ञानाज्ञताभ्यां रहितश्चकास्ति ।
　　　ज्ञानस्वरूपः स्वयमव्ययो यच्छून्यं कथं तत् परमं पदं स्यात् ॥

ekaḥ sa ātmaiva hi turyabhāve jñānājñatābhyāṁ rahitaścakāsti |
jñānasvarūpaḥ svayamavyayo yacchūnyaṁ kathaṁ tat paramaṁ padaṁ syāt ||

In the Supreme State that Self shines alone, free from both knowledge and ignorance. Since He is there as Pure Consciousness, without change, how can that State be a void?

That that State is not a *void* is stated here because some believe that there is no Reality beyond the world.

290.　चैतन्यभासा निजयैव तस्मिन् भात्यात्मरूपं शिवमद्वितीयम् ।
　　　न भासकं तस्य न तेन भास्यं सत्यं किमप्यस्ति तुरीयभावे ॥

caitanyabhāsā nijayaiva tasmin bhātyātmarūpaṁ śivamadvitīyam |
na bhāsakaṁ tasya na tena bhāsyaṁ satyaṁ kimapyasti turīyabhāve ||

Therein the Self shines by His own Light of Consciousness, as the Sole Reality, which is Bliss.

In that Supreme State there is no reality to shed light on Him, nor anything other that could shine by his Light.

291. नोदेति नाप्यस्तमुदेति तस्य चैतन्यदीप्तिः सततैकरूपा ।
आदाय तस्यैव चिदंशलेशं प्रतीयते चेतनवन्मनो हि ॥

nodeti nāpyastamudeti tasya caitanyadīptiḥ satataikarūpā |
ādāya tasyaiva cidaṁśaleśaṁ pratīyate cetanavanmano hi ||

That consciousness-light, which is His Nature, neither rises nor sets, but is ever the same (without change). It is by borrowing a minute particle of His consciousness that the mind appears conscious.

292. मत्वाऽऽत्मनाशास्य पदं तुरीयं बिभ्यत्यमुष्मादविवेकिनो ये ।
वाञ्छन्ति ते नित्यसुखाय गन्तुं लोकान्तरं दिव्यमबुद्धशिष्याः ॥

matvā''tmanāśasya padaṁ turīyaṁ bibhyatyamuṣmādavivekino ye |
vāñchanti te nityasukhāya gantuṁ lokāntaraṁ divyamabuddhaśiṣyāḥ ||

Disciples of non-sages, fearing that in the Supreme State the Self will cease to be, wish to go to some other celestial world, for the sake of eternal happiness.

293. लोको यथाऽयं भविता मृषैव तथैव लोका अनृताः परे च ।
आत्मैव लोकः खलु बुद्धपुंसः स एव तस्माद् गदितः
स्वयं सन् ॥

loko yathā'yaṁ bhavitā mṛṣaiva tathaiva lokā anṛtāḥ pare ca |
ātmaiva lokaḥ khalu buddhapuṁsaḥ sa eva tasmād gaditaḥ svayaṁ san ||

As this world is unreal, so the other worlds also are unreal. For the Sage (who is in the Supreme State) the Self is Himself the world, and hence that World is real in its own right.

Hence sages are free from all worldly attractions.

294. किं नो धनेन प्रजयाऽपि येषां आत्मैव लोको भवतीति बुद्धाः ।
नापि प्रवृत्तिं न च वा निवृत्तिं वाञ्छन्ति संशान्तसमस्तकामाः ॥

kiṁ no dhanena prajayā'pi yeṣām ātmaiva loko bhavatīti buddhāḥ |
nāpi pravṛttiṁ na ca vā nivṛttiṁ vāñchanti saṁśāntasamastakāmāḥ ||

"What for do we need wealth or offspring when the Self is Himself the world?" So thinking, the sages, whose desires have all subsided, care not for action, nor for inaction.

295. एकः स बोधात्मक एव सत्यो बोधः प्रपञ्चाकृतिरज्ञतैव ।
बोधात् प्रपञ्चाकृतिकात् प्रपञ्चो भिन्नो यतो नास्त्यत एव मिथ्या ॥

ekaḥ sa bodhātmaka eva satyo bodhaḥ prapañcākṛtirajñataiva |
bodhāt prapañcākṛtikāt prapañco bhinno yato nāstyata eva mithyā ||

That Self, who is Consciousness, is alone real; the consciousness which has the world-form is ignorance (not true knowledge); and since the world does not exist apart from that world-form-consciousness, it is unreal.

The question then arises, Is this Ignorance real? It is answered thus:-

296. अज्ञानमेतत् तमसा समानं न शक्यमस्तीति तु वक्तुमेतत् ।
तमो न यद्वत् सहते प्रकाशमज्ञानमेवं सहते न बोधम् ॥

ajñānametat tamasā samānaṁ na śakyamastīti tu vaktumetat |
tamo na yadvat sahate prakāśamajñānamevaṁ sahate na bodham ||

This ignorance is like darkness; it cannot be said that it exists. As darkness does not bear the light so this Ignorance does not bear (the Light of) Right Awareness.

But the question arises, wherein does this Ignorance subsist, when it appears. The answer is given next.

297. प्रतीयतेऽज्ञानमिदं परस्मिन् प्रपञ्चरूपं सदिवाज्ञमर्त्यैः ।
सत्ये सुवर्णे रुचकान्यसन्ति सद्वत् प्रतीतानि यथा भवन्ति ॥

pratīyate'jñānamidaṁ parasmin prapañcarūpaṁ sadivājñamartyaiḥ |
satye suvarṇe rucakānyasanti sadvat pratītāni yathā bhavanti ||

This Ignorance, which has the world-form, appears as real to the ignorant ones, in the Supreme Being (who is Consciousness), as jewels, which are unreal, appear as real in gold (which is relatively real).

Here the simile of gold and jewels is used, and it is usually supposed that both are real; but here the jewels are described as unreal. Why is it so described?

298. सत्यं सुवर्णं रुचकान्यसन्तीत्येतत् कथं स्यादिति चेद् गुरोर्नः ।
दार्ष्टान्तिकं विश्वमिदं मृषेति सन्दर्शनायात्र पदप्रयोगः ॥

satyaṁ suvarṇaṁ rucakānyasantītyetat kathaṁ syāditi ced gurornaḥ |
dārṣṭāntikaṁ viśvamidaṁ mṛṣeti sandarśanāyātra padaprayogaḥ ||

If it be asked. 'How is it said that gold is real, but jewels are unreal', (the answer is that) the words are used here by our Guru in order to show that the world, which is the subject of comparison, is unreal.

Can this be done, it may be asked. It is thus answered.

299. दार्ष्टान्तिकस्य स्फुटबोधनाय सर्वोऽपि दृष्टान्त उदीर्यते यत् ।
विवक्षितार्थावगतिर्यथा स्यात् तथैव दृष्टान्तनिवेदनानि ॥

dārṣṭāntikasya sphuṭabodhanāya sarvo'pi dṛṣṭānta udīryate yat |
vivakṣitārthāvagatiryathā syāt tathaiva dṛṣṭāntanivedanāni ||

Since a simile is used for conveying a clear knowledge of the subject of the teaching, the simile is so presented as to convey the intended meaning.

The propriety of thus presenting this simile is next shown.

300. सुवर्णमासन् रुचकानि पूर्वं तदेव मध्येऽपि तदेव चान्ते ।
सत्यं सुवर्णं रुचकान्यपेक्ष्य विनश्वरत्वाद्रुचकानि मिथ्या ॥

suvarṇamāsan rucakāni pūrvaṁ tadeva madhye'pi tadeva cānte |
satyaṁ suvarṇaṁ rucakānyapekṣya vinaśvaratvādrucakāni mithyā ||

The jewels were (only) gold before; they are only that in the middle, and they are that in the end also. As compared to the jewels, gold is (relatively) real and because the jewel-forms are transient, they are unreal.

This is in accordance with the Vedantic definition of reality, which is here stated once more.

301.   अनित्यतैवात्र मृषात्वलिङ्गं सत्यत्वमुक्तं खलु नित्यतैव ।
अतोऽज्ञता तज्जमिदं च विश्वं रज्ज्वामहिर्यद्वदसत्यमेव ॥

anityataivātra mṛṣātvaliṅgaṁ satyatvamuktaṁ khalu nityataiva |
ato'jñatā tajjamidaṁ ca viśvaṁ rajjvāmahiryadvadasatyameva ||

Here impermanence alone is the test of unreality; permanence itself is affirmed as (the quality of) reality. Hence (it follows) that ignorance and the world which is born of it, are unreal, exactly like the serpent seen in a rope.

This has been discussed and settled in a previous context.

Another analogy is used next to explain the teaching.

302.   पटे प्रकाशेन युते यथा वा मृषैव चित्राण्यचले चलन्ति ।
तद्वज्जगच्चित्रततिश्च सेयमायाति संयाति मृषैव सत्ये ॥

paṭe prakāśena yute yathā vā mṛṣaiva citrāṇyacale calanti |
tadvajjagaccitratatiśca seyamāyāti saṁyāti mṛṣaiva satye ||

Or, as the moving pictures, pass across the unmoving lighted screen (in a cinema show), so the series of pictures, namely the world, comes and goes on (the substratum), the Real (which is unmoving).

This is the simile used in *'Forty Verses on Reality'* in the very beginning, immediately after the first two benedictory verses.

303.   द्रष्टा चलच्चित्रततेर्विभिन्नो द्रष्टा जगच्चित्रततावभिन्नः ।
विशेष एवं जगतोऽस्ति यस्मात् सद्रष्टृकस्यास्य मृषात्वसिद्धिः ॥

draṣṭā calaccitratatervibhinno draṣṭā jagaccitratatāvabhinnaḥ |
viśeṣa evaṁ jagato'sti yasmāt sadraṣṭṛkasyāsya mṛṣātvasiddhiḥ ||

(But) in respect of the moving pictures the seer is distinct from them, whereas in the world pictures the seer is included. Thus the world differs (from the cinema show); the result is that the world and its seer (the individual) are both unreal.

304.   यथा चलच्चित्रततेर्विरामे पटप्रकाशोऽस्ति विशुद्ध एवम् ।
मृषाजगच्चित्रततेर्विरामे शिष्येत शुद्धा चितिरात्मरूपा ॥

yathā calaccitratatervirāme paṭaprakāśo'sti viśuddha evam |
mṛṣājagaccitratatervirāme śiṣyeta śuddhā citirātmarūpā ||

Just as the light of the screen remains clear (of the shadow pictures) when those moving pictures have ceased, so too when the series of world-pictures cease, the Consciousness, which is the Self, will remain clear, (as the Sole Reality).

The unreality of the world is further highlighted by the world-appearance being made up of a series of momentary pictures, as is shown next.

305. प्रतिक्षणं नूतनमेव चित्रं वीक्ष्यापि सर्वं मनुते यथैकम् ।
तथैकमज्ञो मनुते हि वीक्ष्य प्रतिक्षणं नूतनमेव विश्वम् ॥

pratikṣaṇaṁ nūtanameva citraṁ vīkṣyāpi sarvaṁ manute yathaikam |
tathaikamajño manute hi vīkṣya pratikṣaṇaṁ nūtanameva viśvam ||

As at every instant of time the spectator, seeing only a new picture, assumes that what he sees is one, so the ignorant one, seeing an utterly new world every instant, assumes that what he sees is one continuous world.

This mistaken view concerns the seer's own body also. From this it follows that the seer who is only a reflection in the three bodies of the seer (the soul), is unreal — that is, as unreal as the spectacle, the world.

The world-appearance is possible only because the Real Self, who is Consciousness, is present as Substratum.

306. आधारवस्त्रेऽपि तदीयभासा यथा चलच्चित्रततिर्विभाति ।
एवं प्रपञ्चोऽपि सदात्मरूपे तदीयसंवित्प्रभयैव भाति ॥

ādhāravastre'pi tadīyabhāsā yathā calaccitratatirvibhāti |
evaṁ prapañco'pi sadātmarūpe tadīyasaṁvitprabhayaiva bhāti ||

As the succession of moving pictures shines only on the screen and by its light, so the world shines only on the Real Self and by His Light of Consciousness.

307. आत्मा स्वतः सन्नत एव हेतोर्नैव स्वतः सत्यमिदं हि विश्वम्‌ ।
विज्ञेयमेवं जगतो मृषात्वं सत्ताऽऽत्मनश्चापि चिदात्मकस्य ॥

ātmā svataḥ sannata eva hetornaiva svataḥ satyamidaṃ hi viśvam |
vijñeyamevaṃ jagato mṛṣātvaṃ sattā"tmanaścāpi cidātmakasya ||

Just for this reason the Real Self is real in His own right; this world is not at all real in its own right: thus should be understood the unreality of the world and the reality of the Self, who is Pure Consciousness.

There is a distinction to be noted between the popular sense of the word 'real' and its sense in Advaitic Vedanta philosophy, which has already been expounded.

The next topic to be studied is the mental impression that time and space are objective realities. These two are inseparable from the world-appearance, and hence the world would continue to be taken as real if these two are taken to be so.

308. देशेन कालेन विभक्तमेव स्वप्ने मनो जागरिते समानम्‌ ।
अवैति देहादिसमस्तदृश्यमतो विचार्याऽस्त्यनयोश्च सत्ता ॥

deśena kālena vibhaktameva svapne mano jāgarite samānam |
avaiti dehādisamastadṛśyamato vicāryā'styanayośca sattā ||

The mind knows all visible objects, the physical body and all the rest, equally in dream and in waking, as divided up in space and in time, and hence it is necessary to inquire whether these two are real (or not).

309.   त्रयं मनोमात्रमिदं प्रदिष्टं देशोऽपि कालोऽपि निमित्तयोगः ।
पाश्चात्यदेशीयविपश्चिताऽस्ति कान्ताभिधानेन सुयुक्तिवादैः ॥

trayaṁ manomātramidaṁ pradiṣṭaṁ deśo'pi kālo'pi nimittayogaḥ |
pāścātyadeśīyavipaścitā'sti kāntābhidhānena suyuktivādaiḥ ||

These three, namely space, time and causality, have been shown to be only mental, by an occidental philosopher named Kant by means of good reasons.

310.   सर्वानुभूत्याऽपि सुषुप्तिभावे बुद्धानुभूत्याऽपि तुरीयभावे ।
मृषात्वमेतत् प्रकटीकरोति स्फुटं मुमुक्षोर्भगवान् गुरुर्नः ॥

sarvānubhūtyā'pi suṣuptibhāve buddhānubhūtyā'pi turīyabhāve |
mṛṣātvametat prakaṭīkaroti sphuṭaṁ mumukṣorbhagavān gururnaḥ ||

Bhagavan Sri Ramana, our Guru, makes it clear to the seekers of Deliverance, from the experience of all men in deep sleep, and from the experiences of sages in the Supreme State, that these three are unreal.

311.   सुषुप्तिभावे मनसि प्रलीने तुरीयभावे मनसि प्रणष्टे ।
न कोऽपि जानाति हि देशकालौ मनोमयं तद्द्वितयं हि तस्मात् ॥

suṣuptibhāve manasi pralīne turīyabhāve manasi praṇaṣṭe |
na ko'pi jānāti hi deśakālau manomayaṁ taddvitayaṁ hi tasmāt ||

Because no one knows space and time, in deep sleep wherein the mind is latent, and in the Supreme State, wherein the mind is lost, therefore these two are only mental.

312. मनः सविश्वं सृजति द्वयं च स्वप्ने यथा जागरिते तथैव ।
ताभ्यां विना वेत्ति मनो न किञ्चिदेष स्वभावो मनसो हि नित्यः ॥

manaḥ saviśvaṁ sṛjati dvayaṁ ca svapne yathā jāgarite tathaiva |
tābhyāṁ vinā vetti mano na kiñcideṣa svabhāvo manaso hi nityaḥ ||

As in the dream state, so in waking, the mind creates these two along with the world; without them the mind knows nothing; this is the enduring nature of the mind.

313. देहोऽहमित्यज्ञतयैव मर्त्यो देशेऽपि कालेऽस्म्यहमित्यवैति ।
देशे भवामो न हि नापि काले देहा वयं चेदुभयोर्भवेम ॥

deho'hamityajñatayaiva martyo deśe'pi kāle'smyahamityavaiti |
deśe bhavāmo na hi nāpi kāle dehā vayaṁ cedubhayorbhavema ||

Only because of the Ignorance 'I am the body' man has the awareness 'I am in space and time': really we are not in space, nor in time; if we were bodies, then (and only then) would we be in them.

314. देहा वयं नो न च देहिनो वा जीवा वयं नैव कदाऽप्यभूम ।
अस्मासु तौ द्वौ मनसोपक्लृप्तौ ह्यविद्यया यद्वदिदं समस्तम् ॥

dehā vayaṁ no na ca dehino vā jīvā vayaṁ naiva kadā'pyabhūma |
asmāsu tau dvau manasopakḷptau hyavidyayā yadvadidaṁ samastam ||

We are not bodies, nor do we own them, since we never became souls. Space and time are created in US by the mind, because of the Ignorance, just like all these things.

It may be asked when we shall be rid of this delusion of the objective reality of space and time. The answer is given in the next verse, according to Bhagavan Sri Ramana, our Guru.

315. मनोऽहमो जन्मभुवं विमृग्य लभेत शान्तिं यदि तुर्यभावे ।
तदा निगीर्येत सदात्मनैव सहाहमा तद्द्वितयं सविश्वम् ॥

mano'hamo janmabhuvaṁ vimṛgya labheta śāntiṁ yadi turyabhāve |
tadā nigīryeta sadātmanaiva sahāhamā taddvitayaṁ saviśvam ||

If the mind, by the Quest of its Source, attains Peace in the Supreme State, then these two will be swallowed up by the Real Self Himself, along with the Ego, and the world.

316. मायामयं कारणकार्यरूपं सदेशकालं बत विश्वमेतत् ।
न विक्रियामेति कदाचिदात्मा देशेन कालेन निमित्ततो वा ॥

māyāmayaṁ kāraṇakāryarūpaṁ sadeśakālaṁ bata viśvametat |
na vikriyāmeti kadācidātmā deśena kālena nimittato vā ||

The whole world, which is composed of causes and effects, together with space and time, are illusory. The Real Self never undergoes change, whether by space or by time, or by causality.

317. सदैकधैवाच्युत एक आत्मा कालातिगो देशविवर्जितश्च ।
पूर्णः प्रबुद्धैरनुभूयते यत् स एव सत्यो न तु किञ्चिदन्यत् ॥

sadaikadhaivācyuta eka ātmā kālātigo deśavivarjitaśca |
pūrṇaḥ prabuddhairanubhūyate yat sa eva satyo na tu kiñcidanyat ||

Since the One Real Self (of all), who is ever the same, never swerving from His True Nature, transcending time and devoid of space, and hence infinite, is experienced by the sages, He alone is the Real, nothing else.

The three divisions of time, namely the past, the present and the future, are next dealt with and shown to be unreal.

318. भूतोऽपि भावी च भवन्नितीमे कालस्य भेदा अपि नैव सत्याः ।
भूतोऽपि भावी भवदाश्रयौ च भवन् स्वकाले भवतो ह्युभौ च ॥

bhūto'pi bhāvī ca bhavannitīme kālasya bhedā api naiva satyāḥ |
bhūto'pi bhāvī bhavadāśrayau ca bhavan svakāle bhavato hyubhau ca ||

Also the divisions of time, namely past, present and future, are not at all real. The past and the future are dependent upon the present, and are themselves present in their own times.

319. अतो भवन्नेव समस्तकालो वाचैव कुर्वन्ति विभागमेवम् ।
आत्मस्वरूपं खलु नित्यसत्यमतो भवन्नाम तदेव नान्यत् ॥

ato bhavanneva samastakālo vācaiva kurvanti vibhāgamevam |
ātmasvarūpaṁ khalu nityasatyamato bhavannāma tadeva nānyat ||

Thus all time is only present; men make this division only by words; the Eternal Reality is indeed the Real Self alone. Hence He alone is present, nothing else.

320. इच्छेदतस्तत्त्वममुष्य बोद्धुं तुरीयभावाधिगमेन साधुः ।
चर्चेह भूतस्य च भाविनोऽपि विनैकसङ्ख्यां गणनेति दिष्टा ॥

icchedatastattvamamuṣya boddhuṁ turīyabhāvādhigamena sādhuḥ |
carceha bhūtasya ca bhāvino'pi vinaikasaṅkhyāṁ gaṇaneti diṣṭā ||

Hence the aspirant must aim at experience of the Truth of that Self by attaining the Supreme State; the discussion of the past and of the future is declared to be like trying to count without knowledge of the number 'one'.

321. अस्त्येकसङ्ख्यैव न काचिदन्या सङ्ख्याः समस्ताश्च
तदात्मिका हि ।
अस्त्येवमात्माकृतिका चिदेव तदात्मकं सर्वमिदं च विश्वम् ॥

astyekasaṅkhyaiva na kācidanyā saṅkhyāḥ samastāśca tadātmikā hi |
astyevamātmākṛtikā cideva tadātmakaṁ sarvamidaṁ ca viśvam ||

Only the number 'one' exists, and none else, because all numbers are modifications of it. In the same way, the Consciousness, which is the Self, alone exists, and the whole world is only He.

322. यथैकसङ्ख्यामवगम्य सम्यक् सङ्ख्यां समस्तामवगन्तुमीष्टे ।
ज्ञात्वैवमेकम् निजतत्त्वमेव जानन्ति बुद्धा जगतोऽपि तत्त्वम् ॥

yathaikasaṅkhyāmavagamya samyak saṅkhyāṁ samastāmavagantumīṣṭe |
jñātvaivamekam nijatattvameva jānanti buddhā jagato'pi tattvam ||

As one becomes able, by knowing the number one, to know all the numbers, so, after knowing the Truth of themselves, the sages come to know the truth of the world also.

323. बोधः स्वतोऽन्यस्य विना स्वबोधमबोध एवेति गुरुर्ब्रवीति ।
स्वस्मिन्नबुद्धे सति वेत्ति यद्यत् तत्तद्विजानात्ययथावदेव ॥

bodhaḥ svato'nyasya vinā svabodhamabodha eveti gururbravīti |
svasminnabuddhe sati vetti yadyat tattadvijānātyayathāvadeva ||

Knowledge of anything other than the Self without knowing the Truth of oneself, the Guru says, is only ignorance. Whatever one knows without right awareness of the Self, all that he knows only contrary to the truth.

324. स्वस्मिन् विबुद्धे निजमार्गणेन बोद्धुं स्वतोऽन्यन्न हि किञ्चिदस्ति ।
बुद्धस्य भात्यात्मतयैव सर्वमात्मा ततः सर्व इति प्रसिद्धः ॥

svasmin vibuddhe nijamārgaṇena boddhuṁ svato'nyanna hi kiñcidasti |
buddhasya bhātyātmatayaiva sarvamātmā tataḥ sarva iti prasiddhaḥ ||

When by the Quest of the Self, that Self is known, there remains nothing else to be known. To the Sage all things shine only as the Self, and hence the Self is well known as the All (in the Vedantas).

325.   सत्यात्मभावे स्थितिमेव तस्मात् सर्वज्ञतां श्रीरमणो ब्रवीति ।
       सर्वज्ञतां यां गणयन्त्यबुद्धाः सैषाऽज्ञतैवेत्यपि वक्ति सोऽयम् ॥

satyātmabhāve sthitimeva tasmāt sarvajñatāṁ śrīramaṇo bravīti |
sarvajñatāṁ yāṁ gaṇayantyabuddhāḥ saiṣā'jñataivetyapi vakti so'yam ||

Therefore Bhagavan Sri Ramana says that Omniscience is only the State of Being the Real Self; He also says that what is considered as omniscience by the Ignorant is only ignorance.

How the Self is the All is next stated.

326.   नेदं शरीरात् पृथगस्ति विश्वं नेदं शरीरं मनसोऽस्ति भिन्नम् ।
       सत्यात्मनो नास्ति मनो विभिन्नमात्मैव तस्मादखिलं च विश्वम् ॥

nedaṁ śarīrāt pṛthagasti viśvaṁ nedaṁ śarīraṁ manaso'sti bhinnam |
satyātmano nāsti mano vibhinnamātmaiva tasmādakhilaṁ ca viśvam ||

This world is not other than the body; this body is not distinct from the mind; the mind does not exist apart from the Real Self; therefore the Self is all the world.

327.   अहं पुरा जन्मनि कीटगासमितः परं चापि कथं भवेयम् ।
       ईदृग्विचारा बत मुग्धतैव न जन्म लेभे हि कदाचिदात्मा ॥

aham purā janmani kīdṛgāsamitaḥ param cāpi katham bhaveyam |
īdṛgvicārā bata mugdhataiva na janma lebhe hi kadācidātmā ||

"How was I in my previous birth, and how shall I be in the next birth?" such inquiries are only (due to) ignorance, because the Self was never born.

328.	व्यष्टेः समष्टेरपि चिन्तनानि निरर्थकान्येव मुमुक्षुपुंसाम् ।
चिन्ताः समस्ताः प्रभवन्ति यस्य तन्मूलचिन्तैव हि मुक्तिदात्री ॥

vyaṣṭeḥ samaṣṭerapi cintanāni nirarthakānyeva mumukṣupuṁsām |
cintāḥ samastāḥ prabhavanti yasya tanmūlacintaiva hi muktidātrī ||

Thinking about the totality and the distinct units (individuals) are vain for the seekers of Deliverance; Only the inquiry as to the source of him (the ego) who is interested in the totality and the units will lead to Deliverance.

329.	प्रश्नाः क्रियन्तेऽत्र मुधैव मर्त्यैः सृष्टं जगत् केन कथं च पूर्वम् ।
का नाम माया कतमाऽप्यविद्या कतं न्वभूज्जीव इति प्रमादात् ॥

praśnāḥ kriyante'tra mudhaiva martyaiḥ sṛṣṭam jagat kena katham ca pūrvam |
kā nāma māyā katamā'pyavidyā katam nvabhūjjīva iti pramādāt ||

Vainly questions are posed by the deluded ones. "By whom, and how, was the world created in the beginning?" "What is Maya?" "What is Ignorance?" "How did the individual soul come into being?" due to forgetting the main thing needing to be inquired into.

The secret of creation is briefly stated next.

330.   दृष्टेर्न सृष्टिः पृथगस्ति काचिद् दृष्टिश्च सृष्टिर्द्वयमेकमेव ।
       सा दृष्टिरज्ञानमयीति हेतोस्तस्याः प्रहाणं निधनं हि सत्यम् ॥

drṣṭerna srṣṭiḥ prṭhagasti kācid drṣṭiśca srṣṭirdvayamekameva |
sā drṣṭirajñānamayīti hetostasyāḥ prahāṇaṁ nidhanaṁ hi satyam ||

There is no creation apart from seeing; seeing
and creation are one and the same; and because
that seeing is due to the Ignorance, to cease seeing
is the truth of dissolution (of the world).

Maya is next explained.

331.   मायाभिधाना परशक्तिरेव मनस्सु बुद्धीन्द्रियबोधरूपम् ।
       विचित्रमेतं सृजति प्रपञ्चं स सत्यवद् गृह्यत एव मुग्धैः ॥

māyābhidhānā paraśaktireva manassu buddhīndriyabodharūpam |
vicitrametaṁ srjati prapañcaṁ sa satyavad grhyata eva mugdhaiḥ ||

It is the Might of the Supreme Being, called
Maya, which takes the form of sense-perception
and thereby creates this varied world, and the
deluded ones are persuaded that it is real.

Ignorance of the individual is related to the Power of
illusion that belongs to the Supreme Being. There is no other
explanation of creation.

It is next shown that engaging in these inquiries
postpones the main thing, the Quest of the Real Self, which
is the main thing to be engaged in.

332. सद्वद्विचारेण मृषात्मकस्य सत्यात् प्रमादो भविता ध्रुवं हि ।
न च प्रमादादपरोऽस्ति मृत्युः स्वो नष्टकल्पोऽस्ति हि तेन साधोः ॥

sadvadvicāreṇa mṛṣātmakasya satyāt pramādo bhavitā dhruvaṁ hi |
na ca pramādādaparo'sti mṛtyuḥ svo naṣṭakalpo'sti hi tena sādhoḥ ||

Inquiring into unrealities, taking them as real, leads to forgetting of the Real (Self). And there is no death other than this forgetting, because thereby the Self is almost lost to the seeker.

The urgency of seeking the Self is next pointed out.

333. अस्मिन्नवेदीद्यदि जन्मनि स्वं तदैव सत्यं पुरुषस्य सत्यम् ।
न चेदवेदीदिह जन्मनि स्वं तस्यावृतं स्यादनृतेन सत्यं ॥

asminnavedīdyadi janmani svaṁ tadaiva satyaṁ puruṣasya satyam |
na cedavedīdiha janmani svaṁ tasyāvṛtaṁ syādanṛtena satyaṁ ||

If the aspirant knows the Self in this (very) life, then and only then, for him the Real is real. If in this life he fails to know the Self, for him the Real (Self) remains concealed by the unreal.

334. तद्देशकालावनृतौ विदित्वा विहाय विश्वं च समस्तमेव ।
इच्छेदधिष्ठानसदेव बोद्धुं स्वात्मस्वरूपं निजमार्गणेन ॥

taddeśakālāvanṛtau viditvā vihāya viśvaṁ ca samastameva |
icchedadhiṣṭhānasadeva boddhuṁ svātmasvarūpaṁ nijamārgaṇena ||

Therefore the aspirant, being firmly convinced that space and time are unreal, should give up the whole world and seek to know the Substratum, the Self, through the Quest of his own True Nature.

The next topic dealt with is the duality of Free Will and Fate.

335.   कर्ताऽस्म्यहं कर्मफलस्य भोक्तेत्येवं नरो यो मनुते स एव ।
धीदैवयोर्भेदमवैति सत्यं कर्ताऽपि भोक्ता न तु सत्य आत्मा ॥

kartā'smyaham karmaphalasya bhoktetyevam naro yo manute sa eva |
dhīdaivayorbhedamavaiti satyam kartā'pi bhoktā na tu satya ātmā ||

Only he that thinks "I am the doer of actions and the recipient of the fruits of actions" takes the distinction between the Intellect (Will) and Fate as real; but the Self is neither the doer nor the recipient of the fruits of actions.

336.   इष्टं यदा कर्मफलं तदानीं बलीयसीं बुद्धिमवैति दैवात् ।
यद्यन्यथा कर्मफलं भवेत्तु दैवं बलीयो मनुते तदानीम् ॥

iṣṭam yadā karmaphalam tadānīm balīyasīm buddhimavaiti daivāt |
yadyanyathā karmaphalam bhavettu daivam balīyo manute tadānīm ||

When the fruit of action is pleasant, man thinks that the Will is stronger than Fate. But when the fruit of action is otherwise, he thinks that Fate is stronger.

That this difference is unreal is then shown.

337. देवं भवेत् पूर्वकृतं हि कर्म धिया कृतं कर्म समस्तमेव ।
धीदैवयोर्द्वन्द्वमतो मृषैव तयोर्विरोधः कथमस्तु सत्यः ॥

daivaṁ bhavet pūrvakṛtaṁ hi karma dhiyā kṛtaṁ karma samastameva |
dhīdaivayordvandvamato mṛṣaiva tayorvirodhaḥ kathamastu satyaḥ ||

Fate is only action done before, and all action is done by the Will. Hence the pair of will and fate is only unreal. How can their antagonism be real?

338. धीदैवयोर्मूलमहङ्कृतिर्यत् स्वान्वेषणात् सा यदि नाशमीयात् ।
धीदैवयोर्द्वन्द्वमिदं विनश्येन्न वेत्ति धीदैवभिदां प्रबुद्धः ॥

dhīdaivayormūlamahaṅkṛtiryat svānveṣaṇāt sā yadi nāśamīyāt |
dhīdaivayordvandvamidaṁ vinaśyenna vetti dhīdaivabhidāṁ prabuddhaḥ ||

Since the root of (both) Will and Fate is the ego, this pair will cease to appear when the ego dies by the pursuit of the Quest of the Real Self, (and hence) the Sage is not aware of the distinction between Free Will and Fate.

339. बुद्धोऽमनस्को गलिताभिमानः सङ्कल्पशून्योऽपि भवेन्न कर्ता ।
भोक्ताऽपि नासौ भविता कदाऽपि न वेत्ति धीदैवभिदामतोऽसौ ॥

buddho'manasko galitābhimānaḥ saṅkalpaśūnyo'pi bhavenna kartā |
bhoktā'pi nāsau bhavitā kadā'pi na vetti dhīdaivabhidāmato'sau ||

The Sage, who has no mind and hence free from attachments and without a (personal) Will, does not become a doer of actions, nor does he reap the fruits of actions; therefore he is not aware of the distinction between Free Will and Fate.

340. स्वोऽबुद्धमर्त्यस्य च नित्यबुद्धो न सज्जते कर्मसु नैति मोहम् ।
तत्सन्निधानेन तु लब्धसंज्ञा प्रवर्तते धीः स्वगुणानुरूपम् ॥

svo'buddhamartyasya ca nityabuddho na sajjate karmasu naiti moham |
tatsannidhānena tu labdhasañjñā pravartate dhīḥ svaguṇānurūpam ||

Even in the case of an ignorant one, the Real Self is ever enlightened, and hence does not engage in actions, nor suffer delusion. But in His Presence the intellect becomes endowed with consciousness and is active according to the qualities that dominate it.

This is important. The Real Self remains unaffected, being Ever-Free. It is only the mind (or Intellect) that is ignorant and bound.

341. चिन्तामतो दैवधियोर्विहाय सांसारिकीं चापि समस्तचिन्ताम् ।
ब्रह्मात्मकं केवलमात्मतत्त्वं यतेत बोद्धुं निजमार्गणेन ॥

cintāmato daivadhiyorvihāya sāṁsārikīṁ cāpi samastacintām |
brahmātmakaṁ kevalamātmatattvaṁ yateta boddhuṁ nijamārgaṇena ||

Therefore the aspirant must cease from thoughts of the worldly life, and strive to become aware of the Truth of the Self, which is the same as the Brahman, by means of the Quest of that Self.

Then the truth about the individual soul, who is called the *jiva*, is discussed.

342.　जीवाभिधानो जगदीक्षको यस्तस्मिन्निगूढं जगतोऽस्य तत्त्वम् ।
उदेत्ययं चेदुदियाच्च विश्वं लीयेत विश्वं लयमेत्ययं चेत् ॥

jīvābhidhāno jagadīkṣako yastasminnigūḍhaṁ jagato'sya tattvam |
udetyayaṁ cedudiyācca viśvaṁ līyeta viśvaṁ layametyayaṁ cet ||

It is in the seer of the world, called the jiva, that the truth of the world lies, (because) when he arises, the world also appears, and when he goes into latency, the world also does the same.

343.　तत्तत्त्वमस्यैव निजानुभूत्या जानन् प्रबुद्धः समवैति विश्वं ।
अन्ये तु देहात्मधियाऽभिभूता विश्वं विजानन्त्ययथावदेव ॥

tattattvamasyaiva nijānubhūtyā jānan prabuddhaḥ samavaiti viśvam |
anye tu dehatmadhiyā'bhibhūtā viśvaṁ vijānantyayathāvadeva ||

Therefore the Sage, knowing the truth of the ego by the Direct Experience of the Real Self, becomes aware of the truth of the world. The rest, being overwhelmed by the belief that the body is the Self, entertain a false view of the world.

344.　जीवोऽज्ञतायाः प्रथमं स्वरूपं जीवोऽङ्कुरः संसृतिदुर्द्रुमस्य ।
विभूतिरस्यैव जगत् समस्तं नाशोऽन्ततश्चास्य विमुक्तिभावः ॥

jīvo'jñatāyāḥ prathamaṁ svarūpaṁ jīvo'ṅkuraḥ saṁsṛtidurdrumasya |
vibhūtirasyaiva jagat samastaṁ nāśo'ntataścāsya vimuktibhāvaḥ ||

The soul is the primary form of the Ignorance; it is the sprout which grows into the poison-tree of the worldly life. All this world is only its expanded form. The State of Deliverance is just its final extinction.

345. तमेनमर्थं सुगतो गुरुश्चाप्यूचे तथा शङ्करदेशिकेन्द्रः ।
ब्रूतेऽपि चास्मद्गुरुरर्थमेनं वेदान्तसारोऽप्ययमर्थ एव ॥

tamenamartham sugato guruścāpyūce tathā śaṅkaradeśikendraḥ |
brūte'pi cāsmadgururarthamenaṃ vedāntasāro'pyayamartha eva ||

The Guru Sugata (Buddha) taught this truth; also the great teacher Sankara taught the same; our own Guru also tells us the same; and this is also the essence of the Vedantas.

346. विश्वं स्वदृश्यं न विना कदाऽपि द्रष्टाऽस्य जीवो भवति प्रतीतः ।
जीवो न कोऽप्यस्ति सुषुप्तिभावे मनोमयोऽयं हि यथाऽस्य दृश्यम् ॥

viśvaṃ svadṛśyaṃ na vinā kadā'pi draṣṭā'sya jīvo bhavati pratītaḥ |
jīvo na ko'pyasti suṣuptibhāve manomayo'yaṃ hi yathā'sya dṛśyam ||

The soul, who is seer of the world, is never known apart from his spectacle, the world. There is no soul in the state of deep sleep. Hence like his spectacle (the world), he also is only a mental creation.

347. सहैव देहेन भवेत् प्रतीतो जीवाभिधोऽयं खलु सर्वदाऽपि ।
मृतौ च देहस्य न पूर्वदेहं जहात्यनादाय हि देहमन्यम् ॥

sahaiva dehena bhavet pratīto jīvābhidho'yaṁ khalu sarvadā'pi |
mṛtau ca dehasya na pūrvadehaṁ jahātyanādāya hi dehamanyam ||

The soul is always known only along with the body. Even when the body dies, he does not leave it without taking hold of another body.

348. जीवोऽयमेवं वपुषोऽपृथक्त्वादन्तर्भवत्येव जगत्स्वरूपे ।
नित्यत्वमस्यैव तु कल्पयन्ति शिष्या अबुद्धस्य गुरोरबुद्धाः ॥

jīvo'yamevaṁ vapuṣo'pṛthaktvādantarbhavatyeva jagatsvarūpe |
nityatvamasyaiva tu kalpayanti śiṣyā abuddhasya gurorabuddhāḥ ||

Since thus the soul is not separable from the body, he is only part and parcel of the world. But unenlightened men who are disciples of unenlightened gurus, ascribe immortality to this same (mythical) person.

349. विना विचारं बत जीवमेनम् देहीति चात्मेत्यपि मन्यमानाः ।
संसारिताद्यानपि चास्य धर्मानारोपयन्त्यात्मनि नित्यमुक्ते ॥

vinā vicāraṁ bata jīvamenam dehīti cātmetyapi manyamānāḥ |
saṁsāritādyānapi cāsya dharmānāropayantyātmani nityamukte ||

Assuming, without inquiry, that this soul is the owner of the body and the real Self, they ascribe to that Self the qualities of worldliness and all else which pertain only to this soul.

350. अतो मतानि प्रभवन्ति नाना सत्यात्मनः सर्वमतातिगस्य ।
बद्धं तमेनं बत मन्यमानाश्चरन्त्यनेकानपि योगमार्गान् ॥

ato matāni prabhavanti nānā satyātmanaḥ sarvamatātigasya |
baddhaṁ tamenaṁ bata manyamānāścarantyanekānapi yogamārgān ||

From this error arise various creeds
concerning the Real Self, who transcends all the
creeds. Believing Him to be bound, they follow
various paths of Yoga to free Him from bondage!

351. कर्तृत्वभोक्तृत्वशरीरिताद्याः संसारिता चाप्युत जीवधर्माः ।
धर्मा न ते शुद्धचिदात्मकस्य सत्यात्मनः सङ्गविवर्जितस्य ॥

kartṛtvabhoktṛtvaśarīritādyāḥ saṁsāritā cāpyuta jīvadharmāḥ |
dharmā na te śuddhacidātmakasya satyātmanaḥ saṅgavivarjitasya ||

The doing of actions, the reaping of their
fruits, ownership of the body and the like, as well
as worldliness are the attributes of the soul. They
are not attributes of the Real Self, who is only Pure
Consciousness and is unrelated (to the world).

352. स्वं जीवभूतं बत मन्यते यो देहात्मभावो न हि तस्य नष्टः ।
बोधात्मतां स्वस्य न बुध्यते यस्तस्यानिवार्यो वपुरात्मभावः ॥

svaṁ jīvabhūtaṁ bata manyate yo dehātmabhāvo na hi tasya naṣṭaḥ |
bodhātmatāṁ svasya na budhyate yastasyānivāryo vapurātmabhāvaḥ ||

He that is, alas, persuaded that he is a soul,
has not got rid of the notion that the body is

himself, (because) for him who does not know (by actual experience) that he is only Consciousness, the belief of identity with the body is inescapable.

353. आत्मा सुषुप्तौ च सुखस्वरूपो लोकैः समस्तैरनुभूयते यत् ।
देहात् पृथक् स्वो भवतीति बोद्धुं शक्नोति धीमान् खलु
सूक्ष्मबुद्धया ॥

ātmā suṣuptau ca sukhasvarūpo lokaiḥ samastairanubhūyate yat |
dehāt pṛthak svo bhavatīti boddhuṁ śaknoti dhīmān khalu sūkṣmabuddhyā ||

Since the Self, who is blissful, is experienced by all in the state of deep sleep, the intelligent man is able to find out, by his subtle intellect, that the Self is other than the body.

354. नाङ्गीकरोति ह्यत एव धीमान् देहात्मतां स्वस्य विचारणायाम् ।
तथाऽप्यविज्ञातनिजस्वरूपो भूयोऽपि देहात्ममतिं करोति ॥

nāṅgīkaroti hyata eva dhīmān dehātmatāṁ svasya vicāraṇāyām |
tathā'pyavijñātanijasvarūpo bhūyo'pi dehātmamatiṁ karoti ||

Therefore it is that the sensible man, when he engages in discrimination, does not accept the notion that the Self is the body. But all the same, because he has not attained Awareness of the Truth of the Real Self, he again confounds the Self with the body.

355. यावन्न जीवत्वमतिर्व्यपैति देहात्मधीर्नैव विनाशमीयात् ।
नश्येत्तु सा तुर्यपदस्य लाभाद्यत्रानुभूयेत परं स्वतत्त्वम् ॥

yāvanna jīvatvamatirvyapaiti dehātmadhīrnaiva vināśamīyāt |
naśyettu sā turyapadasya lābhādyatrānubhūyeta param svatattvam ||

So long as the sense of being a soul does not cease, the sense, 'I am the body' does not become extinct. But it will be extinguished by attaining the Supreme State, wherein the transcendent nature of the Self is experienced.

356. जानाति यः स्वं परमद्वितीयं तुरीयभावे स्थितिमेत्य नित्याम् ।
न तस्य जीवोऽहमिति प्रतीतिः स एव देहात्मधिया विमुक्तः ॥

jānāti yaḥ svam paramadvitīyam turīyabhāve sthitimetya nityām |
na tasya jīvo'hamiti pratītiḥ sa eva dehātmadhiyā vimuktaḥ ||

Only he is free from the notion, 'I am soul', who becomes aware of his real Self as the Supreme Being, the one without a second having attained constant abidance in the Transcendental State; he is also free from the false notion 'I am the body'.

357. देहात्मभावं मनआत्मभावं जीवात्मभावं च मृषेति बुद्ध्वा ।
बोधात्मतां स्वामवगन्तुमिच्छन् यतेत साधू रमणोक्तरीत्या ॥

dehātmabhāvam manaātmabhāvam jīvātmabhāvam ca mṛṣeti buddhvā |
bodhātmatām svāmavagantumicchan yateta sādhū ramaṇoktarītyā ||

The Sadhaka must (therefore) understand that the Self is not the body, not the mind and not the soul, and thereafter strive to become aware (by Experience) of the Self as Pure Consciousness, by following the path taught by Ramana.

358. विचार्यमाणे सति जीवतत्त्वे बुद्धोपदेशैः परिशुद्धबुद्ध्या ।
आविद्यकोऽयं बत जीवनामा न तत्त्वतोऽस्तीति सुबोधमेव ॥

vicāryamāṇe sati jīvatattve buddhopadeśaiḥ pariśuddhabuddhyā |
āvidyako'yaṁ bata jīvanāmā na tattvato'stīti subodhameva ||

If the truth of the soul be investigated with the pure mind, in the light of the teachings of the sages, it will be easily seen that this soul is due to the Ignorance (of the True Self), and (hence) does not really exist.

359. मन्यन्त आत्मद्वितयं च केचिद् भेदेन जीवात्मपरात्मनश्च ।
जीवस्य चात्मेति परं वदन्ति जीवः शरीरं परमस्य चेति ॥

manyanta ātmadvitayaṁ ca kecid bhedena jīvātmaparātmanaśca |
jīvasya cātmeti paraṁ vadanti jīvaḥ śarīraṁ paramasya ceti ||

Some think that there are two selves, making a distinction between the self, which is the soul, and the Self which is the Supreme Being. And they say that the Supreme Being is the Self of the soul, and that the soul is the body of the Supreme Being.

360. जीवात्मतैवं चलमध्रुवं यदात्मा यथार्थः पर एव नान्यः ।
जीवाभिधोऽसन् पर एव सत्य इत्युच्यतेऽस्मद्गुरुणा स्फुटं च ॥

jīvātmataivaṁ calamadhruvaṁ yadātmā yathārthaḥ para eva nānyaḥ |
jīvābhidho'san para eva satya ityucyate'smadguruṇā sphuṭaṁ ca ||

Thus the selfhood of the soul is unsteady and uncertain, and so the Real Self is only the Supreme Being and none else. It has been clearly stated by our Guru that the one called the soul is unreal and that the Supreme Being alone is the Real Self.

361.   मृषात्ववाची खलु जीवशब्दः सत्यत्ववाची परशब्द एव ।
जीवो मृषेत्येवमवेत्य साधुर्जीवात्मभावं प्रयतेत हातुम् ॥

mṛṣātvavācī khalu jīvaśabdaḥ satyatvavācī paraśabda eva |
jīvo mṛṣetyevamavetya sādhurjīvātmabhāvaṁ prayateta hātum ||

The term 'soul' implies unreality; the term 'Supreme' implies reality. The Sadhaka, thus knowing that the soul is unreal, should strive to get rid of the notion 'I am a soul'.

362.   जैवेन रूपेण तमेव देहेष्वनुप्रविष्टं श्रुतयो वदन्ति ।
अतो न जीवोऽस्ति पृथक् परस्मादित्येवमर्थो भवति स्फुटं नः ॥

jaivena rūpeṇa tameva deheṣvanupraviṣṭaṁ śrutayo vadanti |
ato na jīvo'sti pṛthak parasmādityevamartho bhavati sphuṭaṁ naḥ ||

(Also) Revelation says that the Supreme Being Himself entered into the bodies in the form of souls. Hence it is clear to us that the soul is not a distinct entity apart from the Supreme Being.

363.　उदेति जीवो न विलीयते च सत्यात्मनो नैव लयोदयौ स्तः ।
जीवा अनेके च स एक एव सत्येवमात्मा कथमस्तु जीवः ॥

udeti jīvo na vilīyate ca satyātmano naiva layodayau stah |
jīvā aneke ca sa eka eva satyevamātmā kathamastu jīvah ||

The soul appears and vanishes; the Real Self
neither comes into being nor vanishes. The souls
are many, (but) the Supreme Being is only One.
This being so, how can the soul be the Real Self?

364.　विशुद्धचिन्मात्रतया स्वतः सन् न लीयते स्वो हि सुषुप्तिभावे ।
असन् स्वतोऽज्ञानसमुत्थितोऽयं प्रयाति जीवस्तु लयं सुषुप्तौ ॥

viśuddhacinmātratayā svatah san na līyate svo hi suṣuptibhāve |
asan svato'jñānasamutthito'yam prayāti jīvastu layam suṣuptau ||

The (Real) Self, being real in His own right
as Pure Consciousness, does not become lost in
deep sleep. But the Soul, being an outcome of the
Ignorance, and (hence) not real in its own right,
goes into latency in deep sleep.

365.　सुषुप्तिभावे सुखरूपको यो लोकैः समस्तैरनुभूयते च ।
तुरीयभावे परिशिष्यते च शुद्धोऽद्वयः सन् स हि सत्य आत्मा ॥

suṣuptibhāve sukharūpako yo lokaih samastairanubhūyate ca |
turīyabhāve pariśiṣyate ca śuddho'dvayah san sa hi satya ātmā ||

That Supreme Being, who is experienced by
all alike as pure happiness in deep sleep, and is

the Sole Survivor in the Supreme State, as the One without a second, is the Real Self.

366. सुषुप्तिभावेऽप्यहमि प्रलीने तुरीयभावेऽप्यहमि प्रणष्टे।
विभात्यविच्छिन्नतयेत्यसौ स्वो निगद्यतेऽहम्पदलक्षितार्थः ॥

suṣuptibhāve'pyahami pralīne turīyabhāve'pyahami praṇaṣṭe |
vibhātyavicchinnatayetyasau svo nigadyate'hampadalakṣitārthaḥ ||

This Self is declared to be the true meaning of the term 'I', because He shines uninterruptedly, both in the state of deep sleep wherein the ego (the soul) is latent, and in the Supreme State wherein the ego is dead once for all.

367. ब्रह्मात्मकोऽसावहमित्यजस्रं स्वयं विभात्यात्मतया हृदन्तः।
वपुर्मितं जीवमिमं तु तस्मिन् पूर्णे परेऽध्यस्यति हन्त मोहात् ॥

brahmātmako'sāvahamityajasram svayam vibhātyātmatayā hṛdantaḥ |
vapurmitam jīvamimam tu tasmin pūrṇe pare'dhyasyati hanta mohāt ||

That one, who is Brahmam, is Himself ever shining as 'I inside the Heart as the Self. But because of delusion, man confounds Him with this soul, who is only coextensive with the body.

368. अस्मीति बोधं न रुणद्ध्यविद्या बोधोऽहमस्मीति तु बोधमेव।
जानाति सर्वोऽपि हि नैजसत्तां जानाति न स्वं निरुपाधिकं तु ॥

asmīti bodham na ruṇaddhyavidyā bodho'hamasmīti tu bodhameva |
jānāti sarvo'pi hi naijasattām jānāti na svam nirupādhikam tu ||

The Ignorance does not hinder the awareness of 'I am'; it hinders only the Awarenss, 'I am Pure Consciousness'. Every one is aware of his own existence. But none is aware of Oneself as distinct from the veiling sheaths.

369. नाहन्तयोदेति चिदात्मकः स्वो जडो न देहोऽहमिति ब्रवीति ।
मध्ये तयोः कश्चिदुदेत्यबोधे वपुःप्रमाणस्त्वहमित्यसत्यः ॥

nāhantayodeti cidātmakaḥ svo jaḍo na deho'hamiti bravīti |
madhye tayoḥ kaścidudetyabodhe vapuḥpramāṇastvahamityasatyaḥ ||

That Self who is (only) Consciousness does not arise as 'I', the inert body does not say 'I', but between the two there arises someone, who is unreal, as 'I', (but) having the size of the body.

370. अहंस्वरूपा चितिरात्मनो या जडं वपुश्चेत्युभयोश्च योगात् ।
उदेति देहोऽहमिति प्रतीतिः प्रतीतिरेषैव हि जीवरूपम् ॥

ahaṁsvarūpā citirātmano yā jaḍaṁ vapuścetyubhayośca yogāt |
udeti deho'hamiti pratītiḥ pratītireṣaiva hi jīvarūpam ||

By joining together the Consciousness of the Real Self, which has the form of 'I', and the inert body, there arises the sense 'I am the body'. This sense is itself the soul.

371. देहात्मनोरेकतयाऽवगत्या प्रतीयते सत्यवदेष यस्मात् ।
तच्चिज्जडग्रन्थिरिति प्रथाऽस्य भवत्यविद्यापरिकल्पितस्य ॥

dehātmanorekatayā'vagatyā pratīyate satyavadeṣa yasmāt |
taccijjaḍagranthiriti prathā'sya bhavatyavidyāparikalpitasya ||

Since he is believed to be real by confounding the body and the Real Self as one, this soul, a false appearance due to the Ignorance, has the name, 'Knot binding together the Consciousness and the inert (body).'

372. जडेन देहेन कदाऽपि सङ्गः सत्यात्मनो नास्ति यथार्थतस्तु ।
नैवोदभूत् कश्चन जीवनामा नैवाप जीवत्वमसौ च पूर्णः ॥

jaḍena dehena kadā'pi saṅgaḥ satyātmano nāsti yathārthatastu |
naivodabhūt kaścana jīvanāmā naivāpa jīvatvamasau ca pūrṇaḥ ||

But there never was a real joining of the Real Self with the inert body, nor did anyone having the name of 'soul' really come into existence; nor did the All become changed into a soul.

373. स्वयम्प्रकाशं निरपेक्षमेकं चैतन्यमात्माकृतिकं हि सत्यम् ।
चैतन्यमन्यन्न हि किञ्चिदस्तीत्यचित्स्वरूपः खलु जीव एषः ॥

svayamprakāśaṁ nirapekṣamekaṁ caitanyamātmākṛtikaṁ hi satyam |
caitanyamanyanna hi kiñcidastītyacitsvarūpaḥ khalu jīva eṣaḥ ||

One self-shining Consciousness, independent of all else, which is the Real Self, is alone real. There is no other consciousness. Therefore this soul is not consciousness.

374. प्रतीयते चेतनवत्तु जीव आत्मस्वरूपस्य चिदंशयोगात् ।
      अतो हि वेदान्तिन आहुरेनं जीवं चिदाभासमसत्स्वरूपम् ॥

pratīyate cetanavattu jīva ātmasvarūpasya cidaṁśayogāt |
ato hi vedāntina āhurenaṁ jīvaṁ cidābhāsamasatsvarūpam ||

But the soul is taken as being conscious, due to the admixture of the consciousness of the Real Self. Therefore Vedantis call this unreal soul as the illusory consciousness.

375. स्वयं समागत्य यथा विवाहे वदन् वरस्यास्मि सखेति मिथ्या ।
      वधूगृहिभ्यो लभते सपर्यां जीवोऽयमङ्गीक्रियते तथाऽज्ञैः ॥

svayaṁ samāgatya yathā vivāhe vadan varasyāsmi sakheti mithyā |
vadhūgṛhibhyo labhate saparyāṁ jīvo'yamaṅgīkriyate tathā'jñaiḥ ||

Just as someone, coming in uninvited at a marriage, claiming to be a comrade of the bridegroom, obtains honourable reception from the bride's family, so this soul is accepted at its face value by the ignorant.

376. कोऽयं कुतो वेति विचार्यमाणो वधूगृहिभ्यः स्वयमेष धावेत् ।
      धावेत् तथैव स्वयमेष जीवः कोऽयं कुतो वेति विचार्यमाणः ॥

ko'yaṁ kuto veti vicāryamāṇo vadhūgṛhibhyaḥ svayameṣa dhāvet |
dhāvet tathaiva svayameṣa jīvaḥ ko'yaṁ kuto veti vicāryamāṇaḥ ||

The pretended bride-groom's comrade runs away of his own accord as soon as an inquiry is started by the bride's party, questioning 'Who is he? Whence did he come?' In the same way, this soul flees of his own accord when an inquiry is made as to who he is, or whence he has come.

377.   न रूपमस्यास्ति यथार्थतो यत् पिशाचवद् देहगृहे स्थितस्य ।
तद् देहरक्षार्थमयं नियुक्तः पिशाच एवेति गुरुर्ब्रवीति ॥

na rūpamasyāsti yathārthato yat piśācavad dehagṛhe sthitasya |
tad deharakṣārthamayaṁ niyuktaḥ piśāca eveti gururbravīti ||

This soul has really no form of his own, like a ghost haunting a house, this body; therefore (our) Guru says that he is just a ghost appointed to guard the body.

378.   न शिष्यते किञ्चन रूपमस्य तुरीयभावाधिगमे गवेषात् ।
एवं प्रबुद्धो भगवान् गुरुर्नो मृषात्वमस्य प्रकटीकरोति ॥

na śiṣyate kiñcana rūpamasya turīyabhāvādhigame gaveṣāt |
evaṁ prabuddho bhagavān gururno mṛṣātvamasya prakaṭīkaroti ||

Bhagavan Sri Ramana, our Guru, makes clear the unreality of this soul, saying that when the Supreme State is won by the Quest (of the Self) there is no form of this soul found surviving.

379.   आद्या मनोवृत्तिरियं ह्यहन्धीरतोऽन्यधीवृत्तय उद्भवन्ति ।
अतो मनः सूक्ष्मवपुः प्रपञ्चो भवोऽपि बन्धोऽप्ययमेव नान्यत् ॥

ādyā manovṛttiriyaṁ hyahandhīrato'nyadhīvṛttaya udbhavanti |
ato manaḥ sūkṣmavapuḥ prapañco bhavo'pi bandho'pyayameva nānyat ||

The first thought of the mind is this ego-sense; from him arise all other thoughts. Hence this soul is itself mind, the subtle body, the world, wordly life, and bondage – nothing else.

380. बन्धोऽपि बद्धोऽप्ययमेक एव बद्धोऽस्ति नास्मादितरोऽत्र
       कश्चित् ।
       स्वो नित्यमुक्तप्रकृतिर्हि सत्यः स बन्धमापेति कथं नु
       वाच्यम् ॥

bandho'pi baddho'pyayameka eva baddho'sti nāsmāditaro'tra kaścit |
svo nityamuktaprakṛtirhi satyaḥ sa bandhamāpeti kathaṁ nu vācyam ||

Both bondage and the bound one are only this soul; there is no other who can be said to be bound. The Real Self is Ever Free and the Sole Reality. How can it be said that He became bound?

381. अस्मिन्नहन्नामनि जातमात्रे सञ्जायते विश्वमिदम् सहैव ।
       अस्मिन् विलीने लयमेति विश्वं तद्विश्वमस्यैव हि रूपमुक्तम् ॥

asminnahannāmani jātamātre sañjāyate viśvamidam sahaiva |
asmin vilīne layameti viśvaṁ tadviśvamasyaiva hi rūpamuktam ||

As soon as this one named 'I' is born, there is born also along with him the whole world; when he becomes latent, the world also vanishes. Hence the world is said to be his form.

382. नित्यापरोक्षोऽपि सदैव पुंस आत्मा महान् प्रेष्ठ उरुप्रकाशः ।
दुरात्मनाऽहङ्कृतिरूपकेण हृतप्रभो यद्वदलं न भाति ॥३८२॥

nityāparokṣo'pi sadaiva puṃsa ātmā mahān preṣṭha uruprakāśaḥ |
durātmanā'haṅkṛtirūpakeṇa hṛtaprabho yadvadalaṃ na bhāti ||

Though this Great Being, the Real Self, is the
dearest of all and of great splendour, yet He does
not shine unmistakably, his light being stolen, as
it were, by this evil one, who has the ego-form.

383. आच्छादयत्येष मृषात्मकोऽपि सत्यात्मरूपम् खलु जीवनामा ।
अतोऽज्ञपुंसा बहुभिर्विकल्पैर्विकल्पितः स्वोऽस्ति हि
नष्टकल्पः ॥

ācchādayatyeṣa mṛṣātmako'pi satyātmarūpam khalu jīvanāmā |
ato'jñapuṃsā bahubhirvikalpairvikalpitaḥ svo'sti hi naṣṭakalpaḥ ||

Though unreal, this one named the soul
covers up the Truth of the Self; hence the Self,
being wrongly conceived through a variety of false
imaginations, by the ignorant man, is as good as lost.

384. भानुप्रभासञ्जनिताभ्रपङ्क्तिस्तिरोदधात्येव हि भानुरूपम् ।
तिरोदधात्येव तथाऽऽत्मरूपं तस्यैव संवित्प्रभयोदितोऽयम् ॥

bhānuprabhāsañjanitābhrapaṅktistirodadhātyeva hi bhānurūpam |
tirodadhātyeva tathā''tmarūpam tasyaiva saṃvitprabhayodito'yam ||

The mass of clouds, generated by the light
of the sun, does conceal the form of the sun. In

the same way this one (the soul) born as he is by the light of consciousness of the Self, conceals the Self.

This explains why the Real Self remains unknown.

385. किं तेन चोरेण कृतं न पापमात्मापहर्त्रेत्यपि वेदवाणी ।
निन्दत्यहन्धीमुषितात्मतत्त्वं पापेन तेनैव च दूयमानम् ॥

kiṁ tena coreṇa kṛtaṁ na pāpamātmāpahartretyapi vedavāṇī |
nindatyahandhīmuṣitātmatattvaṁ pāpena tenaiva ca dūyamānam ||

Revelation accuses him, who by his ego-sense has stolen the Real Self, and who suffers for that sin, saying: "what sin is there that has not been committed by that thief of the Self?"

386. यदादिमं पापमुदीरयन्ति क्रीस्तानुगा मृत्युकरं नराणाम् ।
कर्माद्यपुंसो न हि तत् परं तु वपुष्यहन्तेति गुरुर्ब्रवीति ॥

yadādimaṁ pāpamudīrayanti krīstānugā mṛtyukaraṁ narāṇām |
karmādyapuṁso na hi tat paraṁ tu vapuṣyahanteti gururbravīti ||

The 'original Sin' affirmed to be the cause of death for men by the Christians, the Master says, is not an act done by the first man, but only the sense 'I am the body'.

387. इदं नरस्यैव हि पापमुक्तं न ह्यस्ति पुंसां नरता सुषुप्तौ ।
देहात्ममत्यैव नरत्वधीर्यत् देहात्मधीरिव हि पापमाद्यम् ॥

idaṁ narasyaiva hi pāpamuktaṁ na hyasti puṁsāṁ naratā suṣuptau |
dehātmamatyaiva naratvadhīryat dehātmadhīreva hi pāpamādyam ||

This sin is said to pertain to man; but men are not men in deep sleep; the sense of being a man is due to identification of oneself with the body; hence the original sin is only this identification of oneself with the body.

388. नष्टिः समस्ताऽप्यगुणः समस्तो दुःखं समस्तं च वपुष्यहन्धीः ।
लाभः समस्तोऽपि गुणः समस्तः सुखं समस्तं च तदीयनाशः ॥

naṣṭiḥ samastā'pyaguṇaḥ samasto duḥkhaṁ samastaṁ ca vapuṣyahandhīḥ |
lābhaḥ samasto'pi guṇaḥ samastaḥ sukhaṁ samastaṁ ca tadīyanāśaḥ ||

All loss, all vice, and all suffering are only the ego-sense; all gain, all virtue and all happiness are the extinction of the ego.

389. आत्माऽज्ञपुंसोऽप्यहमा विनष्टो लब्ध्वाऽपि सर्वं कृपणो हि
सोऽयम् ।
स्वमेव लब्ध्वा त्वहमो विनाशाल्लब्धव्यमन्यन्न हि वीक्षते ज्ञः ॥

ātmā'jñapuṁso'pyahamā vinaṣṭo labdhvā'pi sarvaṁ kṛpaṇo hi so'yam |
svameva labdhvā tvahamo vināśāllabdhavyamanyanna hi vīkṣate jñaḥ ||

To the ignorant one the Self is lost, because of his ego-sense, and (therefore), even if he gains all things, he is but poor. On the other hand the Sage, who has gained Himself by the extinction of the ego, sees nothing else to be gained.

Now the question whether there are many selves is considered.

390.   सत्यं शरीरं बत मन्यमाना आत्मेति मत्वाऽप्युत जीवमेव ।
वेदान्तवाक्यानयथावदेव बुद्ध्वाऽऽत्मनानात्वमुदीरयन्ति ॥

satyaṁ śarīraṁ bata manyamānā ātmeti matvā'pyuta jīvameva |
vedāntavākyānayathāvadeva buddhvā''tmanānātvamudīrayanti ||

Those who think that the body is real and thus come to believe that the soul itself is the Real Self, affirm the plurality of selves, misconceiving the meaning of the texts of the Vedantas.

391.   यद्येक आत्मा द्विविधोऽस्ति दोष एकस्य मुक्तौ सकलस्य मुक्तिः ।
मुच्येत नो कोऽप्यथवेति मुग्धा मुधा वदन्त्यश्रुततुर्यतत्त्वाः ॥

yadyeka ātmā dvividho'sti doṣa ekasya muktau sakalasya muktiḥ |
mucyeta no ko'pyathaveti mugdhā mudhā vadantyaśrutaturyatattvāḥ ||

Deluded men, who have not heard the truth of the Supreme State, argue in vain, saying that if there be only one Self, then there is a dilemma, that either, by the deliverance of one all will be delivered, or none will attain deliverance.

392.   जीवा भवेऽस्मिन् बहवो भवन्तु सत्यात्मनो नैव बहुत्वमिष्टम् ।
नाना मृषैवाप्युत जीवरूपमेकं च सत्यं शिवमात्मरूपम् ॥

jīvā bhave'smin bahavo bhavantu satyātmano naiva bahutvamiṣṭam |
nānā mṛṣaivāpyuta jīvarūpamekaṁ ca satyaṁ śivamātmarūpam ||392||

There is no objection to the souls being conceived as many. But the view of the manyness of the Real Self is unacceptable. The souls are many and unreal; but the Real Self is real, auspicious and only One.

Some of those that affirm the manyness of the Self also say that the selves (souls) are fractions of the Supreme Being, the Self of all. This is next dealt with.

393.   अंशा न सत्या हि चितः परस्य त्वविद्ययाऽंशाः परिकल्पिता हि ।
पदे तुरीये विदुषो विभाति पूर्णाऽविभक्ता च निरंशका सा ॥

aṁśā na satyā hi citaḥ parasya tvavidyayā'ṁśāḥ parikalpitā hi |
pade turīye viduṣo vibhāti pūrṇā'vibhaktā ca niraṁśakā sā ||

There are no real fragments of the One Supreme Consciousness; the fragments appear only because of the Ignorance. To the Sage in the Supreme State that Consciousness shines as one Whole, not divided into parts.

The Experience of the Sage is conclusive on all points. Here is given an utterance of Bhagavan Sri Ramana on this point.

394.   चिदेकका सर्वगता समा च तस्या विभागो विषमोऽज्ञतैव ।
देशो न सत्यो ह्यत एव तस्याः समो विभागोऽपि च नास्ति सत्यः ॥

cidekakā sarvagatā samā ca tasyā vibhāgo viṣamo'jñataiva |
deśo na satyo hyata eva tasyāḥ samo vibhāgo'pi ca nāsti satyaḥ ||

Consciousness is One, omnipresent and equal; its unequal distribution is only an illusion. And because space is unreal, its equal distribution also is unreal.

"One Consciousness, equally distributed everywhere; you through illusion give it unequal distribution; no distribution, no everywhere". These were the words uttered by Bhagavan Sri Ramana to an earnest American Sadhaka, Mr. Hague.

It should be remembered that the Supreme Reality which is the Self, has three unique Names, namely Sat (सत्), Chit (चित्) and Ananda (आनन्द), and is referred to by one, or two, or all the three names together. These names, it is explained by the Bhagavan, must be understood as denying their opposites, and not giving a positive description of the Indescribable. Thus *Sat* means not *Asat* (non-being); *Chit* menas not *Achit* (unconsciousness); and Ananda means not unhappiness.

395. विस्पष्टमेवं गुरुणोपदिष्टा चितः परस्या अविभक्ततैव ।
मुह्यन्त्वबुद्धस्य गुरोस्तु शिष्या अस्माकमत्रास्तु कथं नु मोहः ॥

vispaṣṭamevaṁ guruṇopadiṣṭā citaḥ parasyā avibhaktataiva |
muhyantvabuddhasya gurostu śiṣyā asmākamatrāstu kathaṁ nu mohaḥ ||

Thus it has been clearly taught by the Master that the Supreme Consciousness remains Whole, not divided into parts. Let disciples of non-sages be deluded. How can there be delusion for us on this point?

396.	सिद्धे मृषात्वे सति जीवनाम्नश्चिन्त्ये कथं बन्धविमोचनेऽस्य ।
	न बन्धमुक्ती भवतोऽच्युतस्य पूर्णस्य सत्यात्मन एककस्य ॥

siddhe mṛṣātve sati jīvanāmnaścintye kathaṁ bandhavimocane'sya |
na bandhamuktī bhavato'cyutasya pūrṇasya satyātmana ekakasya ||

Since it is (thus) settled that the one named soul does not exist, how can we think of his bondage or deliverance? There is neither bondage nor deliverance for the Real Self, who remains unswervingly whole and alone (in His Own True State).

This point will be dealt with later.

397.	देहस्य दिक्कालमितस्य चास्य तयोरतीतस्य चिदात्मनश्च ।
	परस्पराध्यासकृताविवेकात् प्रतीयते सत्यवदेष जीवः ॥

dehasya dikkālamitasya cāsya tayoratītasya cidātmanaśca |
parasparādhyāsakṛtāvivekāt pratīyate satyavadeṣa jīvaḥ ||

The soul comes to be taken as real by the failure to discriminate rightly, due to the mutual false identification of the two, namely this body which is limited in space and time and the Self, who is only Consciousness, and unlimited by those two, space and time.

398.	क्वचिच्छरीरेऽहमिति प्रतीत्या तत्सत्यमेवेत्यपि निश्चयेन ।
	पश्यन्ननेकानि वपूंषि सद्ब्रजीवान् पृथक् पश्यति तत्र तत्र ॥

kvaciccharīre'hamiti pratītyā tatsatyamevetyapi niścayena ǀ
paśyannanekāni vapūṃsi sadvajjīvan pṛthak paśyati tatra tatra ǁ

Assuming that one particular body is oneself, then concluding that that body is real, and seeing many (other) bodies as real the ignorant man sees different souls in them.

399. एकः शरीरेष्वनृतेषु सत्यो विभक्तवद्भात्यविभक्त आत्मा ।
पूर्णं तमात्मानमरूपमज्ञो मत्वा सरूपं समवैत्यनेकम् ॥

ekaḥ śarīreṣvanṛteṣu satyo vibhaktavadbhātyavibhakta ātmā ǀ
pūrṇaṃ tamātmānamarūpamajño matvā sarūpaṃ samavaityanekam ǁ

The One Real Self, being really undivided, is taken as being divided into parts in many bodies, which are all unreal. The ignorant one looks upon that Whole, formless Self, as having form and therefore also as many.

400. प्रतिक्षणं नूतनमेव चित्रं पश्यन् यथैकं मनुते तथैव ।
प्रतिक्षणं वीक्ष्य नवं शरीरं तत्सर्वमेकं मनुतेऽज्ञमर्त्यः ॥

pratikṣaṇaṃ nūtanameva citram paśyan yathaikaṃ manute tathaiva ǀ
pratikṣaṇaṃ vīkṣya navaṃ śarīraṃ tatsarvamekaṃ manute'jñamartyaḥ ǁ

As a seer of a cinema-show, seeing a new picture every moment, thinks them all to be one, so the ignorant man seeing a new body every moment, thinks that all of them are one and the same.

In the cinema-show there is a long roll of small pictures which pass successively at a rapid rate between the light inside and the magnifying lens, about 32 pictures being thus projected on the screen successively each second. But the seer thinks he is seeing one single picture all the time, but slowly changing. The world-picture is also made up of a successive stream of separate pictures on the retina (sensitive screen) inside the eye; but the man thinks it is all one continuous spectacle.

401.   एवं सदा नूतन एव देहे जीवं नवं कल्पयतेऽस्य चित्तम् ।
अतो हि बुद्धा निगदन्ति जीवं तमेनमेव क्षणिकं च मिथ्या ॥

evaṁ sadā nūtana eva dehe jīvaṁ navaṁ kalpayate'sya cittam |
ato hi buddhā nigadanti jīvaṁ tamenameva kṣaṇikaṁ ca mithyā ||

Thus all the time his mind is imagining a new soul in a new body every moment. Hence the sages say that this soul is both momentary and unreal.

402.   देहोऽहमित्युत्तमपूरुषं च देहान्तरे मध्यमपूरुषं च ।
अन्यत्र देहे प्रथमं पुमांसं पश्यत्यविज्ञातनिजस्वरूपः ॥

deho'hamityuttamapūruṣaṁ ca dehāntare madhyamapūruṣaṁ ca |
anyatra dehe prathamaṁ pumāṁsaṁ paśyatyavijñātanijasvarūpaḥ ||

The man who has not experienced his own Real Self, thinking 'I am this body' sees himself as I, the first person of grammar, sees another person whom he calls 'you', and in another body sees a third person as 'he'.

Thus the one Real Self becomes 'I' in one body, 'you' in another body and 'he' in a third body. It follows that these distinctions arise from the Primary Ignorance.

403. भिन्नास्त्रिधैवं पुरुषा न सत्या देहोऽहमित्यज्ञतया प्रतीताः ।
नष्टेऽहमि स्वात्मगवेषणेन चिद्रूप आत्मैकक एव भायात् ॥

bhinnāstridhaivaṁ puruṣā na satyā deho'hamityajñatayā pratītāḥ |
naṣṭe'hami svātmagaveṣaṇena cidrūpa ātmaikaka eva bhāyāt ||

These three distinct persons are not real, because they are seen because of the false notion 'I am a body'. When the ego (soul) is lost as the result of the Quest of the Real Self, then only that Self, who is only Consciousness, will shine.

404. प्रत्येति यः स्वं बत जीवभूतं जीवा अनेके विलसन्ति तस्य ।
एवंविधाज्ञानविवर्जितस्य भायान्न बुद्धस्य तु कोऽपि जीवः ॥

pratyeti yaḥ svaṁ bata jīvabhūtaṁ jīvā aneke vilasanti tasya |
evaṁvidhājñānavivarjitasya bhāyānna buddhasya tu ko'pi jīvaḥ ||

To one who thinks of himself as a soul (or a body) a plurality of souls will appear. But to the Sage who is freed from this Ignorance, no soul will appear.

This is next illustrated by the simile of the cinema show.

405. स्त्रियः पुमांसो बहवश्चरन्ति पटप्रकाशे खलु चित्रमात्राः ।
एवं चरन्त्यात्मनि चित्स्वरूपे जीवा अनेके बत चित्रमात्राः ॥

striyaḥ pumāṁso bahavaścaranti paṭaprakāśe khalu citramātrāḥ |
evaṁ carantyātmani citsvarūpe jīvā aneke bata citramātrāḥ ||

On the lighted screen there pass women and men in great number, who are only pictures. So too on the screen, the Consciousness, which is the Real Self, there pass a great many souls, who are only mental projections.

406. पटप्रकाशोपममात्मतत्त्वं चित्रोपमा एव भवन्ति जीवाः।
आत्माद्वयत्वं परमार्थमेवं न बाध्यते जीवबहुत्वभानात् ॥

paṭaprakāśopamamātmatattvaṁ citropamā eva bhavanti jīvāḥ |
ātmādvayatvaṁ paramārthamevaṁ na bādhyate jīvabahutvabhānāt ||

Like the screen-light is the Real Self; like the pictures are the souls. Thus the appearance of a plurality of souls does not affect the final Truth of Experiecne, the Oneness of the Self.

407. आत्मेति जीवस्य विनिश्चयेन प्रत्येति नानात्वमिहात्मनां च।
सत्यं तु नात्मानमवैति पूर्णं मुह्यत्यतो भेददधियाऽपकृष्टः ॥

ātmeti jīvasya viniścayena pratyeti nānātvamihātmanāṁ ca |
satyaṁ tu nātmānamavaiti pūrṇaṁ muhyatyato bhedadhiyā'pakṛṣṭaḥ ||

One believes in the plurality of selves by believing that the soul is the Real Self; but he does not know the Real Self (by Experience), being misled by his belief in multiplicity.

Another simile is next employed to clarify this truth, the plurality of reflections of a single object.

408.	यथा शरावेषु पृथग् जलेषु विभान्त्यनेके प्रतिबिम्बचन्द्राः ।
तथैव देहेषु मनस्सु भान्ति जीवा अनेके प्रतिबिम्बमात्राः ॥

yathā śarāveṣu pṛthag jaleṣu vibhāntyaneke pratibimbacandrāḥ |
tathaiva deheṣu manassu bhānti jīvā aneke pratibimbamātrāḥ ||

As in the waters in separate vessels there appear many different images of the one moon, so in the minds within bodies there appear many souls, which are only reflected images (of the One Real Self).

409.	यथार्थचन्द्रो भविता यथैक आत्मा यथार्थोऽपि तथैक एव ।
यथा च नाना प्रतिबिम्बचन्द्रा विभान्ति नानेव तथैव जीवाः ॥

yathārthacandro bhavitā yathaika ātmā yathārtho'pi tathaika eva |
yathā ca nānā pratibimbacandrā vibhānti nāneva tathaiva jīvāḥ ||

As the real moon is only one, so the Real Self is only One. As there are many reflections of the moon, so there are seen a great many souls.

Now the riddle of Deliverance is solved.

410.	पृथग् जलेन्दोर्निधने विभान्ति यथैव पूर्वं हि जलेन्दवोऽन्ये ।
पृथक् चिदाभासमृतौ तथाऽन्ये पूर्वं यथा भान्ति मृषैव सन्तः ॥

pṛthag jalendornidhane vibhānti yathaiva pūrvaṃ hi jalendavo'nye |
pṛthak cidābhāsamṛtau tathā'nye pūrvaṃ yathā bhānti mṛṣaiva santaḥ ||

As, when one reflected image of the moon is lost, the other images go on appearing as before, so when one pseudo-consciousness (a soul) dies, the others continue to appear as before, though unreal.

411. यो यो विजानाति निजं स्वरूपं तस्मै भवोऽयं विरतिं प्रयाति ।
अन्ये यथापूर्वमिह भ्रमन्ति यावद्विजानन्ति निजं न तत्त्वम् ॥

yo yo vijānāti nijaṁ svarūpaṁ tasmai bhavo'yaṁ viratiṁ prayāti |
anye yathāpūrvamiha bhramanti yāvadvijānanti nijaṁ na tattvam ||

Whoever obtains Awareness of the Real Self, for him this worldly life comes to an end. The others continue to wander here as before, as long as they are not aware of their Real Nature.

412. एषोपमा मन्दमतिभ्य उक्ता तेषां मृषाज्ञानमनूद्य बुद्धैः ।
जीवो मृषैवेत्यवयन्ति ये तु निरर्थकोऽयं भविता विवादः ॥

eṣopamā mandamatibhya uktā teṣāṁ mṛṣājñānamanūdya buddhaiḥ |
jīvo mṛṣaivetyavayanti ye tu nirarthako'yaṁ bhavitā vivādaḥ ||412||

This illustration has been vouchsafed by sages, according to their false knowledge, to men of immature minds. But this discussion can have no meaning at all for those who realise the unreality of the individual soul.

413. स्वप्ने यथा मानसमोहजाता जीवा अनेके विलसन्ति सद्वत् ।
तथाऽज्ञपुंसां विलसन्त्यनेके जीवा इमे जागरितेऽप्यसन्तः ॥

svapne yathā mānasamohajātā jīvā aneke vilasanti sadvat |
tathā'jñapuṁsāṁ vilasantyaneke jīvā ime jāgarite'pyasantaḥ ||

As in dream there appears as real a multitude of souls created by mental delusion, just so appears as real, in waking also, a multitude of these souls.

414. स्वानां बहुत्वं वदतां प्रमाणं निरस्तदोषं न हि किञ्चिदस्ति ।
आत्माद्वयत्वेऽस्त्युभयं प्रमाणं बुद्धानुभूतिश्च तदुक्तयुक्तिः ॥

svānāṁ bahutvaṁ vadatāṁ pramāṇaṁ nirastadoṣaṁ na hi kiñcidasti |
ātmādvayatve'styubhayaṁ pramāṇaṁ buddhānubhūtiśca taduktayuktiḥ ||

There is not even one flawless proof on the side of those that assert the plurality of souls. (But) there is a twofold proof for the Unity of the Real Self, namely the Experience of the Sage and the argument that He has given.

415. अहंस्वरूपेण सदैकधाऽन्तरात्मा शरीरेषु विभाति यस्मात् ।
तत् सर्वदेहेषु स एक एवेत्यस्मद्गुरुः श्रीरमणो ब्रवीति ॥

ahaṁsvarūpeṇa sadaikadhā'ntarātmā śarīreṣu vibhāti yasmāt |
tat sarvadeheṣu sa eka evetyasmadguruḥ śrīramaṇo bravīti ||

Our Guru Sri Ramana says that because the Self shines in the same way, as "I", therefore in all bodies He is One and only One.

Now a warning is given for the benefit of immature aspirants against a misuse of the theoretical knowledge herein so far given. This is taken from Bhagavan Sri Sankaracharya's *'Tatvopadesa'*, wherein it is the last verse.

416.   ध्येया सदैवाद्वयता प्रयत्नाद् वर्तेत नाद्वैतधिया क्रियासु ।
       मन्येत लोकत्रितयेऽद्वयत्वं मन्वीत नैवं गुरुणा तु साकम् ॥

dhyeyā sadaivādvayatā prayatnād varteta nādvaitadhiyā kriyāsu |
manyeta lokatritaye'dvayatvaṁ manvīta naivaṁ guruṇā tu sākam ||

One should meditate upon the Truth of Non-Duality with effort, but should not apply this Truth in his (worldly) activities. (Also) one may think of Non-Duality in respect of all the three worlds, but should not imagine such (non-difference) with the Guru.

The reason is that theoretical knowledge of the Truth of Non-Duality does not avail to destroy the primary Ignorance, so as to raise one to the Egoless State, wherein wrong action would be impossible. So, till that State is won, the Ego would be in command of actions and this warning is therefore necessary.

Next the question is raised and dealt with, as to how the physical body and the world as a whole appear to the Sage.

417.   यथाऽज्ञपुंसां भुवनं विभाति भायात् तथेदं विदुषः कथं नु ।
       येन प्रकारेण विभाति विश्वं बुद्धस्य तं चापि गुरुर्ब्रवीति ॥

yathā'jñapuṁsāṁ bhuvanaṁ vibhāti bhāyāt tathedaṁ viduṣaḥ kathaṁ nu |
yena prakāreṇa vibhāti viśvaṁ buddhasya taṁ cāpi gururbravīti ||

How can the world appear to the Sage in the same way as it does to the ignorant? TheGuru tells us in what way the world appears to the Sage.

The next verse gives the answer briefly, but also clearly.

418. ईशोऽपि जीवा जडवस्तुजातमिति प्रतीतं जगदज्ञमर्त्यैः ।
बुद्धस्य भात्यात्मतया समस्तं ह्यारोपितांशप्रविलापनेन ॥

īśo'pi jīvā jaḍavastujātamiti pratītaṁ jagadajñamartyaiḥ |
buddhasya bhātyātmatayā samastaṁ hyāropitāṁśapravilāpanena ||

The world, which to the ignorant appears as comprising the trinity of God, the souls and the insentient objects, appears as the Self to the Sage, due to the liquidation of the super-imposed false appearance (the world).

This is explained in detail as follows:

419. तत् तुर्यनिष्ठां सहजामवाप्य जीवन् विमुक्तो विनिवृत्तमोहः ।
नात्मेतरत् किञ्चन वीक्षते यत् किमप्यसत् तस्य भवेत् कथं नु ॥

tat turyaniṣṭhāṁ sahajāmavāpya jīvan vimukto vinivṛttamohaḥ |
nātmetarat kiñcana vīkṣate yat kimapyasat tasya bhavet kathaṁ nu ||

Hence (the Sage who) has attained his natural state, which is the Supreme State, and remains in His natural freedom, and is therefore free from delusions, sees nothing other than the Self. How then can he see anything unreal?

420. तत् स्वं शरीरं भुवनं च सत्यं वदेत् प्रबुद्धोऽपि च यद्वदज्ञः ।
भावे द्वयोरस्ति महांस्तु भेदो नारोपितांशो विदुषो हि भाति ॥

tat svaṁ śarīraṁ bhuvanaṁ ca satyaṁ vadet prabuddho'pi ca yadvadajñaḥ |
bhāve dvayorasti mahāṁstu bhedo nāropitāṁśo viduṣo hi bhāti ||

Therefore the Sage, established as he is in his natural state, the Supreme State, would say that the body appearing as His body to others and the world are real. But there is a world of difference in the meaning (of what he says). Because the superimposition does not appear (as real) to the Sage.

Now it may be questioned whether the Sage also, like us, does not need the discrimination between the Real and the unreal. The answer is given below.

421.   मुमुक्षुपुंसे हि विवेकदृष्टिर्विधीयते नैव विमुक्तपुंसः ।
भवेन्मुमुक्षोरविवेकदृष्टिर्न संभवेत् सा खलु बुद्धपुंसः ॥

mumukṣupuṁse hi vivekadṛṣṭirvidhīyate naiva vimuktapuṁsaḥ |
bhavenmumukṣoravivekadṛṣṭirna sambhavet sā khalu buddhapuṁsaḥ ||

The outlook of Discrimination is enjoined (only) on the aspirant for Deliverance, not for Him that has won Deliverance. Confused outlook is possible for the former, not for the latter.

The views that the two have of the body is next explained and distinguished.

422.   देहात्ममत्याऽज्ञजनः सरूपं वपुर्मितं चापि हि मन्यते स्वम् ।
ज्ञो वेत्त्यनन्तं स्वमरूपमेकं भावे भिदैवं भवति द्वयोश्च ॥

dehātmamatyā'jñajanaḥ sarūpaṁ vapurmitaṁ cāpi hi manyate svam |
jño vettyanantaṁ svamarūpamekaṁ bhāve bhidaivaṁ bhavati dvayośca ||

The ignorant one, because of his confounding body with the Self, thinks of himself as with form and extensive with that body. The Sage is aware of the Self as infinite, formless Being; this is the distinction in the meaning of what is said by these two.

423. शरीरमित्यज्ञजनेक्षितं यद् बुद्धस्य भात्यात्मतयैव तद्धि ।
तदेव बुद्धोऽहमिति ब्रवीति ह्युपेक्ष्य बोधेन शरीररूपम् ॥

śarīramityajñajanekṣitaṁ yad buddhasya bhātyātmatayaiva taddhi |
tadeva buddho'hamiti bravīti hyupekṣya bodhena śarīrarūpam ||

What is seen as the 'body' by the ignorant appears to the Sage only as the Self; and He refers to it as 'I', ignoring the body-form through His Right Awareness.

Next it is explained that there is a similar difference in the outlook of the Sage on the world, from that of the ignorant one.

424. सत्यं प्रपञ्चं वदतोर्द्वयोश्च वाक्ये समानेऽपि भिदाऽस्ति भावे ।
अज्ञस्य भेदैर्हि निमीलितं सत् सत्यं यथावद्विदुषस्य भाति ॥

satyaṁ prapañcaṁ vadatordvayośca vakye samāne'pi bhidā'sti bhāve |
ajñasya bhedairhi nimīlitaṁ sat satyaṁ yathāvadviduṣasya bhāti ||

Also, when the two say that the world is real, there is difference in the meaning, though the words are the same. For the ignorant one the Reality is veiled by differences, while to the Sage It appears as it really is.

425. आधारसत्यं जगतोऽविदित्वा समीक्ष्य चारोपितवस्तुजातम् ।
मन्वान एतत् स्वत एव सत्यं ब्रवीति सत्यं जगदित्यविद्वान् ॥

ādhārasatyaṁ jagato'viditvā samīkṣya cāropitavastujātam |
manvāna etat svata eva satyaṁ bravīti satyaṁ jagadityavidvān ||

Unaware of the Substratum of the world-appearance, seeing (only) the superimposed multitude of (inert) objects, and believing that this world of objects is real in its own right, the ignorant one says: 'The world is real'.

426. विभात्यधिष्ठानसदेव शुद्धमनामरूपं विदुषो हि साक्षात् ।
नारोपितं भाति हि तस्य सद्वद् वदेन्मृषा विश्वमसौ कथं नु ॥

vibhātyadhiṣṭhānasadeva śuddhamanāmarūpaṁ viduṣo hi sākṣāt |
nāropitaṁ bhāti hi tasya sadvad vadenmṛṣā viśvamasau kathaṁ nu ||

(On the other hand) to the Sage there shines only the Substratum, which is the Pure Reality, nameless and formless. For Him the superimposition does not appear as real. (That being the case), how can He say that the world is unreal?

427. आच्छादकं विश्वमिदं परस्य स्वाज्ञानसन्दूषितलोचनस्य ।
आच्छाद्यते तेन सता परेण स्वज्ञानसंशोधितलोचनस्य ॥

ācchādakaṁ viśvamidaṁ parasya svājñānasandūṣitalocanasya |
ācchādyate tena satā pareṇa svajñānasaṁśodhitalocanasya ||

This world, which, to the one whose eye is
blinded by unawareness of his own Real Self,
conceals the Supreme Being, is itself concealed, to
the One whose eye is purified by the Right
Awareness of that Self, by that same Supreme Being.

This is the meaning conveyed by the opening verse of
Isa Upanishad.

Supposing that the Sage *does* see the world of names
and forms, it is explained that the Sage's view is unclouded
by the Ignorance.

428. तत्त्वं विजानन् मृगतृष्णिकाया भूयो यथा पश्यति ताममूढः ।
पश्यंस्तथा विश्वमिदं प्रबुद्धो न मन्यते सत्यमिदं यथाऽज्ञः ॥

tattvaṁ vijānan mṛgatṛṣṇikāyā bhūyo yathā paśyati tāmamūḍhaḥ |
paśyaṁstathā viśvamidaṁ prabuddho na manyate satyamidaṁ yathā'jñaḥ ||

Just as one, that has become wise as to the
truth of the mirage, may again see the mirage
without being deluded, so too the Sage, seeing
this world, does not think of it as real, as does the
ignorant one.

Thus there is no comparison at all between the ignorant
man and the Sage. This is shown next.

429. विश्वं यथाऽज्ञैः सदिति प्रतीतं नैवं हि सत्यं तदिदं कथञ्चित् ।
सत्यं यथेदं विदुषो विभाति जानन्त्यबुद्धा न हि तं प्रकारम् ॥

viśvaṁ yathā'jñaiḥ saditi pratītaṁ naivaṁ hi satyaṁ tadidaṁ kathañcit |
satyaṁ yathedaṁ viduṣo vibhāti jānantyabuddhā na hi taṁ prakāram ||

This world is not real in the sense in which it
is believed to be real by the ignorant man.
Ignorant ones do not understand the sense in
which the world is seen (as real) by the Sage.

430. यदज्ञपुंसां बहुभेदभिन्नं सरूपकं स्वान्यदिवावभाति ।
तदेतदात्मैव हि बुद्धपुंसो निरस्तभेदोऽप्युत रूपहीनः ॥

yadajñapuṁsāṁ bahubhedabhinnaṁ sarūpakaṁ svānyadivāvabhāti |
tadetadātmaiva hi buddhapuṁso nirastabhedo'pyuta rūpahīnaḥ ||

That which appears to the ignorant ones as
diversified by a great many differences, as forms
and other than the Self, is only the Self,
undifferentiated and formless, to the Sage.

It is then explained that the teaching about the world is
two-fold, as unreal from one view-point and real from another
view-point.

431. अत्यन्तमिथ्या न हि विश्वमुक्तं नेदं नराश्वादिविषाणतुल्यम् ।
अत्यन्तमिथ्या यदि नैव भायाद् भाति त्वधिष्ठानसदंशयोगात् ॥

atyantamithyā na hi viśvamuktaṁ nedaṁ narāśvādiviṣāṇatulyam |
atyantamithyā yadi naiva bhāyād bhāti tvadhiṣṭhānasadaṁśayogāt ||

It is not taught that the world is completely unreal; it is not (unreal) like the horn of man or horse. If it were wholly unreal, it would not appear at all. But it does appear because of its confusion with its Substratum, the Reality.

The two kinds of unrealities are further explained for the sake of distinction.

432. मिथ्या ह्यधिष्ठानसता विहीनं वन्ध्यासुताद्यं न विभाति किञ्चित्।
मिथ्या ह्यधिष्ठानसति प्रतीतं रज्ज्वां यथाऽहिः सदिवावभाति॥

mithyā hyadhiṣṭhānasatā vihīnaṁ vandhyāsutādyaṁ na vibhāti kiñcit |
mithyā hyadhiṣṭhānasati pratītaṁ rajjvāṁ yathā'hiḥ sadivāvabhāti ||

The unreality which has no substratum, such as the son of a barren woman and the like, does not appear at all. But the unreality which appears on a substratum, like the snake seen in a rope, appears as real.

The presence or absence of a substratum makes all the difference. No one is misled into thinking that a barren woman's son has any existence, because he does not appear at all. On the other hand the snake not only appears, but is believed to be real, because it has a substratum for its appearance; it appears and is for some time at least believed to be real. This distinction is very important for understanding the truth of the world, which is further elucidated in the succeeding verses, in which Bhagavan Sri Ramana's teaching is given.

433. सत्ताऽप्यसत्ताऽप्युभयं च वाच्यं विश्वस्य नास्त्यत्र विरोधलेशः ।
सत्ताऽस्त्यधिष्ठानसदंशयोगान्मिथ्यात्वमारोपितनामरूपैः ॥

satta'pyasatta'pyubhayam ca vācyam viśvasya nāstyatra virodhaleśaḥ |
satta'styadhiṣṭhānasadamśayogānmithyātvamāropitanāmarūpaiḥ ||

Both reality and unreality have to be stated,
in respect of the world, and herein there is not
the least contradiction. It is real because of the
reality of the Substratum, and it is unreal, because
of the super-imposition of names and forms.

All the same, it must not be said that the world exists,
as explained below:

434. सत्यत्वमङ्गीकृतमेवमस्य किं त्वेतदस्तीत्युचितं न वक्तुम् ।
सत्तास्तिते द्वे भवतो विभिन्ने तदुच्यतेऽस्तीति यत् स्वतः सत् ॥

satyatvamaṅgīkṛtamevamasya kim tvetadastītyucitam na vaktum |
sattāstite dve bhavato vibhinne taducyate'stīti yat svataḥ sat ||

Reality (of a soul) is conceded for the world,
but it would not be correct to say that it exists.
'Reality' and 'existence' are quite distinct. That
alone is said to exist, which is real in its own right.

Thus in the language of the Vedanta the term 'Reality'
applies strictly only to that which is real in its own right, not
to what has a borrowed reality, as explained in the next two
verses.

435.	वदन्ति विश्वं व्यवहारसत्यं प्रातीतिकं स्वप्नसमीक्षितं च ।
	ब्रह्माद्वितीयं परमार्थसत्यं मुधा विकल्पास्त इमे हि भेदाः ॥

vadanti viśvaṁ vyavahārasatyaṁ pratītikaṁ svapnasamīkṣitaṁ ca |
brahmādvitīyaṁ paramārthasatyaṁ mudhā vikalpāsta ime hi bhedāḥ ||

They say, the world is pragmatically real, that what is seen in dream is apparently real, and that the One without a second, namely Brahman, is the Supreme Reality. These grades of reality are vain.

These three degrees of reality are spoken of in order to enable weak minds to receive the teaching in stages. But ultimately there is Only One Reality.

436.	एकस्वरूपैव हि सत्यताऽस्ति न सन्ति भेदाः खलु सत्यतायाम् ।
	अतो ह्यसत्यं द्वितयं समानं स्वप्नेक्षितं जागरितेक्षितं च ॥

ekasvarūpaiva hi satyatā'sti na santi bhedāḥ khalu satyatāyām |
ato hyasatyaṁ dvitayaṁ samānaṁ svapnekṣitaṁ jāgaritekṣitaṁ ca ||

Reality is always of one kind; there are no varieties or degrees of reality. Hence what is seen in dream and what is seen in waking are both equally unreal.

The necessity for accepting this teaching is next explained.

437.	विश्वस्य मिथ्यात्वमिहोपदिष्टं स्वान्वेषणात् तुर्यपदस्य लिप्सोः ।
	सत्यं प्रपञ्चं बत मन्यमानो विद्यात् कथं स्वं परमार्थसत्यम् ॥

viśvasya mithyātvamihopadiṣṭaṁ svānveṣaṇāt turyapadasya lipsoḥ |
satyaṁ prapañcam bata manyamāno vidyāt kathaṁ svaṁ
paramārthasatyam ||

The truth of the unreality of the world has here been taught to one that is in earnest to attain the Supreme State by pursuing the Quest of the Real Self. How can one, that believes the world to be real, ever become rightly aware of the Supreme Reality, the Self?

438.   यत् सत्यवत् स्यादनृतस्य भानं ज्ञानेन तस्यास्ति विराम एव ।
संविद्विवस्वान् खलु सत्य आत्मा तत्सन्निधाने कथमस्त्वविद्या ॥

yat satyavat syādanṛtasya bhānaṁ jñānena tasyāsti virāma eva |
saṁvidvivasvān khalu satya ātmā tatsannidhāne kathamastvavidyā ||

When (the sun of) Right Awareness dawns, what happens is only the cessation of the unreal appearing as real. The Real Self being the Sun or Pure, Infinite Consciousness, how can Ignorance exist in His Presence?

439.   अस्त्यज्ञता चेदथ कस्य सेति प्रश्नोऽत्र जागर्ति हि साधकस्य ।
तेनात्मतत्त्वं परिमृग्यते चेदज्ञोऽज्ञता द्वे व्रजतो विनाशम् ॥

astyajñātā cedatha kasya seti praśno'tra jāgarti hi sādhakasya |
tenātmatattvaṁ parimṛgyate cedajño'jñātā dve vrajato vināśam ||

If (it be thought that) Ignorance exists, then there is present for the aspirant the question 'To whom is the Ignorance?' If by that question the Truth of the Self be sought, then the ignorant one and the Ignorance, both become extinct.

440.   अज्ञानमङ्गीक्रियतेऽत्र शास्त्रे जीवाभिधस्यैव हि कल्पितस्य ।
       नैवात्मनोऽङ्गीकृतमेतदस्ति स नित्यबुद्धप्रकृतिर्हि तुर्यः ॥

ajñānamaṅgīkriyate'tra śāstre jīvābhidhasyaiva hi kalpitasya |
naivātmano'ṅgīkṛtametadasti sa nityabuddhaprakṛtirhi turyaḥ ||

Ignorance is accepted in the teaching only as pertaining to the individual soul, who is only a figment of the imagination; it is not accepted as affecting the Real Self, because He is ever enlightened by His own Nature, transcending all the three states of life in the world.

441.   सम्बध्यते नैव सहानृतेन द्वैतप्रपञ्चेन कदाचिदात्मा ।
       देशेन कालेन निमित्ततो वा यथेह रज्जुर्भुजगेन साकम् ॥

sambadhyate naiva sahānṛtena dvaitaprapañcena kadācidātmā |
deśena kālena nimittato vā yatheha rajjurbhujagena sākam ||

Just as the rope is never related in any way to the unreal snake (seen in it), so the Real Self is never related in space, time, or causality with the world of variety, which is unreal.

442.   उक्ता जगत्कारणता परस्य भवत्यसत्यैव हि तत्त्वदृष्ट्या ।
       परस्य शक्तिस्त्रिगुणात्मिका या मायाभिधा कारणमुच्यते सा ॥

uktā jagatkāraṇatā parasya bhavatyasatyaiva hi tattvadṛṣṭyā |
parasya śaktistriguṇātmikā yā māyābhidhā kāraṇamucyate sā ||

The saying that the Supreme Being — (the Real Self) — is the cause of the world is incorrect from the standpoint of the Truth. The true cause of the world is the Might of the Supreme Being, known as Maya.

443. द्वे ब्रह्मणी हि श्रुतिषु प्रसिद्धे निर्बीजकं चापि सबीजकं च ।
निर्बीजकं ब्रह्म तुरीयसंज्ञं सबीजकं शक्तिमदीशरूपम् ॥

dve brahmaṇī hi śrutiṣu prasiddhe nirbījakaṁ cāpi sabījakaṁ ca |
nirbījakaṁ brahma turīyasañjñaṁ sabījakaṁ śaktimadīśarūpam ||

In the sacred lore two forms of the Brahman are mentioned, one the seedless, and the other with seed. The seedless one is the transcendental Supreme Being; the one with seed is God having the Might of Maya.

Which of these two is the Real One? The answer is as follows:

444. स्वभावतो निश्चल एक आत्मा नृत्यं करोतीव तयाऽऽत्मशक्त्या ।
लीना यदा सा त्वचलस्वरूपे भायादसौ निश्चल एककः सन् ॥

svabhāvato niścala eka ātmā nṛtyaṁ karotīva tayā''tmaśaktyā |
līnā yadā sā tvacalasvarūpe bhāyādasau niścala ekakaḥ san ||

The One Self, who is by nature moveless, appears to dance because of His Own Might. But when that Might merges into that Moveless Essence, then there will shine the One Moveless Self as the Sole Reality.

So the cause of variety is the Might called Maya. What about this Maya?

445. मायेयमुक्ता व्यवहारदृष्ट्या मिथ्याजगत्कारणपृच्छकानाम् ।
मायाऽपि तत्कार्यमिदं जगच्च द्वयं च मिथ्या परमार्थदृष्ट्या ॥

māyeyamuktā vyavahāradṛṣṭyā mithyājagatkāraṇapṛcchakānām ।
māyā'pi tatkāryamidaṁ jagacca dvayaṁ ca mithyā paramārthadṛṣṭyā ॥

Maya is stated (as the cause) to those who ask what is the cause of this world, which really is unreal. (But) from the standpoint of the Reality both of these, namely Maya and its effect, the world, are equally unreal.

446. का नाम माया कतमाऽस्त्यविद्या सृष्टं जगत्केन कथं च पूर्वम् ।
कथं न्वभूज्जीव इति स्म मोहात् प्रश्नाः क्रियन्तेऽत्र मुधैव मर्त्यैः ॥

kā nāma māyā katamā'styavidyā sṛṣṭaṁ jagatkena kathaṁ ca pūrvam ।
kathaṁ nvabhūjjīva iti sma mohāt praśnāḥ kriyante'tra mudhaiva martyaiḥ ॥

Questions, such as these, are posed by vain men, namely; "What is Maya? What is the Ignorance? By whom and how was the world created in the beginning? How did the individual soul come into being?

These questions have no basis and need no answer. The final answer to all such questions is the Awareness of the Real Self in the Egoless State. In that State, these and other questions will not arise, because the questioner, the ego-mind, will not survive in that State.

447. मायेदृशी यन्निधनान्मुमुक्षुर्लभेत निष्ठां निजसत्स्वरूपे ।
न वेत्ति बुद्धोऽपि तदीयरूपं सा प्रेक्ष्यमाणैव हि नाशमेति ॥

māyedṛśī yannidhanānmumukṣurlabheta niṣṭhāṃ nijasatsvarūpe |
na vetti buddho'pi tadīyarūpaṃ sā prekṣyamāṇaiva hi nāśameti ||

Maya is that by whose destruction the aspirant for Deliverance becomes established in his True State. Even the Sage does not know Its true nature, because It perishes when looked at.

This is the meaning of a verse from the Yoga Vasishtha.* Strictly speaking, Maya is the totality of Samsara, consisting of the Ignorance, which is the Ego-sense, and its expanded form, the mind and its creation, the universe. These do not survive in the True State of the Real Self.

448. मनस्तया ब्रह्म न पर्यणंसीत् जगत्तया ब्रह्म न पर्यणंसीत् ।
ब्रह्मास्ति नैजामलचित्स्वरूपादप्रच्युतं कालदिगाद्यतीतम् ॥

---

* The verse is as follows:

ईदृशी राम मायेयं या स्वनाशेन हर्षदा ।
न लक्ष्यते स्वभावोऽस्याः प्रेक्ष्यमाणैव नश्यति ॥

īdṛśī rāma māyeyaṃ yā svanāśena harṣadā |
na lakṣyate svabhāvo'syāḥ prekṣyamāṇaiva naśyati ||

manastayā brahma na paryaṇaṁsīt jagattayā brahma na paryaṇaṁsīt |
brahmāsti naijāmalacitsvarūpādapracyutaṁ kāladigādyatītam ||

The Supreme Being did not become Mind; neither did It become the world. It remains unswerving from Its True Nature as Pure (unmodified) Consciousness, transcending Time, Space, and the rest.

449.   नाभूज्जगन्न प्रलयं व्रजेद्वा नैवोदभूत् कश्चन जीवनामा।
न बद्धमुक्तौ न च साधको वा सर्वोत्तमं सत्यमिदं निरुक्तम्॥

nābhūjjaganna pralayaṁ vrajedvā naivodabhūt kaścana jīvanāmā |
na baddhamuktau na ca sādhako vā sarvottamaṁ satyamidaṁ niruktam ||

The world did not come into being, nor is it going to be destroyed; no one, called the individual soul, really was born; there is neither a bound one, nor one that has become free; nor is there any aspirant. This is the most excellent Truth that has been clarified.

This is the Truth of Non-Becoming, demonstrated by the Sage Gaudapadacharya, in his Mandukya Karikas, which is strictly in agreement with the Experience of all the sages. This is further explained.

450.   यथा चलच्चित्रततिप्रसृत्या नाधारवस्त्रं भजते विकारम्।
न विक्रियामेति तथा परात्मा प्रतीयमाने सति च प्रपञ्चे॥

yathā calaccitratatiprasṛtyā nādhāravastram bhajate vikāram |
na vikriyāmeti tathā parātmā pratīyamāne sati ca prapañce ||

Just as the supporting screen is not affected by the series of pictures passing over it, so the Supreme Being is not affected, even while the Cinema of the world is being seen.

This is what Bhagavan Sri Ramana says at the very beginning of his Ulladu Narpadu (Forty Verses on Reality), where He employed the simile of the cinema show. The show begins with a Lighted Screen. On this is projected a series of pictures passing at great speed, so that the pictures are not seen separately. The screen does not become wet by the appearance of water, nor is it burned by an appearance of fire. At the end the lighted screen alone remains. So is this world-show. The Lighted Screen represents the Real Self, who is both Reality and Consciousness.

451.   श्रीशङ्कराचार्यवरेण सोऽयं सिद्धान्त उक्तोऽस्त्यसकृत् स्फुटं च ।
अनेकधा स्पष्टमिमं ब्रवीति बुद्धो गुरुः श्रीरमणोऽपि साधोः ॥

śrīśaṅkarācāryavareṇa so'yaṁ siddhānta ukto'styasakṛt sphuṭaṁ ca ।
anekadhā spaṣṭamimaṁ bravīti buddho guruḥ śrīramaṇo'pi sādhoḥ ॥

This Truth (of Non-Becoming) has been unmistakably stated many times by the Great Guru, Sri Sankaracharya. Also Sri Ramana, the Guru, has stated this Truth clearly in a variety of ways, for the benefit of the aspirant.

452.   उक्तं हि तेनास्ति तुरीयमेव सत्यं तदन्यत् त्रितयं मृषेति ।
उक्तं च सत्यस्य सदाऽद्वयत्वं द्वैतस्य नित्यं च मृषात्वमेव ॥

uktaṁ hi tenāsti turīyameva satyaṁ tadanyat tritayaṁ mṛṣeti ।
uktaṁ ca satyasya sadā'dvayatvaṁ dvaitasya nityaṁ ca mṛṣātvameva ॥

Indeed by Him it has been said that the (so-called) Fourth State is alone real, and the other three — (the states of waking, dream and dreamless sleep) — are always unreal. Also it has been declared by Him that the Real is always only One, and that manifoldness is always unreal.

This has been set forth in detail in the very beginning. The Truth of Non-becoming is implicit in these teachings.

453.　न किञ्चनेह त्वदृतेऽस्ति सत्यं त्वमेककः कालदिगाद्यतीतः।
अपास्य मिथ्याभ्रममास्स्व शान्त इत्यात्मनिष्ठा
गदिताऽस्ति तेन॥

na kiñcaneha tvadṛte'sti satyaṁ tvamekakaḥ kāladigādyatītaḥ |
apāsya mithyābhramamāssva śānta ityātmaniṣṭhā gaditā'sti tena ||

"There is nothing else real, apart from Thyself; Thou art the Only One, transcending Time, space and so on. Throw off the delusion of Ignorance and remain at Peace," — thus did He teach the State of True Being of the Self.

454.　मत्स्थानि भूतानि न तत्त्वदृष्ट्या मदीयमायैव समस्तमेतत्।
इत्यात्मनोऽजातिमुवाच सत्यां गीतासु कृष्णो भगवान्
स्वयं च॥

matsthāni bhūtāni na tattvadṛṣṭyā madīyamāyaiva samastametat |
ityātmano'jātimuvāca satyāṁ gītāsu kṛṣṇo bhagavān svayaṁ ca ||

"In Truth the creatures are not in Me; all this is only My Maya" — thus did Bhagavan Krishna Himself tell the Truth of the Non-Becoming of the Real Self in the Gita.

455. पूर्णात्मतां स्वामजहत् परं सत् स्वमायया पूर्णमिदं बभूव ।
       बुद्धस्य पूर्णात्मतयैव भातीत्यजातिरुक्ता श्रुतिशीर्षवाचा ॥

pūrṇātmatāṁ svāmajahat paraṁ sat svamāyayā pūrṇamidaṁ babhūva |
buddhasya pūrṇātmatayaiva bhātītyajātiruktā śrutiśīrṣavācā ||

"The Supreme Reality, without losing Its Fullness of Being, by Its own Maya became this complete (universe); to the Sage It appears only as Fullness," — thus the Upanishad also has stated the Truth of Non-Becoming.

Then are given the five verses of Bhagavan Sri Ramana's Tamil Ekatma-Panchakam.

456. विस्मृत्य यत् स्वं वपुरात्ममत्या भ्रान्त्वाऽप्यसङ्ख्येषु
       भवेषु चान्ते ।
       स्वतत्त्वबोधाद् भवति स्व एव स स्वप्नलोकाटनतः प्रबोधः ॥

vismṛtya yat svaṁ vapurātmamatyā bhrāntvā'pyasaṅkhyeṣu bhaveṣu cānte |
svatattvabodhād bhavati sva eva sa svapnalokāṭanataḥ prabodhaḥ ||

The forgetting of one's own Real Self, due to the belief that the body is oneself, then after innumerable births (in bodies), finally becoming his own Real Self by Awareness of the Truth of the One Self, is just (like) waking from a dream of world-wandering.

In a dream one may go through a world-tour and in the dream itself return home and lie down in one's own bed; but when he awakes he knows that it was all a dream. In the same way all of one's Samsaric reincarnations are only a long-drawn out dream, at the end of which only the Self remains, unaffected by all this. There is a difference here, because it was not the Self that dreamed, but only the ego-mind.

In the second verse the quest of '*Who am I?*' is ridiculed, logically enough.

457.   यथा मनुष्यो मधुपानमत्तः कोऽहं नु कुत्राहमिति प्रपृच्छन् ।
आत्मैव सन्नेवमिहाज्ञमर्त्यः कोऽहं कुतोऽहं न्विति पृच्छति
स्वम् ॥

yathā manuṣyo madhupānamattaḥ ko'haṁ nu kutrāhamiti prapṛcchan |
ātmaiva sannevamihājñamartyaḥ ko'haṁ kuto'haṁ nviti pṛcchati svam ||

As one who has become inebriated through drunkenness, who asks (passers-by) "Who am I" or "Wherefrom am I" so the ignorant man asks himself "Who am I" or "Whence am I", being all the time only the Real Self.

Here the difference is that the drunken man puts the question to others, but the Sadhaka puts the question to his own ignorant false self; the Real Self remaining unaffected all along.

458.   अस्त्यात्मनोऽन्तर्वपुरित्यबुद्ध्वा तस्मिञ्जडेऽस्मीत्यभिमन्यते यः ।
मन्येत चित्रस्थमसौ तदीयमाधारभूतं बत वस्त्रमेव ॥

astyātmano'ntarvapurityabuddhvā tasmiñjaḍe'smītyabhimanyate yaḥ ǀ
manyeta citrasthamasau tadīyamādhārabhūtaṁ bata vastrameva ǀǀ

He, who, not knowing that the body is in the Self, and so believes that He, the Self, is in the body, is the same as the one who thinks that the screen, which is the support of the pictures, is in the pictures.

Herein the relation of supporter and the supported is turned topsy-turvy.

459. स्वर्णात् पृथग् भूषणमस्ति किं नु
स्वस्मात् पृथक् किं नु शरीरमस्ति ।
शरीरमेव स्वमवैत्यबुद्धः शुद्धं स्वमेव स्वमवैति बुद्धः ॥

svarṇāt pṛthag bhūṣaṇamasti kiṁ nu svasmāt pṛthak kiṁ nu śarīramasti ǀ
śarīrameva svamavaityabuddhaḥ śuddhaṁ svameva svamavaiti buddhaḥ ǀǀ

Is the jewel separate from gold? Is the body separate from the Self? The ignorant one believes that his body is himself; the Sage knows only the Real Self as the Self.

Here the Truth is that the One Self is the *Substratum* of all appearances. This has been explained before. In the True State there is no superimposition, only the Substratum remains, but is no longer a Substratum.

460. तमेकमात्मानमनादिसत्यं मौनोपदेशाद् गुरुरादिमोऽपि ।
निबोधयामास कथं नु कोऽपि वाचा वदन् बोधयितुं समर्थः ॥

tamekamātmānamanādisatyaṁ maunopadeśād gururādimo'pi |
nibodhayāmāsa kathaṁ nu ko'pi vācā vadan bodhayituṁ samarthaḥ ||

Since the Primal Guru Himself taught this beginningless Self only by Silence, who is there that can teach that Self by speech?

So this is the Rationale of the Silent Teaching by God as Dakshinamurti, the First Guru. Rightly to teach the Self is to be perfectly Quiet. That is Teaching By Being only the Self, without ego and without mind. He who likewise remains as the Self, mindless and egoless, understands this Silent Teaching.

Thus the Truth of Non-becoming is confirmed.

The knowledge thus far imparted is only preparatory to the teaching of the Means of obtaining the Right Awareness. It is not itself that Awareness.

461. इत्यात्मतत्त्वं बहुधोदितं चाप्यनुक्तमेवानुभवैकवेद्यम् ।
तां स्वानुभूतिं निरुणद्धि चित्तं निरूढदेहात्मधिया मुमुक्षोः ॥

ityātmatattvaṁ bahudhoditaṁ cāpyanuktamevānubhavaikavedyam |
tāṁ svānubhūtiṁ niruṇaddhi cittaṁ nirūḍhadehātmadhiyā mumukṣoḥ ||

Even though the Truth of the Self has been stated in many ways, it remains untold, because it can be known only by actual Experience. That Experiential Awareness of the Self is prevented by the mind, due to the firmly established conviction, 'I am the body', for the aspirant to Deliverance.

462.　श्रुत्वैव चैवं विमलान्तरङ्गाः सद्योऽपि निष्ठां सहजां लभेरन् ।
अन्यैस्त्वहङ्कारविनाशनाय सुसाधनं किञ्चिदनुष्ठितव्यम् ॥

śrutvaiva caivaṁ vimalāntaraṅgāḥ sadyo'pi niṣṭhāṁ sahajāṁ labheran |
anyaistvahaṅkāravināśanāya susādhanaṁ kiñcidanuṣṭhitavyam ||

By listening in this way alone, those minds which have been purified from worldly attachments, at once get firmly established in the Natural State, as the Real Self. But others need to go through some excellent process for the extinction of the ego-sense.

463.　अन्तर्हृदि स्वं विमलं विशोकं जिज्ञासयाऽन्विष्य लभेत
शान्तिम् ।
इति श्रुतिर्वक्ति गुरुश्च मार्गं ऋजुं स्वरूपानुभवाय साधोः ॥

antarhṛdi svaṁ vimalaṁ viśokaṁ jijñāsayā'nviṣya labheta śāntim |
iti śrutirvakti guruśca mārgaṁ ṛjuṁ svarūpānubhavāya sādhoḥ ||

"One should seek the Self, who is Pure and free from sorrow within the Heart, by Resolve to know Him, and thereby aim at Peace", — so the ancient Revelation, and the Guru, describe the Direct Path for the Experience of the Truth of the Real Self.

464.　जिज्ञासनं नाम निगद्यतेऽत्र निजस्वरूपानुभवस्य लिप्सा ।
तयैव हि स्वात्मगवेषणेऽस्मिन्नन्तर्मुखत्वं भविता मुमुक्षोः ॥

jijñāsanaṁ nāma nigadyate'tra nijasvarūpānubhavasya lipsā |
tayaiva hi svātmagaveṣaṇe'sminnantarmukhatvaṁ bhavitā mumukṣoḥ ||

The 'Resolve to Know', mentioned here, is the intention to win Experience of one's own Self; only by such intention can the aspirant turn his mind inwards in this Quest of one's own Self.

465.　श्रुतिप्रसिद्धं भवनं परस्य सत्यात्मभूतस्य हृदाख्यमस्ति ।
　　　स एव सर्वं हि कथं नु तस्य निर्दिश्यते स्थानमिदं हृदाख्यम् ॥

śrutiprasiddhaṁ bhavanaṁ parasya satyātmabhūtasya hṛdākhyamasti |
sa eva sarvaṁ hi kathaṁ nu tasya nirdiśyate sthānamidaṁ hṛdākhyam ||

There is mentioned in the ancient Revelation the dwelling place of the Supreme One, named the Heart. He himself being all there is, how can the Heart be designated as His dwelling place?

The explanation follows.

466.　प्रज्ञास्वरूपं हृदयं हि सत्यं प्रज्ञास्वरूपः स च सत्य आत्मा ।
　　　अतः स आत्मा हृदयं हि सत्यं प्रतिष्ठितं सर्वमिदं हि तस्मिन् ॥

prajñāsvarūpaṁ hṛdayaṁ hi satyaṁ prajñāsvarūpaḥ sa ca satya ātmā |
ataḥ sa ātmā hṛdayaṁ hi satyaṁ pratiṣṭhitaṁ sarvamidaṁ hi tasmin ||

The real Heart is just Consciousness in its native purity, and the Self also is that Consciousness. So it follows that the Self is Himself the Heart, and all creation is established in Him (as the Substratum).

467. तथाऽपि बुद्धा निगमान्तवाचो विधातुमन्तर्मुखतां गवेषे ।
      अन्तः शरीरे निलयं हृदाख्यं दिशन्ति तस्यानिलयस्य पुंसः ॥

tathā'pi buddhā nigamāntavāco vidhātumantarmukhatāṁ gaveṣe |
antaḥ śarīre nilayaṁ hṛdākhyaṁ diśanti tasyānilayasya puṁsaḥ ||

And yet the sages and the Vedantas teach that
the One, who has really no dwelling place, has a
dwelling place called the Heart inside the body,
in order to cause the inward-turning of the mind
in the Quest.

The necessity of this inward-turning is then shown.

468. बहिर्मुखान्येव किलेन्द्रियाणि यतः प्रपञ्चेन निमील्यते स्वः ।
      उपाय उन्मीलयितुं स्वरूपं स्वान्वेषणेऽन्तर्मुखतैव साधोः ॥

bahirmukhānyeva kilendriyāṇi yataḥ prapañcena nimīlyate svaḥ |
upāya unmīlayituṁ svarūpaṁ svānveṣaṇe'ntarmukhataiva sādhoḥ ||

The sense-organs are turned only outwards,
that being the reason for the Self being covered over
by the world. The means for uncovering the true
nature of that Self is only the inward turning (of the
mind), of the aspirant in the Quest of that Self.

That is the meaning of an Upanishadic verse.*

---

*   पराञ्चि खानि व्यतृणत् स्वयम्भूस्तस्मात् पराङ् पश्यति नान्तरात्मन् ।
     कश्चिद्धीरः प्रत्यगात्मानमैक्षदावृत्तचक्षुरमृतत्वमिच्छन् ॥(क.उ.)]

parāñci khāni vyatṛṇat svayambhūstasmāt parāṅ paśyati nāntarātman |
kaściddhīraḥ pratyagātmānamaikṣadāvṛttacakṣuramṛtatvamicchan || (ka. u .)

469.　बन्धस्य मुक्तेरिदमन्तरं हि सन्दर्शितं स्वानुभवेन बुद्धैः ।
　　　बद्धस्य पुंसः समुदेत्यहन्ता नोदेत्यहन्ता तु विमुक्तपुंसः ॥

bandhasya mukteridamantaraṁ hi sandarśitaṁ svānubhavena buddhaiḥ |
baddhasya puṁsaḥ samudetyahantā nodetyahantā tu vimuktapuṁsaḥ ||

The difference between bondage and Deliverance has been shown (thus) by the sages in accordance with their own Experience: "The bound one suffers from the arising of the ego-sense; the ego-sense does not arise in the case of the One that is Free.

470.　नित्यापरोक्षोऽपि सदैव जन्तोरात्मा महान् प्रेष्ठ उरुप्रकाशः ।
　　　दुरात्मनाऽहङ्कृतिरूपकेण हृतप्रभो यद्वदलं न भाति ॥

nityāparokṣo'pi sadaiva jantorātmā mahān preṣṭha uruprakāśaḥ |
durātmanā'haṅkṛtirūpakeṇa hṛtaprabho yadvadalaṁ na bhāti ||

Though the Great Being, the Self, is ever present, dearly beloved and of great effulgence, it is as if His effulgence is dimmed by the evil one, the Ego, so that He does not shine sufficiently, so as to be recognized.

471.　देहोऽहमस्मीत्यनुभूतिरूपो भवत्यबोधः खलु बन्धरूपः ।
　　　बोधोऽहमस्मीति विनाऽनुभूतिं कथं नु नीयेत विनाशमेषः ॥

deho'hamasmītyanubhūtirūpo bhavatyabodhaḥ khalu bandharūpaḥ |
bodho'hamasmīti vinā'nubhūtiṁ kathaṁ nu nīyeta vināśameṣaḥ ||

Ignorance consists in the awareness which consists in the experience 'I am the body'. How can this experiential awareness be just brought to end once for all, without the experiential awareness, "I am the Pure Consciousness"?

Because the Ignorance, which is itself bondage, consists in an experiential awareness, even though wrong, it can be extinguished only by the Right Awareness, which is also an Experience. Mere inferential knowledge, usually called Knowledge of something absent — *Parokshajnanam* — is wholly ineffectual for winning Deliverance. The Sadhana as taught by Bhagavan Sri Ramana is the Direct Path to that Experience. This Sadhana is now to be explained.

472. देहोऽहमस्मीति समुद्भवन्ती धीरेव रूपं खलु जीवनाम्नः ।
सत्यांशमस्यैव विविच्य साधुर्गवेषयेज्जन्मभुवं तदीयम् ॥

deho'hamasmīti samudbhavantī dhīreva rūpaṁ khalu jīvanāmnaḥ |
satyāṁśamasyaiva vivicya sādhurgaveṣayejjanmabhuvaṁ tadīyam ||

The thought that arises in the form, 'I am the body,' is itself the form in which the individual soul has experience. The aspirant must seek the source wherefrom it arises, after separating from it the fraction of it which is real.

473. नात्यन्तमिथ्या खलु जीव एष नायं हि वन्ध्यातनयस्य तुल्यः ।
आत्माह्यधिष्ठानतयास्ति तस्मान्मृषाऽपि सन् सत्यवदेव भाति ॥

nātyantamithyā khalu jīva eṣa nāyaṁ hi vandhyātanayasya tulyaḥ |
ātmāhyadhiṣṭhānatayā'sti tasmānmṛṣā'pi san satyavadeva bhāti ||

This individual is not altogether unreal; he is not so in the same sense as the barren woman's son is unreal. The Real Self is present as the Substratum on which the sense of an individual soul is superimposed, and hence even though unreal, he is taken to be real.

This distinction is very important, as will be seen. Everyone knows that there is no barren woman's son, mare's horn, and so on, because these notions have no substratum. On the other hand the rope-snake, the silver in the mother-of-pearl, etc. are capable of being imagined to be seen, because these have a substratum, as explained before. So the individual soul comes to be taken as existing, though he really does not exist, as taught before.

The question then is what is the substratum on which the appearance of an individual soul is superimposed. This and other pertinent questions are answered in the verses that follow.

474. सत्यांश एतस्य हि जीवनाम्नः सत्यात्मचैतन्यमहंस्वरूपम् ।
आदाय सत्यांशमिमं मुमुक्षुर्भवेत् समर्थो निजमार्गणाय ॥

satyāṁśa etasya hi jīvanāmnaḥ satyātmacaitanyamahaṁsvarūpam |
ādāya satyāṁśamimaṁ mumukṣurbhavet samartho nijamārgaṇāya ||

The element of Reality of the 'soul', which is the "I", is the consciousness, which is the Nature of the Real Self. By taking hold of this element of

Reality the seeker of Deliverance is enabled to engage in the Quest of that Self.

475.   अस्यासदंशं वपुरादिसर्वं विहाय शिष्टां निरुपाधिकां ताम् ।
सत्यात्मनो दीधितिवत् सुसूक्ष्मामहंस्वरूपां चितिमाददानः ॥

asyāsadaṁśaṁ vapurādisarvaṁ vihāya śiṣṭāṁ nirupādhikāṁ tām |
satyātmano dīdhitivat susūkṣmāmahaṁsvarūpāṁ citimādadānaḥ ||

476.   श्वा स्वामिनं स्वं सुमुपैति यद्वत् तद्गन्धमादाय गवेषयित्वा ।
लभेत यत्किञ्चन मग्नवस्तु निमज्ज्य यद्वत् सलिले तथा वा ॥

śvā svāminaṁ svaṁ sumupaiti yadvat tadgandhamādāya gaveṣayitvā |
labheta yatkiñcana magnavastu nimajjya yadvat salile tathā vā ||

477.   अस्याहमो जन्मभुवं स्वतत्त्वं विमृग्य कोऽहं नु कुतोऽहमेषः ।
इति स्वतत्त्वानुबुभूषयाऽन्तर्निमज्ज्य निष्ठां सहजां लभेत ॥

asyāhamo janmabhuvaṁ svatattvaṁ vimṛgya ko'haṁ nu kuto'hameṣaḥ |
iti svatattvānububhūṣayā'ntarnimajjya niṣṭhāṁ sahajāṁ labheta ||

Giving up the element of unreality of this soul, namely the body and all the rest of it, and fixing the mind on the consciousness of the Self, having the form of 'I', which is extremely subtle like a ray of the Real Self, the seeker should dive into the Heart, seeking the place of birth of this "I"-sense (the ego) with the question 'Who am I', or 'Whence is this I?' like the dog that rejoins his master, seeking him by following his scent, or as a diver dives into water, to recover something that has fallen therein, and thereby attain one's own Real State.

478. बहिर्मुखत्वं निजमार्गणेऽस्मिन् व्रजेन्मनश्चेद्विषयाभिमुख्यात् ।
पुनर्मनोऽन्तर्मुखमेव कुर्यात् साधुः प्रयत्नात् प्रविलापदृष्ट्या ॥

bahirmukhatvaṁ nijamārgaṇe'smin vrajenmanaścedviṣayābhimukhyāt |
punarmano'ntarmukhameva kuryāt sādhuḥ prayatnāt pravilāpadṛṣṭyā ||

If during this quest of one's own Self the mind turns outwards, due to attachment to sense objects, the seeker should turn it inwards again by merging the world in the Self.

This is explained next:—

479. तरङ्गफेनादिकमब्धिमात्रं स्वाप्नं जगत् स्वप्नदृगेव यद्वत् ।
सर्वं जगच्चाप्यहमेव नान्यदिति प्रतीतिः प्रविलापदृष्टिः ॥

taraṅgaphenādikamabdhimātraṁ svāpnaṁ jagat svapnadṛgeva yadvat |
sarvaṁ jagaccāpyahameva nānyaditi pratītiḥ pravilāpadṛṣṭiḥ ||

"Just as waves, foam, etc. are only the ocean, and as the dream-world is only the seer of the dream, and nothing else, so the whole world is only Myself and nothing else". This view is the merging of the world in the Self.

Another method is as follows:

480.   कस्येदमेवं विषयाभिमुख्यमिति स्वतत्त्वस्य दिदृक्षया वा ।
       अन्तर्मुखीकृत्य पुनः पुनश्च मनो नियुञ्जीत गवेषयोगे ॥

kasyedamevaṁ viṣayābhimukhyamiti svatattvasya didṛkṣayā vā |
antarmukhīkṛtya punaḥ punaśca mano niyuñjīta gaveṣayoge ||

Or he should bring the mind back again and again (as often as necessary) and re-engage it in the Quest by the resolve to become aware of the Truth of oneself, by means of the question: "Who is he, that has the attachment to sense-objects"?

481.   कदा नु निष्ठां सहजां लभेयेत्येवं निरुत्साहमना विषीदन् ।
       भक्तोऽथवा स्वात्मगवेषयोगी स्वयं विमुक्तेर्निरुणद्धि मार्गम् ॥

kadā nu niṣṭhāṁ sahajāṁ labheyetyevaṁ nirutsāhamanā viṣīdan |
bhakto'thavā svātmagaveṣayogī svayaṁ vimukterniruṇaddhi mārgam ||

The devotee or the Seeker of the Self who becomes discouraged by the thought, 'When shall I attain the Natural State', thereby hinders progress on the Path to Deliverance.

482.   उत्साहसन्तोषयुतेन भाव्यं मुमुक्षुणा सात्त्विकमानसेन ।
       अनुस्मरन् कालमृषात्वमुक्तं मनो नियुञ्जीत गवेषयोगे ॥

utsāhasantoṣayutena bhāvyaṁ mumukṣuṇā sāttvikamānasena |
anusmaran kālamṛṣātvamuktaṁ mano niyuñjīta gaveṣayoge ||

The aspirant for Deliverance must be full of enthusiasm, with his mind in the Sattvic mood, and should engage in this Quest, remembering the teaching that Time is unreal.

483. प्रश्नस्य कोऽस्मीति सदैव साधोर्द्वाराणि सर्वत्र च सम्भवन्ति ।
द्वारेण केनापि गवेषणेऽस्मिन् मनो नियुञ्जीत पुनः पुनश्च ॥

praśnasya ko'smīti sadaiva sādhordvārāṇi sarvatra ca sambhavanti |
dvāreṇa kenāpi gaveṣaṇe'smin mano niyuñjīta punaḥ punaśca ||

Always and everywhere there are doorways for getting at the question 'Who am I?'. By any one of these the seeker must again and again engage the mind in this Quest.

The nature of the answer to this question is next indicated.

484. नास्योत्तरं काचन बुद्धिवृत्तिर्न वेत्ति धीस्तं खलु तुर्यसत्यम् ।
अस्योत्तरं स्वानुभवस्तुरीये नष्टेऽहमि प्रष्टरि जीवनाम्नि ॥

nāsyottaraṃ kācana buddhivṛttirna vetti dhīstaṃ khalu turyasatyam |
asyottaraṃ svānubhavasturīye naṣṭe'hami praṣṭari jīvanāmni ||

The answer to this question is not an intellectual conclusion. The (proper) answer to it is only the Experience of the Real Self in the Supreme State, arising on the death of the ego, the questioner, named the "individual self" (the soul).

485. यो निर्विकल्पः सहजः समाधिस्तत्रैव भायात् स्फुटमात्मतत्त्वम् ।
अन्यत्र धीवृत्तिविमिश्रितत्वाद् भायाद्यथावन्न हि सत्य आत्मा ॥

yo nirvikalpaḥ sahajaḥ samādhistatraiva bhāyāt sphuṭamātmatattvam |
anyatra dhīvṛttivimiśritatvād bhāyādyathāvanna hi satya ātmā ||

The Real Self will shine as He really is, only
in the thought-free Natural State of the Self. In
other states the Real Self will not shine as He
really is, due to its being mixed up with
intellectual views (or beliefs).

Another hindrance to success in the Quest is now stated.

486. नियुक्तमेवं तु मनो गवेषे लीयेत चेन्निष्फल एव यत्नः ।
लयात् प्रबोध्याथ पुनश्च साधुर्मनो नियुञ्जीत मनोगवेषे ॥

niyuktamevaṁ tu mano gaveṣe līyeta cennisphala eva yatnaḥ |
layāt prabodhyātha punaśca sādhurmano niyuñjīta manogaveṣe ||

If the mind thus engaged in the Quest
becomes unconscious (as in deep sleep), the effort
so far made becomes unfruitful. (So) the seeker
should awaken the mind from this unconsciousness
and again engage it in the Quest.

What is needed is not unconsciousness of the mind, but
its complete extinction. This is next stated as clearly pointed
out by Bhagavan Sri Ramana in His Upadesa Sara.

487. नाशो लयश्चेत्युभयप्रकारो मनोनिरोधो गुरुणास्ति दिष्टः ।
मनोलयस्यानिलरोधनाद्या भवन्त्युपाया हठयोगमार्गे ॥

nāśo layaścetyubhayaprakāro manonirodho guruṇā'sti diṣṭaḥ |
manolayasyānilarodhanādyā bhavantyupāyā haṭhayogamārge ||

Mental quiescence has been explained by the Guru as being of two kinds, as latency in unconsciousness and final extinction. In Hatha Yoga there are many methods of attaining unconsciousness, such as suspension of the breath.

The difference between these two is then explained.

488.　मनो विलीनं सह वासनाभिर्भवाय पश्चात् पुनरुद्धवेद्धि ।
नष्टं मनश्चेन्निजमार्गणेन निर्वासनं भर्जितबीजवत् स्यात् ॥

mano vilīnaṁ saha vāsanābhirbhavāya paścāt punarudbhaveddhi |
naṣṭaṁ manaścennijamārgaṇena nirvāsanaṁ bharjitabījavat syāt ||

The mind, when it has gone into latency together with its habits of activity, will later become active again to produce the worldly life. The mind that has been extinguished will lose its habits of action and thus become like seed that has been roasted.

As roasted seed does not sprout, so the mind that has become extinct cannot lead to rebirth.

489.　बध्नात्यविद्या बत वासनाभिः स्वाज्ञं हि ता एव मनः स्वरूपम् ।
गवेषणे स्याद्यदि जागरूकं मनस्तु तासां भविताऽथ नाशः ॥

badhnātyavidyā bata vāsanābhiḥ svājñaṁ hi tā eva manaḥ svarūpam |
gaveṣaṇe syādyadi jāgarūkaṁ manastu tāsāṁ bhavitā'tha nāśaḥ ||

Ignorance binds the ignorant one by means of (these) habits. If the mind remains wide-awake in the Quest, then there will ensue the destruction of the habits.

490. ज्ञानोदयः स्यान्मनसो विनाशान्नष्टासु सर्वास्वपि वासनासु ।
मुक्तिर्निरुक्ताऽखिलवासनानामात्यन्तिको नाश इति प्रबुद्धैः ॥

jñānodayaḥ syānmanaso vināśānnaṣṭāsu sarvāsvapi vāsanāsu |
muktirniruktā'khilavāsanānāmātyantiko nāśa iti prabuddhaiḥ ||490||

Right awareness dawns on the complete extinction of the mind, whereby all the mental habits also are lost. Deliverance is affirmed by all sages to be none other than the final and complete destruction of the mental habits.

Apart from latency there is another obstacle, namely craving for sense-pleasures; it is next pointed out.

491. क्षुरस्य धारा निशिता यथैवं मार्गो ह्ययं स्वात्मविचारनामा ।
रागो लयश्चेत्युभयं विहाय तिष्ठेत् सदैकाग्रधिया गवेषे ॥

kṣurasya dhārā niśitā yathaivaṃ mārgo hyayaṃ svātmavicāranāmā |
rāgo layaścetyubhayaṃ vihāya tiṣṭhet sadaikāgradhiyā gaveṣe ||491||

Like the keen edge of a razor is this Quest of the Real Self. So one should overcome both desire and latency and keep the mind concentrated in the Quest.

The uniqueness of this method, the Quest, is next explained.

492. अन्येषु योगेषु हि जीवनामा सन् कोऽपि कर्मादिकदोषयुक्तः ।
अस्तीति मत्वैव च दोषहीनं विधातुमेनं यतते च योगी ॥

anyeṣu yogeṣu hi jīvanāmā san ko'pi karmādikadoṣayuktaḥ |
astīti matvaiva ca doṣahīnaṁ vidhātumenaṁ yatate ca yogī ||492||

In all the other yogas it is assumed that there is an entity called 'Soul', having defects, namely action and the rest and the yogi makes efforts to make him free from those defects.

493. कर्मित्वनाशाय च कर्मयोगो विभक्तिनाशाय च भक्तियोगः ।
वियोगनाशाय च राजयोगोऽप्यबोधनाशाय च बोधयोगः ॥

karmitvanāśāya ca karmayogo vibhaktināśāya ca bhaktiyogaḥ |
viyoganāśāya ca rājayogo'pyabodhanāśāya ca bodhayogaḥ ||493||

For eradicating the defect of being an actor, there is the yoga of action; for getting rid of separateness (from God) there is the yoga of Devotion; for the cure of the defect of difference there is the yoga of mind-control; and for the eradication of Ignorance there is the Yoga of Right Awareness.

These yogas are ridiculed by pointing out the truth of the Real Self.

494.   स एव साक्षात् पुरुषः परः सन् स्वस्मात् पृथक् स्वं गणयन्नबुद्धः ।
तेनैक्यमिच्छन् यतते च योगैर्हास्यं हि तस्मादितरत् किमस्ति ॥

sa eva sākṣāt puruṣaḥ paraḥ san svasmāt pṛthak svaṁ gaṇayannabuddhaḥ |
tenaikyamicchan yatate ca yogairhāsyaṁ hi tasmāditarat kimasti ||

Being himself the same as the Supreme Being, the ignorant man, thinking himself to be someone other than He, through delusion, tries to become one with Him by various Yogas! What else is there, more absurd?

The superiority of the Quest is then shown.

495.   आदाय जीवस्य चिदंशमेव तन्मूलभूतात्मगवेषणेन ।
निर्दोष आत्मैव हि भात्यनन्तो न शिष्यते कश्चन तत्र जीवः ॥

ādāya jīvasya cidaṁśameva tanmūlabhūtātmagaveṣaṇena |
nirdoṣa ātmaiva hi bhātyananto na śiṣyate kaścana tatra jīvaḥ ||

When, by taking hold of the consciousness-element of the soul, the Quest is made of the Self, the root of that soul, that Self, who is free from all defects shines alone; there the soul does not survive.

496.   अतो महायोगसमाख्यकोऽयं नान्योऽस्य योगस्य समोऽधिको वा ।
अन्तर्भवन्त्यत्र समस्तयोगा अङ्गानि ते ह्यस्य यथोचितं स्युः ॥

ato mahāyogasamākhyako'yaṁ nānyo'sya yogasya samo'dhiko vā |
antarbhavantyatra samastayogā aṅgāni te hyasya yathocitaṁ syuḥ ||

Hence this (Quest) is named the Great Yoga; there is no other Yoga, equal to this, or greater. All the Yogas are included in, and may be used as auxiliaries to this one, as may be found suitable.

497.   जीवोदयस्थानगवेषणं यत् स एक एवाखिलयोगमार्गाः ।
स कर्मयोगोऽप्युत भक्तियोगः स राजयोगोऽप्युत बोधयोगः ॥

jīvodayasthānagaveṣaṇaṁ yat sa eka evākhilayogamārgāḥ |
sa karmayogo'pyuta bhaktiyogaḥ sa rājayogo'pyuta bodhayogaḥ ||

This Yoga, the Quest of the source of the soul, is itself all the Yogas; it is the yoga of Action, the yoga of Devotion, the yoga of Restraining the mind and also the yoga of Right Awareness.

This quest of the Real Self, it is next pointed out, is not to be practiced as a meditation.

498.   प्रश्नस्वरूपो हि गवेष एष न ध्यानवत् साधनमेतदुक्तम् ।
हृन्मज्जनं सम्भवति ह्यनेन प्रश्नेन न ध्यानपरम्पराभिः ॥

praśnasvarūpo hi gaveṣa eṣa na dhyānavat sādhanametaduktam |
hṛnmajjanaṁ sambhavati hyanena praśnena na dhyānaparamparābhiḥ ||

Since this Quest has the form of a Question, it is not to be practised as a mode of meditation. By this question, the mind dives into the Heart, which it does not do by any series of meditations.

499. केचिन्निदिध्यासनमाचरन्ति श्रुत्वाऽपि मत्वाऽपि निजं स्वरूपम् ।
अन्यो हि मार्गोऽयमुतान्य एव स्वान्वेषरूपो रमणोपदिष्टः ॥

kecinnididhyāsanamācaranti śrutvā'pi matvā'pi nijaṁ svarūpam |
anyo hi mārgo'yamutānya eva svānveṣarūpo ramaṇopadiṣṭaḥ ||

Some practise continuous meditation on the Truth of one's own self, after listening to and reflecting upon that Truth. This method is other than the Quest of the Self taught by Bhagavan Sri Ramana.

The method taught by Bhagavan Sri Ramana is not an affirmation, but a question. The threefold process is further explained.

500. ब्रह्मात्मनोस्तत् त्वमसीत्यभेदश्छान्दोग्यवेदान्तनिरूपितोऽस्ति ।
अभेद एष प्रतिपाद्यते च वाच्यार्थलक्ष्यार्थविवेचनेन ॥

brahmātmanostat tvamasītyabhedaśchāndogyavedāntanirūpito'sti |
abheda eṣa pratipādyate ca vācyārthalakṣyārthavivecanena ||

In the Chhandogya Upanishad the identity of the Supreme Being and the Real Self is taught by the sentence, 'Thou art That'. This identity is confirmed by distinguishing between the literal and the intended meanings (of the terms used).

The terms 'Thou' and 'That', if taken in the literal sense, tend to show that there can be no such identity. Hence the intended meanings are sought, so that the identity may be accepted as true. The identity is not of the apparent self, but of the Real Self, with the Supreme Being. At the same time the Supreme Being is not the Personal God of the theists, but the Impersonal Being of the Upanishads. Both are of the Nature of Consciousness, and it is this Consciousness that is the real essence of both. Thus the Identity is true.

It has been assumed by the traditional school of Advaita Vedanta that this sentence conveys an injunction to meditate on the teaching. Actually, as Bhagavan Sri Ramana says, the sentence states only a fact. The acceptance of it as a fact is not enough. And meditation is no better. What is needed is to verify the fact by reaching and remaining in the Mind-free state, called also the Natural State. What He has said is the following:-

501. वाक्येऽत्र तच्छब्दनिवेदितस्य चर्चां विना त्वम्पदलक्षितस्य ।
सत्यात्मनस्तत्त्वगवेषणस्य कर्तव्यतां श्रीरमणो ब्रवीति ॥

vākye'tra tacchabdaniveditasya carcāṁ vinā tvampadalakṣitasya |
satyātmanastattvagaveṣaṇasya kartavyatāṁ śrīramaṇo bravīti ||

Sri Ramana says that, without an enquiry as to the intended meaning of the term 'That', in the sentence, one should make a Quest of the Truth of the Real Self, who is indicated by the term 'Thou'.

This Quest leads upto the mind-free state wherein the Real Self shines unhindered by the veil of ignorance, which is the Ego, the false self. Then it will be realized that there is only one entity, which is the Real Self and also the Impersonal Supreme Being of the Upanishads.

Bhagavan Sri Ramana calls the Quest the *Direct Path*. It bye-passes the meditation mentioned before.

502. एवं गवेषेण भवेन्मुमुक्षोर्हन्मज्जनात् स्वानुभवस्तुरीये ।
न स्यान्निदिध्यासनमस्य कार्यं नानेन कार्यं मननं च दीर्घम् ॥

evaṁ gaveṣeṇa bhavenmumukṣorhṛnmajjanāt svānubhavasturīye |
na syānnididhyāsanamasya kāryaṁ nānena kāryaṁ mananaṁ ca dīrgham ||

By this Quest the Aspirant obtains the Direct Experience of the Real Self in the Transcendental State (beyond the three states of the Ignorance). For him that has thus succeeded in this Quest, there is no need for the continuous Meditation nor the prolonged Reflection (mentioned before).

It is here taken for granted that the aspirant accepts the teaching of the Identity as true, because of his faith in the Guru, who has that Experience, and is therefore a competent witness of that Truth.

So there is no injunction to meditate in the sentence cited.

503. श्रुत्योदिते तत्त्वमसीति वाक्ये ध्यानं न किञ्चिद्विहितं हि साधोः ।
उक्ता परस्यैव तुरीयभावे बुद्धेन सत्यात्मतयाऽनुभूतिः ॥

śrutyodite tattvamasīti vākye dhyānaṁ na kiñcidvihitaṁ hi sādhoḥ |
uktā parasyaiva turīyabhāve buddhena satyātmatayā'nubhūtiḥ ||

In the Sentence of the ancient Revelation, 'Thou art That', no meditation has been enjoined. What is said by implication is that in the Egoless State the Sage (who has won that State) has the Experience of the Impersonal Being as identical with his own Real Self.

504. तत्त्वं स्वकं यन्निरुपाधिकं तद् ब्रह्मेति वेदान्तगिरा सुसिद्धे ।
ब्रह्मात्मनोरेकतयाऽनुभूत्यै स्वान्वेषणात् किं करणीयमन्यत् ॥

tattvam svakam yannirupādhikam tad brahmeti vedāntagirā susiddhe |
brahmātmanorekatayā'nubhūtyai svānveṣaṇāt kim karaṇīyamanyat ||

Since it is settled by the sentence of the Vedanta that one's own Real Self, disentangled from the veiling sheaths, is the Supreme Reality (the Impersonal Being) what else is there for attaining the Experience of the Identity of that Reality and the Self, except the Quest of that Self?

This is obvious, says Bhagavan Sri Ramana. The real meaning of the text, 'Thou art That', is next set forth according to the spirit of His teachings.

505. विहाय देहात्ममतिं विमृग्य स्वमेव बुद्ध्वा हृदि निष्ठितस्य ।
भात्यात्मरूपः पर एव साक्षादित्यर्थको हि श्रुतिशीर्षवाणी ॥

vihāya dehātmamatim vimṛgya svameva buddhvā hṛdi niṣṭhitasya |
bhātyātmarūpaḥ para eva sākṣādityarthakā hi śrutiśīrṣavāṇī ||

The meaning of that Vedantic Text is this, that if one gives up the notion 'I am the Body', seeks the Self, becomes aware of His True Nature and is thus firmly fixed in the Heart, then for him the Supreme-Being Himself shines as the Real Self.

Has the meditation on the Truth any use at all?

506.   निजस्वरूपस्य गवेषणं यत् साक्षाद् भवेत् साधनमेतदेव ।
उक्तं निदिध्यासनमङ्गमस्य देहात्मधीनिर्मथनाय साधोः ॥

nijasvarūpasya gaveṣaṇaṁ yat sākṣād bhavet sādhanametadeva |
uktaṁ nididhyāsanamaṅgamasya dehātmadhīnirmathanāya sādhoḥ || .

The Quest of the Truth of the Self is alone the Direct Path to the Right Awareness of the Self. The meditation spoken of is a preliminary aid to this Quest, for breaking up the idea of the body as the Self (which is the hindrance to the Quest).

This is what Bhagavan Sri Ramana has said. In the way shown the meditation is useful for those who are not able to free themselves from their ego-sense, by which the body is identified as the Self.

The obstacles that may lie on the path are next dealt with.

507.   हृन्मज्जनं स्वात्मगवेषणेऽस्मिन् न सम्भवेद् दुर्बलमानसस्य ।
वृत्तिष्वनेकासु विभज्यमानं नितान्तमल्पं मनसो बलं हि ॥

hṛnmajjanaṁ svātmagaveṣaṇe'smin na sambhaved
    durbalamānasasya |
vṛttiṣvanekāsu vibhajyamānaṁ nitāntamalpaṁ manaso balaṁ hi ||

The diving (of the mind) into the Heart in this Quest of the Self does not occur for him with a weak mind. The mind's strength, being subdivided among innumerable thoughts, is insignificant.

One-pointedness of the mind is needed. A mind that is one-pointed will be strong enough for this purpose. Curbing of the vanity of thoughts is the expedient to be adopted.

508.   एकाग्रता या मनसो गवेषे मनोबलं नाम तदेव नान्यत् ।
ईदृग् बलं यस्य भवेत् स एव धीरः स्वधीरक्षणकौशलेन ॥

ekāgratā yā manaso gaveṣe manobalaṁ nāma tadeva nānyat |
īdṛg balaṁ yasya bhavet sa eva dhīraḥ svadhīrakṣaṇakauśalena ||

The one-pointedness of the mind in the Quest itself is the strength of mind that is needed, and nothing else. He, who has this strength, is called 'Valiant', because he has the skill to protect his intellect from being frittered away (on a variety of thoughts).

509.   ध्यानेन वर्धेत मनोबलं यत् तद् ध्यानमङ्गं निजमार्गणस्य ।
ध्यानान्मनो निश्चलतां प्रसाध्य ततः स्वतत्त्वम् मृगयेत धीरः ॥

dhyānena vardheta manobalaṁ yat tad dhyānamaṅgaṁ nijamārgaṇasya |
dhyānānmano niścalatāṁ prasādhya tataḥ svatattvam mṛgayeta dhīraḥ ||

By the practice of meditation mental strength (one-pointedness) will be intensified. Therefore meditation is an aid to the Quest. First achieving motionlessness of the mind by meditation, the valiant aspirant must seek the Truth of one's own self.

Then the question arises, what is to be taken as the object of meditation.

510. अहंस्वरूपा चितिरात्मनो या सर्वोत्तमं ध्येयमिदं मुमुक्षोः ।
मज्जेदनेनैव मनो हृदन्त इत्यस्मदाचार्यवरोपदेशः ॥

ahaṁsvarūpā citirātmano yā sarvottamaṁ dhyeyamidaṁ mumukṣoḥ |
majjedanenaiva mano hṛdanta ityasmadācāryavaropadeśaḥ ||

The best of all possible objects for meditation is the consciousness, having the form 'I', which is the Essence of the Real Self, for the seeker of Deliverance. By this meditation alone, the mind will naturally dive into the Heart. Such is the teaching of our Great Guru.

'I', He has pointed out, is the Name of that Impersonal Being, the subject matter of the Vedantas. He has said that this Name is even holier than the Pranava (Om).

An alternative method for stilling the mind's thoughts, as recommended by Bhagavan Sri Ramana, is stated.

511. शान्तिं नयन् केवलकुम्भकेन चित्तं विना पूरकरेचकाभ्याम् ।
सज्जेत चेत् स्वात्मगवेषयोगे हृन्मजनं स्यान्मनसो मुमुक्षोः ॥

śāntiṁ nayan kevalakumbhakena cittaṁ vinā pūrakarecakābhyām |
sajjeta cet svātmagaveṣayoge hṛnmajjanaṁ syānmanaso mumukṣoḥ ||

(Or) if the aspirant to Deliverance stills the mind by pure *Kumbhaka*, without *puraka* and *rechaka*, and thus engages in the Quest, then his mind will dive into the Heart.

Ordinary pranayama consists of the three parts, breathing in (Puraka), retaining the breath within

(Kumbhaka), and breathing out (Rechaka). But here the middle part (kumbhaka) alone is recommended as a means of stilling the mind. This may be mastered by steady practice. This is called Kevala Kumbhaka.

The same process is prescribed in the Yoga Vasishta, as quoted below:

512.   देहं पृथक्कृत्य निजस्वरूपे विश्रम्य तिष्ठेद्यदि चित्स्वरूपे ।
अहम्मतिस्तस्य विनाशमेतीत्येवं वसिष्ठो भगवानवोचत् ॥

deham pṛthakkṛtya nijasvarūpe viśramya tiṣṭhedyadi citsvarūpe |
ahammatistasya vināśametītyevaṁ vasiṣṭho bhagavānavocat ||

Bhagavan Vasishtha has said: 'If one separates the body (from oneself) and remains at rest in one's own self, which is consciousness, then his ego-sense perishes'.

That is, he attains the Egoless State.

What happens when the Quest is thus persisted in, long enough?

513.   आत्मानमन्विष्य मनः कयाऽपि शक्त्या गृहीतं हृदये निमज्जेत् ।
तत्रात्मनश्चित्प्रभया निगीर्णं मनोऽहमा साकमुपैति नाशम् ॥

ātmānamanviṣya manaḥ kayā'pi śaktyā gṛhītaṁ hṛdaye nimajjet |
tatrātmanaścitprabhayā nigīrṇaṁ mano'hamā sākamupaiti nāśam ||

The mind, seeking the Self, being taken hold of by some mysterious Power (from within) dives into the Heart; there the mind, being consumed by the consciousness-Light of the Self, ceases to exist, along with the ego.

What is this Power?

514.   शक्तिः कृपाख्या खलु सा परस्य सत्यात्मभूतस्य हृदि स्थितस्य ।
विद्यामयी सा हि समर्प्य तस्यै स्वमेव साधुर्भविता कृतार्थः ॥

śaktiḥ kṛpākhyā khalu sā parasya satyātmabhūtasya hṛdi sthitasya |
vidyāmayī sā hi samarpya tasyai svameva sādhurbhavitā kṛtārthaḥ ||

That Power is indeed the Grace of God, who is the Real Self in the Heart. She is of the Nature of Right Awareness. By yielding up oneself to Her, the Aspirant becomes blessed (beyond measure).

The State thus reached is the Highest. It is further described.

515.   ज्ञानाग्निना विश्वमिदं प्रदग्धं सहाहमा यत्र महाश्मशाने ।
चिद्व्योम्नि तत्राहमहन्तयाऽऽत्मा सदाशिवो नृत्यति केवलः
सन् ॥

jñānāgninā viśvamidaṁ pradagdhaṁ sahāhamā yatra mahāśmaśāne |
cidvyomni tatrāhamahantayā"tmā sadāśivo nṛtyati kevalaḥ san ||

In that great burning ground, the sky of Pure Consciousness, where, by the Fire of Right Awareness, this universe, along with the ego is consumed, dances, the Ever-Auspicious Real Self, the Sole Reality, in the form of 'I', 'I'.

This Fire consumes the whole of creation with its Root, the Ego, leaving not even ashes. The Real Self is said to be dancing, to indicate the Bliss of that State.

So there is no dance in the literal sense.

516. तदेव चिद्व्योम हि तत्स्वरूपं नृत्येदसौ तत्र कथं न्वरूपः ।
आनन्दरूपत्वममुष्य दिष्टमेवं हि तन्निश्चलनृत्यमेव ॥

tadeva cidvyoma hi tatsvarūpaṁ nṛtyedasau tatra kathaṁ nvarūpaḥ |
ānandarūpatvamamuṣya diṣṭamevaṁ hi tanniścalanṛtyameva ||

That same Sky of Consciousness being His real Nature, how can He, being Formless, dance there? By this (metaphor) it is shown that His Form is Bliss, and that the Dance is only without movement.

517. न तत्र मायास्ति न काऽप्यविद्या न देशकालौ न च कोऽपि जीवः ।
तस्मिन् पदे निर्मलचित्स्वरूप आत्मैक एवास्ति न किञ्चिदन्यत् ॥

na tatra māyā'sti na kā'pyavidyā na deśakālau na ca ko'pi jīvaḥ |
tasmin pade nirmalacitsvarūpa ātmaika evāsti na kiñcidanyat ||

In that State there is no Maya, nor Avidya (Ignorance) nor space, nor time, nor any individual called the 'soul'. There, only the Real Self, having the form of Pure Consciousness, exists and nothing else.

This state of Aloneness is called Kaivalya.

Maya and Avidya are mutually dependent. Neither can exist without the other. So both are lost in this conflagration. This has been definitely stated in one of the Hymns to Sri Arunachala by Bhagavan Sri Ramana.

518.   मायाभिधाना परमेशशक्तिः सर्वं जगद्यत्परिणाम एव ।
नष्टैव सेयं ह्यचले परस्मिन् साकं स्वकार्यैरपि तुर्यभावे ॥

māyābhidhānā parameśaśaktiḥ sarvam jagadyatpariṇāma eva |
naṣṭaiva seyam hyacale parasmin sākam svakāryairapi turyabhāve ||

In that Transcendental State, the Power of God, named Maya, whose expanded form is the whole world, is wholly lost in that Moveless Supreme One, along with the whole of Her creation.

For him that dwells eternally in that Supreme State, there is neither Maya nor Avidya nor the world.

519.   विभात्यतस्तुर्यपदे प्रशान्ते सत्यात्मरूपं प्रतिबन्धहीनम् ।
तस्मिन् पदे स्वात्मतयाऽवशिष्टो निगद्यते मुक्त इति प्रबुद्धैः ॥

vibhātyatasturyapade praśānte satyātmarūpam pratibandhahīnam |
tasmin pade svātmatayā'vaśiṣṭo nigadyate mukta iti prabuddhaiḥ ||

Therefore in that Supreme State of Peace, there shines, unhindered, the true form of the Real Self. The one that survives in that State as his own Real Self, is designated by the sages as the Free One.

Bondage being due to the false identification of the body as the Self, it is lost, when the ego-sense is lost. There is no more any false identification.

The mind is lost. But therewith is lost also the pairs of pleasure and pain. This is illustrated as follows:-

520. सुदुःखिता स्त्री श्वशुरस्य गेहे मातुगृहि शान्तिमुपैति यद्वत् ।
एवं मनः संसृतिदुःखतप्तं निवृत्य मूलं निजमेव शान्तम् ॥

suduḥkhitā strī śvaśurasya gehe māturgṛhe śāntimupaiti yadvat |
evaṁ manaḥ saṁsṛtiduḥkhataptaṁ nivṛtya mūlaṁ nijameva śāntam ||

Just as a woman, suffering intolerably in her father-in-law's house, obtains peace in her mother's house, so the mind, harried by 'samsaric' suffering, wins Peace by returning to its Source, the (Real Self).

What about the unfree souls in the world? Does the Free One see them, and is he anxious for them?

521. यथा नरः स्वप्नसमुत्थितः सन् स्वाप्नं जनं पश्यति नैव कञ्चित् ।
अज्ञाननिद्रोत्थित एवमेको न वीक्षते कञ्चिदपि स्वतोऽन्यम् ॥

yathā naraḥ svapnasamutthitaḥ san svāpnaṁ janaṁ paśyati naiva kañcit |
ajñānanidrotthita evameko na vīkṣate kañcidapi svato'nyam ||

As a man awaking from a dream does no more see any of the dream-persons, so the one, who has awakened from the sleep of Ignorance and who is therefore alone as the Sole Reality, does not see any one as other than his own Real Self.

In all persons alike, the Real Self is unaffected. Ignorance and bondage are not for Him, but for the mind or the ego, the imaginary individual soul, who never had any real existence.

522.   यस्तन्मयानन्दनिमग्न आस्ते स्वान्यस्य बोधेन विनाऽद्वयत्वे ।
पदं तदीयं सहजं प्रशान्तं धीगोचरत्वं भजतां कथं नु ॥

yastanmayānandanimagna āste svānyasya bodhena vinā'dvayatve |
padaṁ tadīyaṁ sahajaṁ praśāntaṁ dhīgocaratvaṁ bhajatāṁ kathaṁ nu ||

How can that State, the Natural State of Peace, become knowable by the intellect — that State of Him who dwells engrossed in the Bliss of that Self, having no knowledge of others as different from Himself?

Just as that State is unthinkable by the intellect, so too is the one who has won that State and dwells eternally therein.

523.   विनष्टचित्तं निजसत्यभावे विनष्टदेहं च विनष्टलोकम् ।
ज्ञातुं प्रबुद्धं भविता समर्थः स्वबुद्धिशक्त्यैव कथं नु मर्त्यः॥

vinaṣṭacittaṁ nijasatyabhāve vinaṣṭadehaṁ ca vinaṣṭalokam |
jñātuṁ prabuddhaṁ bhavitā samarthaḥ svabuddhiśaktyaiva kathaṁ
nu martyaḥ ||

How can any man understand, by the unaided power of his own intellect, the one who is mindless, bodiless and worldless in his own Real Nature and fully enlightened?

The One who is established in that State of Deliverance is called a Sage, or Prabuddha or Buddha. He cannot be known because he has none of the attributes of an individual. He is One with the Eternal Subject, the Supreme Reality, and so cannot be made an object for any one to know.

524. अलक्षणं तन्न मनोऽपि मन्तुं शक्नोति तुर्यं न वचोऽपि वक्तुम् ।
अतन्निरासेन तु बोधयन्ति वेदान्तवाचोऽपि हि तत्स्वरूपं ॥

alakṣaṇaṁ tanna mano'pi mantuṁ śaknoti turyaṁ na vaco'pi vaktum |
atannirāsena tu bodhayanti vedāntavāco'pi hi tatsvarūpaṁ ||

Because that Transcendental State has no peculiar marks or features, the mind cannot think of it, nor words describe it. The words of the Vedantas teach Its real Nature only by negating whatever is not That.

The Vedantas never try to give a *positive* description. Even those sentences that seem to give such a description are interpreted as distinguishing It from things that can be visualized or thought of.

That unthinkable One is for that reason infinite, unlimited.

525. वाचाऽपि वक्तुं मनसाऽपि मन्तुं शक्यं यदल्पं खलु तत्समस्तम् ।
अगोचरत्वान्मनसो धियोऽपि भूमेति जानन्ति तमात्मनिष्ठाः ॥

vācā'pi vaktuṁ manasā'pi mantuṁ śakyaṁ yadalpaṁ khalu tatsamastam |
agocaratvānmanaso dhiyo'pi bhūmeti jānanti tamātmaniṣṭhāḥ ||

Whatever is describable in words or thinkable by the mind, is for that reason finite. Because the

Real Self is beyond the reach of the mind and the intellect, therefore those that are established in the Self call it the Infinite.

Only the Infinite is Blissful, not the finite, says the Chandogya Upanishad.

526.　यद्यत् प्रबुद्धैर्निगमान्तवाक्यैः सत्यं परं प्रत्युपदिष्टमस्ति ।
तत्तत्फलं शिष्यमृषाग्रहाणां निरास एवेति वदन्ति बुद्धाः ॥

yadyat prabuddhairnigamāntavākyaiḥ satyaṁ paraṁ pratyupadiṣṭamasti |
tattatphalaṁ śiṣyamṛṣāgrahāṇāṁ nirāsa eveti vadanti buddhāḥ ||

Whatever is said, concerning the Supreme Reality by the Sages or by the Vedantas, has for its purpose only the removal of the mistaken notions of the disciples.

No positive statements can be made. The ultimate teaching is by Silence.

527.　सीता यथा दाशरथिं दिदेश निषेधनादन्यनृपात्मजानाम् ।
तथात्मनो रूपमतन्निरासैर्वेदान्तवाचः प्रतिपादयन्ति ॥

sītā yathā dāśarathiṁ dideśa niṣedhanādanyanṛpātmajānām |
tathātmano rūpamatannirāsairvedāntavācaḥ pratipādayanti ||

Just as Sita indicated Rama by negating all the other princes, so the Vedantas indicate the Truth of the Self by negating all else (that could be mistakenly believed to be the Self)

528. अर्थो न वेद्यो न च वेदनीयः स्वयम्प्रभः केवल एक आत्मा ।
तमोनिरासेन विना न किञ्चित् गुरूपदेशैः क्रियते हि साधोः ॥

artho na vedyo na ca vedanīyaḥ svayamprabhaḥ kevala eka ātmā |
tamonirāsena vinā na kiñcit gurūpadeśaiḥ kriyate hi sādhoḥ ||

Since the self-shining, Solitary One Self is a thing neither to be known, nor to be (directly) taught, therefore nothing is done for the aspirant by the teachings of the Guru, except to free him from his Ignorance.

Ignorance causes him to identify something as the Self, which is not That.

Since the Self shines by His Own Consciousness-Light, there is no need to do anything more. In the Egoless State, the Real Self cannot be mistaken, because therein He alone survives.

The darkness (ignorance) that conceals the Self is just the visible and tangible world seen by the outward-going mind, it is shown next.

529. ज्ञानात्मकः स्वो हि तिरोहितोऽज्ञैः प्रापञ्चिकज्ञानमयैस्तमोभिः ।
तमांसि तान्येव गुरूपदेशा निरस्य साधुं हि कृतार्थयन्ति ॥

jñānātmakaḥ svo hi tirohito'jñaiḥ prāpañcikajñānamayaistamobhiḥ
tamāṁsi tānyeva gurūpadeśā nirasya sādhuṁ hi kṛtārthayanti ||

Since the Self who is of the Nature of (Pure) Consciousness, is concealed by the ignorant by the darkness, which consists of worldly knowledge, the teachings of the Guru bless the aspirant by removing that knowledge-ignorance.

Nothing more need be done when the false notion of a serpent is removed; the real rope reveals itself. So too, when the veiling false knowledge is removed, the Self shines by His own Light of Consciousness.

Another simile, given by Bhagavan Sri Ramana, is here given:

530. यथाऽवकाशं जनयेन्न कोऽपि निरोधकापाकरणं विहाय ।
तथाऽऽत्मलाभाय न कार्यमन्यद्धित्वा मृषाज्ञाननिरासमस्ति ॥

yathā'vakāśaṁ janayenna ko'pi nirodhakāpākaraṇaṁ vihāya |
tathā''tmalābhāya na kāryamanyaddhitvā mṛṣājñānanirāsamasti ||

As one has nothing to do, for creating an empty space, except to remove the encumbering unwanted lumber, so for obtaining the Self, nothing more is needed than the removal of the false knowledge.

Bhagavan Sri Ramana has said that the process of knowing the Self is really a process of unlearning, because the Self is never unknown. Being the Self it cannot remain unknown. The Awareness of the Self is there already and always. It only needs to be relieved from the confusing false views.

The Self has not been lost. There is only the notion that it has been lost.

531. लब्धव्य आत्मा भविता कथं नु नासौ विनष्टः खलु तत्त्वदृष्ट्या ।
येनाहमाऽऽत्माऽस्ति तु नष्टकल्पो
नाशस्तदीयो भविताऽऽत्मलाभः ॥

labdhavya ātmā bhavitā katham nu nāsau vinaṣṭaḥ khalu tattvadṛṣṭyā |
yenāhamā"tmā'sti tu naṣṭakalpo nāśastadīyo bhavitā"tmalābhaḥ ||

How can the Self be something to be obtained? From the Truth's point of view He was never lost. The gaining of the Self, that is spoken of, is only the death of the ego, by whom the Self was as good as lost (though not really lost).

It is also said by Bhagavan Sri Ramana that the Truth is rightly taught only by Silence. This is explained next.

532. परा च पश्यन्त्युत मध्यमा च वाग् वैखरी चेति चतुःप्रकारा ।
       सा वाक् परा नाम तु मौनमेव तदेव रूपं च सतः परस्य ॥

parā ca paśyantyuta madhyamā ca vāg vaikharī ceti catuḥprakārā |
sā vāk parā nāma tu maunameva tadeva rūpaṁ ca sataḥ parasya ||

Speech is fourfold, as transcendent, seeing, medium and articulate speech. That transcendent speech is only Silence. And that Silence is itself the true nature of the Supreme Reality.

533. वाग् वैखरी मध्यमवाक्प्रसूता वाग् वीक्षमाणाऽस्ति तदीयमाता ।
       तस्याः परा वागिति सुप्रसिद्धा वाक् सैव मौनं परचित्स्वरूपम् ॥

vāg vaikharī madhyamavākprasūtā vāg vīkṣamāṇā'sti tadīyamātā |
tasyāḥ parā vāgiti suprasiddhā vāk saiva maunaṁ paracitsvarūpam ||

The articulate form of speech was born of the medium speech; its mother is the Seeing speech;

that its mother is the Transcendent speech, is well known. That same Supreme Speech is Silence, the form of the Supreme Consciousness.

So the grossest form of speech, being the great grand daughter of the Silence it cannot reach the Real Self.

534.   व्याख्या यथार्थाऽप्युत मौनमेव स्थितस्य बुद्धस्य पदे तुरीये ।
वाग् वैखरी भेदमतिप्रसूता वदेत् परं तं कथमस्तभेदम् ॥

vyākhyā yathārthā'pyuta maunameva sthitasya buddhasya pade turīye|
vāg vaikharī bhedamatiprasūtā vadet param tam kathamastabhedam ||

True Speech is really only the Silence of the Sage, who is the eternal dweller in the Transcendental State. How can gross speech, born of the belief in difference, speak of the Supreme One, wherein differences are lost?

535.   अतो हि मौनेन दिदेश रूपमात्मस्वरूपस्य गुरुः पुराणः ।
मौनेन वाचो मनसोऽपि पूर्वे शिष्या अबुध्यन्त तदीयरूपम् ॥

ato hi maunena dideśa rūpamātmasvarūpasya guruḥ purāṇaḥ |
maunena vāco manaso'pi pūrve śiṣyā abudhyanta tadīyarūpam ||

Therefore the most Ancient Guru taught the Truth of the Self by Silence. And, by achieving silence of speech and of mind, those ancient disciples (of that Guru) became aware of that Truth.

Here the reference is to the incarnation of God as Dakshinamurti, the God of Right Awareness, dwelling in that State of Awareness. The disciples, Sanaka, Sanandana, Sanatana and Sanat Kumara attained the Supreme State by being silent, just like their Guru.

536. गुरोः प्रबुद्धस्य हि मौनभावात् स्वयं प्रबुद्धाश्च भवन्ति सन्तः ।
वाचोपदेशाः प्रभवन्ति नैव तत्त्वं परं बोधयितुं यथावत् ॥

guroḥ prabuddhasya hi maunabhāvāt svayaṁ prabuddhāśca bhavanti santaḥ |
vācopadeśāḥ prabhavanti naiva tattvaṁ paraṁ bodhayituṁ yathāvat ||

Well-qualified disciples became themselves sages by the silent Teaching of their Guru. Teaching by words does not avail to impart True Knowledge of the Real Self.

The greatness of the Guru's Silence is next indicated.

537. गुरोः प्रबुद्धस्य यदस्ति मौनं शक्तिस्तदीया न हि मानमेति ।
मौनोपदेशः परमो हि तस्मात् तेनैव साधोर्हि मनःप्रशान्तिः ॥

guroḥ prabuddhasya yadasti maunaṁ śaktistadīyā na hi mānameti |
maunopadeśaḥ paramo hi tasmāt tenaiva sādhorhi manaḥpraśāntiḥ ||

The power there is in the Silence of the Guru is immeasurable. Hence teaching by Silence is the highest there is. Thereby alone does the aspirant's mind obtain peace.

There is the question about initiation. What is true initiation?

538. दीक्षा त्रिधोक्ता गुरुणा प्रयोज्या निरीक्षणध्यानकराभिमर्शाः ।
गुरोस्तु मौनस्तिथिसंप्रयुक्तां ब्रवीति दीक्षां परमां गुरुर्नः ॥

dīkṣā tridhoktā guruṇāa prayojyā nirīkṣaṇadhyānakarābhimarśāḥ |
gurostu maunastithisamprayuktāṁ bravīti dīkṣāṁ paramāṁ gururnaḥ ||

It is said that Initiation is of three forms, namely looking, thinking and touch with the hand. But the highest initiation (Diksha) consists in the Guru remaining in the Supreme Silence, says our Guru (Ramana Bhagavan).

The Supreme State is called Silence.

539. मौनोपदेशादपि मौनभावे स्थित्वैव लभ्या भवतीत्यतश्च ।
मौनं पदं तं निगदन्ति बुद्धा मौनी वदन्नेव च सम्प्रबुद्धः ॥

maunopadeśādapi maunabhāve sthitvaiva labhyā bhavatītyataśca |
maunaṁ padaṁ taṁ nigadanti buddhā maunī vadanneva ca
samprabuddhaḥ ||

Because that State is taught by Silence and also because it is attained by remaining in Silence (Stillness of Mind), It is called Silence. The Sage is in Silence always, even when He speaks.

The last statement is difficult to understand. It will be better understood when Bhagavan Sri Ramana's Teaching about the Natural State (Sahaja Samadhi) is explained.

This Enlightenment is the subject of many questions. One of these is, "Will it remain permanent, or will it be lost later"?

540.   सकृद्विभातं पदमव्ययं तच्चैतन्यभानोः प्रभयैव तस्य ।
अतः प्रमादाच्च्युतिरात्मभावान्न बुद्धपुंसो भविता कदाचित् ॥

sakṛdvibhātaṁ padamavyayaṁ taccaitanyabhānoḥ prabhayaiva tasya |
ataḥ pramādāccyutirātmabhāvānna buddhapuṁso bhavitā kadācit ||

That eternal State is ever-shining by the Light of the sun of Consciousness, the Real Self; hence there is no possibility of the enlightened Sage swerving from that Natural State of the Self due to forgetting at any time afterwards.

The reason is that when the Right Awareness dawns by following the Direct Path, the ego and mind merge and are once for all lost in that Self. It is otherwise when some sort of bliss is experienced as a result of yoga independently. Yoga by itself does not lead up to egolessness.

Does the world survive after the egolessness is established?

541.   अत्ता समस्तस्य चराचरस्याप्यात्मेति वेदान्तगिरा यदुक्तम् ।
निर्दिश्यते तेन तदीयभासा ग्रासोऽस्य विश्वस्य तमोमयस्य ॥

attā samastasya carācarasyāpyātmeti vedāntagirā yaduktam |
nirdiśyate tena tadīyabhāsā grāso'sya viśvasya tamomayasya ||

The statement of the Vedantic Text, that the Self swallows up the moving and the moveless means that the world, which is only Darkness, is consumed by the Effulgence of that Self.

The Upanishads thus clearly state that the world, being only darkness cannot possibly survive in the presence of the Light of Right Awareness.

The very same truth has been expressed by Bhagavan Sri Ramana in the first verse of His Arunachala Pancharatnam, which is paraphrased below.

542.   निगीर्य सर्वं घनविश्वरूपं चैतन्यभासा निजया परात्मा ।
एकोऽद्वयो भात्यरुणाचलेश इति स्वरूपं गुरुणाऽस्ति गीतम् ॥

nigīrya sarvaṁ ghanaviśvarūpaṁ caitanyabhāsā nijayā parātmā |
eko'dvayo bhātyaruṇācaleśa iti svarūpaṁ guruṇā'sti gītam ||

The essential Nature of the Self has been sung by the Bhagavan Guru thus: The Supreme Self, named Arunachalesa, shines alone without a second, having swallowed this solid seeming universe by His Own Consciousness-Light.

Thus is confirmed the statement that creation is composed of Darkness (Ignorance) alone, and has no substantial reality even now, when ignorance and ego are rampant.

An inaccuracy of statement that is unavoidably made is corrected next.

543.   ब्रह्मात्मभावं प्रतिपद्य तुर्ये विमुच्यते स्वो भवबन्धपाशात् ।
इत्येष वादो न भवेद्यथार्थो नहि स्वरूपाच्च्युतिरात्मनोऽभूत् ॥

brahmātmabhāvaṁ pratipadya turye vimucyate svo bhavabandhapāśāt |
ityeṣa vādo na bhavedyathārtho nahi svarūpāccyutirātmano'bhūt ||

The statement, that the Self, by attaining oneness with the Brahmam, becomes freed from the bondage of samsara is not true, because the Self never fell from His True State.

544. न श्वेतिमानं नवमेति धौतं वस्त्रम् स्वभावो ह्ययमस्य यद्वत् ।
ब्रह्मत्वमात्मा नहि याति बोधात् ब्रह्मत्वमात्मप्रकृतिर्हि नित्यः ॥

na śvetimānaṁ navameti dhautaṁ vastram svabhāvo hyayamasya yadvat |
brahmatvamātmā nahi yāti bodhāt brahmatvamātmaprakṛtirhi nityaḥ ||

Just as (white) cloth does not acquire a new whiteness, whiteness being its nature, so the Self does not become Brahman because the Self is eternally the Brahman by nature.

It is said that for creating the world the Brahman itself became the Self when entering the created bodies. This only means that the Self is never other than the Brahman.

Certain expressions, freely used to designate the Sage are next critically viewed.

545. ब्रह्मज्ञ आत्मज्ञ इति प्रसिद्धे बुद्धस्य पुंसो भवतोऽभिधे द्वे ।
ब्रह्मैव चात्मैव यतः स बुद्धो ज्ञाते उभे तेन कथं भवेताम् ॥

brahmajña ātmajña iti prasiddhe buddhasya puṁso bhavato'bhidhe dve |
brahmaiva cātmaiva yataḥ sa buddho jñāte ubhe tena kathaṁ bhavetām ||

Two names are commonly in use to designate the Sage, namely 'Knower of Brahman' and 'Knower of the Self'. Since the Sage is Himself the Brahman, as well as the Self, how can they become known to the Sage?

Neither of the two, which are identical with each other, can become the object of knowledge. The Self, as the eternal Subject, is not an object of knowing, and the Brahman is therefore not an object. The unknowability of Brahman is due to Its being the Self. So the terms, taken literally, are inapplicable. What then are their proper meanings?

546. अब्रह्मताधीरहितत्वमेव ब्रह्मज्ञतोक्ता न तु काचिदन्या ।
आत्मज्ञता नाम भवेदनात्मन्यात्मत्वमत्या रहितत्वमेव ॥

abrahmatādhīrahitatvameva brahmajñatoktā na tu kācidanyā |
ātmajñatā nāma bhavedanātmanyātmatvamatyā rahitatvameva ||

To be free from the notion 'I am not Brahman' is itself the knowing of the Brahman. Freedom from the notion that anything not the Self is the Self is the (right) knowing of the Self.

The reason is given next.

547. तत्त्वं स्वमन्विष्य परस्य तस्य सत्यात्मनोऽन्नत्वमुपेत्य तुर्ये ।
कथं नु तस्मान्निजसत्स्वरूपात् तिष्ठेत् पृथक् कश्चन बुद्धनामा ॥

tattvaṁ svamanviṣya parasya tasya satyātmano'nnatvamupetya turye |
kathaṁ nu tasmānnijasatsvarūpāt tiṣṭhet pṛthak kaścana buddhanāmā ||

When, by making the Quest of one's Self, one becomes consumed, like food, by that Supreme One, how can any one survive as separate from Him, who could be named a Sage?

The use of some word or other to designate one that has found the Self after Sadhana is necessary and inevitable. But since in this case the success of the Quest involves the loss of the unreal individuality of the seeker, practically all the words available are objectionable as implying something not true.

Another reason, shown next, is that the state is Advaitic.

548. अद्वैतनिष्ठामनुभूय तुर्ये जीवेत् पृथक्त्वेन कथं परस्मात् ।
तद् ब्रह्मनिर्वाणमुदीरितं हि कृष्णेन साक्षात् परमेण पुंसा ॥

advaitaniṣṭhāmanubhūya turye jīvet pṛthaktvena kathaṁ parasmāt |
tad brahmanirvāṇamudīritaṁ hi kṛṣṇena sākṣāt parameṇa puṁsā ||

How can one, after experiencing the Truth of Non-Duality (in that Supreme State), remain separate from the Supreme Being? For that State has been styled, by Sri Krishna, Himself the Supreme One, as Merger into the Brahman.

By this merger there is the loss of individuality.

549. निर्दिश्यते ब्रह्म यथैव शास्त्रे निर्दिश्यते बुद्धपुमांस्तथैव ।
ब्रह्मस्वरूपं खलु संविदेव बुद्धस्वरूपं न ततोऽस्ति भिन्नम् ॥

nirdiśyate brahma yathaiva śāstre nirdiśyate buddhapumāṁstathaiva |
brahmasvarūpaṁ khalu saṁvideva buddhasvarūpaṁ na tato'sti bhinnam ||

In the sacred lore the Sage is described in the same terms as the Brahman Itself is described. Since the True Nature of the Brahman is Pure,

Supreme Consciousness, the true nature of the Sage is not different.

What Bhagavan Sri Ramana has to say on this point is the following:-

550.   नात्मद्वयं कस्यचिदस्ति यस्मात् तद् वेद्मि मामित्यपि नेति हास्ये ।
वेद्यत्वमात्मा न कदाऽपि यातीत्येषाऽस्ति वाणी भगवत्तमस्य ॥

nātmadvayaṁ kasyacidasti yasmāt tad vedmi māmityapi neti hāsye |
vedyatvamātmā na kadā'pi yātītyeṣā'sti vāṇī bhagavattamasya ||

Since no one has two selves, it follows that the sayings, 'I know my Self' and 'I do not know my Self' are both ridiculous. The Self never becomes an object for knowledge. Such is the statement (on this point) made by the Most Holy One.

It may be asked why that State is one of Non-Duality. The answer is the following.

551.   अद्वैतनिष्ठेत्युदिताऽस्ति सेयमुपाधिनिर्मुक्तनिजस्वरूपे ।
यतो न तस्मात् पृथगस्ति पूर्णं ब्रह्माभिधानं परसत्यमेकम् ॥

advaitaniṣṭhetyuditā'sti seyamupādhinirmuktanijasvarūpe |
yato na tasmāt pṛthagasti pūrṇaṁ brahmābhidhānaṁ parasatyamekam ||

This State of being one's own True Self freed from all limiting superimpositions (the sheaths) is called the State of Non-Duality, because therein the Supreme Sole Reality, the Infinite Brahman, is not other than that Self.

An incidental question is whether this State of Non-Duality came into existence for the first time at the end of the Quest, or had been existing all along.

552.   अद्वैतता सा विदुषाऽनुभूता सत्यात्मनस्तुर्यपदाधिगत्या ।
       न साधनाभ्यासबलेन सिद्धा सत्यात्मनः सा खलु नित्यसिद्धा ॥

advaitatā sā viduṣā'nubhūtā satyātmanasturyapadādhigatyā |
na sādhanābhyāsabalena siddhā satyātmanaḥ sā khalu nityasiddhā ||

That State of Non-Duality of the Real Self, experienced by the Sage by attaining the Supreme State, is not the fruit of the practice of sadhana, but is the eternal Nature of that Self.

The following view, held by some, is next stated and discussed.

553.   द्वैतं भवेत् सत्यमिदं हि तावद् यावद् भवेत् साधनतत्परत्वम् ।
       सिद्धौ भवेदद्वयतोद्भवस्तु द्वैतप्रणाशादिति केचिदाहुः ॥

dvaitaṁ bhavet satyamidaṁ hi tāvad yāvad bhavet sādhanatatparatvam |
siddhau bhavedadvayatodbhavastu dvaitapraṇāśāditi kecidāhuḥ ||

Some say that this Duality (variety) will remain real so long as one is engaged in practising sadhana, but that when the goal is reached, Non-Duality will come into being by the extinction of the Duality.

These thinkers seek to reconcile the Dvaitic and Advaitic teachings.

554.   नेमे विजानन्ति तु तुर्यतत्त्वं कालातिगं चानुदितप्रपञ्चम् ।
अद्वैतमाद्यन्तविवर्जितं हि द्वैतं सदिक्कालमसत् सदैव ॥

neme vijānanti tu turyatattvam kālātigam cānuditaprapañcam |
advaitamādyantavivarjitam hi dvaitam sadikkālamasat sadaiva ||

These men do not know the Truth of the Transcendental State, beyond (Space and) Time, and wherein the world has not come into being. Non-Duality has neither beginning nor end. Duality, with space and time, is unreal always.

Herein the whole discussion about the world, and the teaching of Non-Becoming are relevant, and also the discussion whether bondage is real, which comes later.

What then is the use of Sadhana?

555.   मिथ्याभ्रमस्यैव विराम उक्तः शास्त्रे मुमुक्षोरहमो विनाशात् ।
सत्यं न बोधेन विनाशमीयान्न भासते किञ्चिदसत् तुरीये ॥

mithyābhramasyaiva virāma uktaḥ śāstre mumukṣorahamo vināśāt |
satyam na bodhena vināśamīyānna bhāsate kiñcidasat turīye || 555 ||

In the sacred lore it is said that, by the extinction of the ego, there is, for the aspirant to Deliverance, cessation of his delusion. What is real cannot be destroyed by Right Awareness, nor will anything unreal shine (as real) in the Supreme State.

The extreme doctrine of the Dvaitis is next stated and refuted.

556.   द्वैतं भवेत् सत्यमिदं सदैव ज्ञानेऽपि नैवास्य भवेद्विनाशः ।
अद्वैतसिद्धिर्न भवेत् कदाऽपीत्येषा मतिर्दूरतरैव साधोः ॥

dvaitaṁ bhavet satyamidaṁ sadaiva jñāne'pi naivāsya bhavedvināśaḥ |
advaitasiddhirna bhavet kadā'pītyeṣā matirdūrataraiva sādhoḥ ||

The conclusion (of the Dvaitis) that this Duality is always real, that it will not cease to exist even when Right Awareness dawns, and that Non-Duality will never be achieved, is much farther away for the aspirant (than the one stated before).

What Bhagavan Sri Ramana says on this point is next set forth.

557.   सत्या सदैवाद्वयताऽत्मनोऽसौ स्वान्वेषणे सत्यपि चात्मलाभे ।
लब्धोऽभवद्यो दशमो गवेषात् पूर्वं च सोऽयं दशमो हि नान्यः ॥

satyā sadaivādvayatā''tmano'sau svānveṣaṇe satyapi cātmalābhe |
labdho'bhavadyo daśamo gaveṣāt pūurvaṁ ca so'yaṁ daśamo hi nānyaḥ ||

The Non-Duality of the Real Self is true always, both when He was being sought by the Quest, and when He was realized, just as the tenth man, (who was supposed to have been lost), was the tenth man all along, even when he was being sought.

The reference here is to a parable of the loss and the finding of the tenth man in a party of ten. The ten, while travelling, crossed a river and then, one by one, they counted the members to see whether all had safely crossed over. But as each one counted only the others, leaving out himself, they believed that one, the tenth man, was lost, and were bewailing him, when a passerby saw them and asked them the cause of their sorrow. When he was told, he counted them and found all the ten were there. He convinced them of this truth by making them count the blows he would give all of them. There were ten blows and this convinced the men.

558.   जानन्त्यजातिं परवस्तुनो ये माण्डूक्यवेदान्तनिरूप्यमाणाम् ।
तत्त्वे परे निश्चितबुद्धयस्ते मुह्यन्ति नैतादृशमुग्धवादैः ॥

jānantyajātiṁ paravastuno ye māṇḍūkyavedāntanirūpyamāṇām |
tattve pare niścitabuddhayaste muhyanti naitādṛśamugdhavādaiḥ ||

Those that have understood the Truth of the Non-Becoming of the Supreme Reality as taught in Mandukya Vedanta, would not be perplexed by these theories of the ignorant, being firmly convinced of the True Nature of the Supreme Being (as taught by all the sages).

The imperfections that beset life in samsara are transcended, it is shown, in the Supreme State reached by the sages.

559.   न भीतिकामौ भवतोऽद्वयत्वे स्थितस्य बुद्धस्य यथाऽङ्गपुंसः ।
द्वैतेक्षया मोहितमानसानां नृणामुभे कामभयेऽनिवार्ये ॥

na bhītikāmau bhavato'dvayatve sthitasya buddhasya yathā'jñapuṁsaḥ |
dvaitekṣayā mohitamānasānāṁ nṛṇāmubhe kāmabhaye'nivārye ||

For the Sage who dwells in the State of Non-Duality fear and desire do not arise, as for the ignorant one. Desire and fear are unavoidable for those that are deluded by seeing differences.

560. भीतिर्द्वितीयाद्धि भवेदितीदं भीत्यास्पदं द्वैतमिदं प्रदिष्टम् ।
भेदप्रतीत्या मुषितात्मभावो नात्येति भीतिं खलु कोऽपि जन्तुः ॥

bhītirdvitīiyāddhi bhaveditīdaṁ bhītyāspadaṁ dvaitamidaṁ pradiṣṭam ।
bhedapratītyā muṣitātmabhāvo nātyeti bhītiṁ khalu ko'pi jantuḥ ॥

By the sentence 'Fear arises from a second entity', it has been shown that this (seeing of) Duality is the cause of fear. No creature, whose real Self has been stolen (as it were) by the belief in (the reality) of differences, is ever free from fear.

561. विद्वानगम्ये मनसोऽपि वाचामानन्दरूपात्मनि मोदमानः ।
बिभेत्यसौ नैव कुतश्चनेति श्रुत्योदिता निश्चलता तुरीये ॥

vidvānagamye manaso'pi vācāmānandarūpātmani modamānaḥ ।
bibhetyasau naiva kutaścaneti śrutyoditā niścalatā turīye ॥

"The Sage, who is immersed in the ecstasy of the Blissful Real Self, who is beyond the scope of mind and speech, is not afraid from any cause whatever". Thus the Revelation teaches that the Sage in the Supreme State is unmoved from His State of Peace (by any cause).

562.   नोदेति कामोऽपि हि कोऽपि तुर्ये मृतो ह्ययं
             कामयिताऽहमाख्यः ।
       सर्वांश्च कामान् समकालमेव लब्ध्वेव बुद्धोऽस्ति हि नित्यतृप्तः ॥

nodeti kāmo'pi hi ko'pi turye mṛto hyayaṁ kāmayitā'hamākhyaḥ |
sarvāṁśca kāmān samakālameva labdhveva buddho'sti hi nityatṛptaḥ ||

For Him that is established in the Supreme state, desires also do not arise, because therein the desirer, the Ego, has ceased to exist. The Sage (in that State) is ever contented, as if He had obtained simultaneously enjoyment of all possible desires at one stroke.

This is from the Taittiriya Vedanta. What is meant is that all the happiness that is possible in the worldly life is contained, in a minute fraction of that Bliss of the Brahman.

563.   आत्मैव सर्वं हि तदीयलाभे लब्धव्यमन्यन्न हि किञ्चिदस्ति ।
       तदाप्तकामो गदितोऽप्यकामः शास्त्रे प्रबुद्धोऽस्ति हि यद्वदीशः ॥

ātmaiva sarvaṁ hi tadīyalābhe labdhavyamanyanna hi kiñcidasti |
tadāptakāmo gadito'pyakāmaḥ śāstre prabuddho'sti hi yadvadīśaḥ ||

Since the Real Self is all that is, nothing remains for the Sage to be won, when that Self is won. Hence in the sacred lore, the Sage is spoken as one who has attained and enjoyed all objects of desire, and is therefore desireless, just like God Himself.

It must be remembered that God is really *impersonal*, as the Brahman, so that the Personal God is only a modification of It.

564. साक्षात्कृतं येन निजं स्वरूपं स कस्य कामाय च किं समिच्छन्।
तप्येत देहात्मधियेति वक्ति बुद्धस्य कामानुदयं श्रुतिर्हि ॥

sākṣātkṛtaṁ yena nijaṁ svarūpaṁ sa kasya kāmāya ca kiṁ samicchan |
tapyeta dehātmadhiyeti vakti buddhasya kāmānudayaṁ śrutirhi ||

By the sentence, 'For whose desire and desiring what object would that One suffer from identification with the body, who has experienced the Truth of His own Self?', Revelation shows that for the Sage desires do not arise.

565. देहात्मना संस्थित एव कामी बुद्धस्तु देहात्मधिया विमुक्तः।
स्वकं शरीरं समवैति बुद्धः शरीरमन्यस्य यथा तथैव ॥

dehātmanā saṁsthita eva kāmī buddhastu dehātmadhiyā vimuktaḥ |
svakaṁ śarīraṁ samavaiti buddhaḥ śarīramanyasya yathā tathaiva ||

"Only that man has desires, who identifies himself with the body". But the Sage has become free from the thought, 'I am the body'. The Sage looks upon His own body as if it were the body of another.

The first sentence in the above is a quotation from the Viveka-Chudamani.

Another powerful reason is that the Sage is by Nature eternally happy with the Bliss of the Real Self. This has been stated and explained before.

But the Bliss of the Sage does not cause bondage, as shown below.

566.	सुखस्य नास्वादनमस्ति तुर्ये सुखित्वदुःखित्वमती न तत्र ।
	सुखस्य दुःखस्य विलक्षणं तत् तुर्यं पदं द्वन्द्वविवर्जितत्वात् ॥

sukhasya nāsvādanamasti turye sukhitvaduḥkhitvamatī na tatra |
sukhasya duḥkhasya vilakṣaṇaṁ tat turyaṁ padaṁ dvandvavivarjitatvāt ||

In the Supreme State there is no tasting of
Bliss; for there the sense of being happy or
miserable cannot arise. Because in that state
there are no pairs of opposites, the Bliss of the
Sage is not like the pleasure and misery (of
samsara).

The explanation is that while, in samsara, pleasures
are from external objects, in the Natural State the Bliss is
the very Nature of the Self, who is identical with the Para-
Brahman.

This difference is related to another, which is dealt with
next.

567.	न शिष्यते कश्चन तत्र कोशः स्वरूपसङ्कोचकरोऽज्ञपुंसाम् ।
	अखण्ड आत्मा निरुपाधिको हि विराजते तत्र वियत्समानः ॥

na śiṣyate kaścana tatra kośaḥ svarūpasaṅkocakaro'jñapuṁsām |
akhaṇḍa ātmā nirupādhiko hi virājate tatra viyatsamānaḥ ||

In that State none of the sheaths remain
whereby for the ignorant, the Real Self becomes
circumscribed and finitised. For therein the Self
is infinite like the sky, free from the limiting factors
(the sheaths).

It is the sheaths that create the false sense of finiteness for the soul.

The Buddhistic teaching of Nirvana is next compared with this State.

568. निर्वाणसंज्ञां सुगतो गुरुर्यां दिदेश निष्ठां भवदुःखहन्त्रीम् ।
कोशे समस्ते गलिते तुरीये पदे स्थितिः सेति गुरुर्जगाद ॥

nirvāṇasañjñāṁ sugato gururyāṁ dideśa niṣṭhāṁ bhavaduḥkhahantrīm |
kośe samaste galite turīye pade sthitiḥ seti gururjagāda || 568 ||

The Guru has said that the State of Nirvana which puts an end to all samsaric sufferings, which was taught by (Bhagavan) Buddha, is only the remaining in the Supreme State (taught here), on the falling off of all the sheaths.

So the Buddhist Goal is the same as the State of Deliverance taught in the Vedantas.

It is next shown that by the Experience of the True Nature of the Self, doubts become impossible.

569. न संशायानामुदयोऽस्ति तत्र पुमान् प्रबुद्धः स्थितधीर्हि नित्यम् ।
आस्ते स सङ्कल्पविकल्पहीनः प्रशान्तगम्भीरतयाऽस्तचेताः ॥

na saṁśayānāmudayo'sti tatra pumān prabuddhaḥ sthitadhīrhi nityam |
āste sa saṅkalpavikalpahīnaḥ praśāntagambhīratayā'stacetāḥ ||

In that State doubts do not arise, since the Sage is ever firm in His Awareness of the True Self. There He remains without affirmations and

vacillations, immersed in the depths of Peace, the
mind having become extinct.*

It is next shown that, in that State, death is transcended.

570. आद्यन्तहीनं स्वमवेत्य बोधात् स मृत्युमत्येत्यपि सम्प्रबुद्धः ।
पुमानबुद्ध्वाऽमृतमात्मतत्त्वं नात्येति मृत्युं बत कोऽपि लोके ॥

ādyantahīnaṁ svamavetya bodhāt sa mṛtyumatyetyapi samprabuddhaḥ |
pumānabuddhvā'mṛtamātmatattvaṁ nātyeti mṛtyuṁ bata ko'pi loke ||

Becoming aware of the Real Self, who has
neither beginning nor end, the Sage transcends
Death. Surely no one in the world transcends
death without experiencing the Truth of the Self
as Deathless.

571. लेभे जनिं यः परमे स्वमूले विचार्य कस्मादहमित्युदारः ।
स एव जातः स च नित्यजातो नवो नवोऽयं सततं मुनीन्द्रः ॥

lebhe janiṁ yaḥ parame svamūle vicārya kasmādahamityudāraḥ |
sa eva jātaḥ sa ca nityajāto navo navo'yaṁ satataṁ munīndraḥ ||

---

* This is expressed in the oft-quoted Upanishadic Text.
भिद्यते हृदयग्रन्थिश्छिद्यन्ते सर्वसंशयाः ।
क्षीयन्ते चास्य कर्माणि तस्मिन् दृष्टे परावरे ॥ उ.

bhidyate hṛdayagranthiśchidyante sarvasaṁśayāḥ |
kṣīyante cāsya karmāṇi tasmin dṛṣṭe parāvare || u .
"The Heart's Knot is cut, all doubts are dispelled, all karmas
expire when that Supreme Being is realized."

That exalted one who has obtained birth in his own source, the Supreme One, by inquiring 'Whence am I', is alone born. He is born once for all and is ever new, the Lord of the Munis (God).

This is explained later.

572.   इत्येवमाचार्यवरेण दिष्टा ब्रह्मात्मभावे सहजे स्थितस्य ।
निष्ठा परा सर्वविकारहीना निरामया कालदिगाद्यतीता ॥

ityevamācāryavareṇa diṣṭā brahmātmabhāve sahaje sthitasya |
niṣṭhā parā sarvavikārahīnā nirāmayā kāladigādyatītā ||

Thus, by the Great Guru, has been taught the Supreme State of Him that is established in His Own Natural State, in perfect Identity with the Brahman, free from disease, beyond Time and Space.

The body itself is disease, says Bhagavan Sri Ramana. So True Health is to be aware that the body is not the Self. So bodily disease does not detract from the perfectly healthy State of the Sage, as we all know.

The truth about birth and death is next discussed.

573.   अज्ञस्य लोके मरणाय जन्म मृतिस्तदीया जननाय भूयः ।
तस्मादिमे जन्ममृती मृषैवेत्यस्मभ्यमुक्तं भगवत्तमेन ॥

ajñasya loke maraṇāya janma mṛtistadīyā jananāya bhūyaḥ |
tasmādime janmamṛtī mṛṣaivetyasmabhyamuktaṁ bhagavattamena ||

For the ignorant one in the world, birth is for dying, and his death is for being born again.

Hence it has been said for us by the Most Holy
One that this birth and this death are unreal.

Each cancels the other and so samsara is without end.

574.   मृतिर्यथार्था त्वहमो विनाशो जनिर्यथार्था सहजात्मनिष्ठा ।
       द्वन्द्वैर्विमुक्तं पदमव्ययं तद् यत्रैकतां जन्ममृती भजेते ॥

mṛtiryathārthā tvahamo vināśo janiryathārthā sahajātmaniṣṭhā |
dvandvairvimuktaṁ padamavyayaṁ tad yatraikatāṁ janmamṛtī bhajete ||

Real death is death of the ego. Real birth is
to dwell in one's own Natural State. In that State,
wherein pairs of opposites have no existence, birth
and death have become one.

Another aspect of the Supreme State is next discussed.

575.   अद्वैतभावे स्थितिमेत्य नित्यां भेदान् कथं पश्यतु सम्प्रबुद्धः ।
       भेदाकुलं भाति यदज्ञपुंसां विश्वं तदात्मैव हि बुद्धपुंसः ॥

advaitabhāve sthitimetya nityāṁ bhedān kathaṁ paśyatu samprabuddhaḥ |
bhedākulaṁ bhāti yadajñapuṁsāṁ viśvaṁ tadātmaiva hi buddhapuṁsaḥ ||

How can the Sage, who is for ever established
in the State of Non-Duality, become aware of
differences? The World, which appears to the
ignorant as riddled with differences, is to the Sage
only the Self.

576. अभेददृष्टिः समदर्शनं चेत्येतद् द्वयं यद् विदुषो वदन्ति ।
तद् भेददृष्ट्या रहितत्वमेव न केवलत्वे खलु वीक्षणानि ॥

abhedadṛṣṭiḥ samadarśanaṁ cetyetad dvayaṁ yad viduṣo vadanti |
tad bhedadṛṣṭyā rahitatvameva na kevalatve khalu vīkṣaṇāni ||

The two attributes that some speak of as pertaining to the Sage, namely 'seeing of non-difference' and 'equal vision', amount only to this, that he is free from the vision of differences, because in the Solitary State there are no seeings.

577. स्वमेव सर्वत्र च नित्यबुद्धं बुद्धः पुमान् पश्यति न स्वतोऽन्यम् ।
तन्मन्यतेऽज्ञं कमपीह नासौ सर्वे प्रबुद्धा हि तदीयदृष्ट्या ॥

svameva sarvatra ca nityabuddhaṁ buddhaḥ pumān paśyati na svato'nyam |
tanmanyate'jñaṁ kamapīha nāsau sarve prabuddhā hi tadīyadṛṣṭyā ||

In all persons the Sage sees only the Real Self who is eternally aware of the Truth, not some one other than Himself. Hence He does not look upon any one as ignorant. In His sight all are sages.

This was exactly what Bhagavan Sri Ramana was heard to say. This brings out the uniqueness of the Sage. He does not look down upon any one or anything, as inferior to Himself.

Now the question of the actions of Sages is taken up.

578. यथा चरेत् कश्चन सुप्त एव तथैव बुद्धो जगति क्रियासु ।
दृश्येत जानन्निव लोकभेदान् भेदानजानन्नपि सर्वदैव ॥

yathā caret kaścana supta eva tathaiva buddho jagati kriyāsu |
dṛśyeta jānanniva lokabhedān bhedānajānannapi sarvadaiva ||

As one who is asleep may go about or act, so the Sage, in actions in the world, may be seen as if he were aware of worldly differences, without really being aware of them always.

This point will become clear later on while dealing with the distinction between the yogic (Kevala) Samadhi and the Natural (Sahaja) Samadhi of the Sage.

The crucial test of the Sage, by which He is distinguished from the ignorant is next given.

579. बुद्धस्य चाज्ञस्य भिदा स्फुटा स्यान्निन्दा नुतिश्चेत्युभयोश्च दृश्या ।
द्वयोर्न भेदं समवैति बुद्धो द्वन्द्वं मृषेदं खलु यद्यदन्यत् ॥

buddhasya cājñasya bhidā sphuṭā syānnindā nutiścetyubhayośca dṛśyā |
dvayorna bhedaṁ samavaiti buddho dvandvaṁ mṛṣedaṁ khalu yadvadanyat ||

The difference between a Sage and an ignorant one can be plainly seen in respect of censure and praise. The Sage does not know the difference between the two, since (for Him) this pair of opposites is unreal, like all others.

580. विज्ञाय वेदान्तनिगूढमर्थं विहाय विश्वं तृणवत् समस्तम् ।
अप्राप्य निष्ठां निजसत्यभावे स्वस्यैव तत्त्वस्य गवेषणेन ॥

vijñāya vedāntanigūḍhamarthaṁ vihāya viśvaṁ tṛṇavat samastam |
aprāpya niṣṭhāṁ nijasatyabhāve svasyaiva tattvasya gaveṣaṇena ||

581.   अलुप्तदेहात्ममतिर्विमुह्यन् यः सत्यवज्जीवभिदामवैति ।
यात्येव सोऽयं ह्यवशोऽपि दास्यं वाराङ्गनाया नुतिनामिकायाः ॥

aluptadehātmamatirvimuhyan yaḥ satyavajjīvabhidāmavaiti |
yātyeva so'yaṁ hyavaśo'pi dāsyaṁ vārāṅganāyā nutināmikāyāḥ ||

Having well understood the subtle meanings of the Vedantas and renounced the whole world as mere trash, but not having attained permanent abode in the Natural State of the Real Self by pursuing the Quest of the Truth thereof and therefore not free from the sense of identity of the body with the Self, being therefore subject to the delusion of the difference between soul and soul, he inevitably becomes a slave to the harlot named Praise.

This refers to an incident in the life of Sri Sadasiva Brahmendra, who for long lived in the woods, practising Sadhana. Once a co-pupil of his met him in a forest and began praising him for a long time. At last Sadasiva became so elated by it that he exhibited horripilation. Noticing this, the other questioned Sadasiva how such an exalted person could be so affected. Sadasiva replied by a verse in Sanskrit to the effect that even such a one, if he had not reached the Experience of the Real Self, cannot help feeling pleasure from praise. This verse has been translated by Bhagavan Sri Ramana and placed in the Supplement (Anubandha) of the Ulladu Narpadu. That the Sage is not so affected, is next shown.

582. कमप्यजानन् पुरुषं स्वतोऽन्यमप्रच्युतः स्वीयपदात् प्रबुद्धः ।
निन्दानुतिभ्यां न विकारमेति निन्दा नुतिर्वा स्वकृतेव तस्मै ॥

kamapyajānan puruṣaṁ svato'nyamapracyutaḥ svīyapadāt prabuddhaḥ |
nindānutibhyāṁ na vikārameti nindā nutirvā svakṛteva tasmai ||

The Sage, who does not know any one as
other than Himself, and hence never swerving
from His Own True State, is unaffected by censure
or praise, because for Him censure or praise are
as if it were made by Himself.

This is the uniqueness of Egolessness. The Sage is really
bodiless; those that see His body judge Him as if He were
like them.

583. देहीव मर्त्यः परिदृश्यमानो नासौ शरीरी निरहङ्कृतिर्यत् ।
सूक्ष्मं वपुस्तस्य न देहपाते नियाति किन्तु प्रविलीयतेऽत्र ॥

dehīva martyaḥ paridṛśyamāno nāsau śarīrī nirahaṅkṛtiryat |
sūkṣmaṁ vapustasya na dehapāte niryāti kintu pravilīyate'tra || 583

Though He appears as embodied, He is
really bodiless, being egoless. His subtle body does
not survive and go forth somewhere when the
gross body falls, but undergoes disintegration
here.

Adherents of sects, whose doctrines are different, have
raised controversy, stating that the soul remains an individual
after enlightenment, being endowed with a sort of body. On
this point there are two views, one that the liberated soul

has a body always, and another that he has no body, but can assume a body when he pleases. Bhagavan Sri Ramana's teaching is that all forms are unreal, and hence neither of these two is acceptable. This is dealt with below.

584. सत्यं प्रपञ्चं बत मन्यमाना रूपं प्रबुद्धस्य वदन्ति केचित्।
तस्येच्छया ऽरूपिण एव रूपं कदाचन स्यादिति केचिदाहुः।

satyaṁ prapañcaṁ bata manyamānā rūpaṁ prabuddhasya vadanti kecit |
tasyecchayā'rūpiṇa eva rūpaṁ kadācana syāditi kecidāhuḥ |

Some believers in the reality of the world say that the Sage has a body. Others say that the Sage, being bodiless can assume a body if he so pleases.

585. रूपस्य सर्वस्य निदानभूता नष्टा ह्यहन्ता निजतत्त्वबोधात्।
रूपाण्यतोऽसन्ति हि बुद्धपुंसस्तन्मुग्धतैषा बत रूपवार्ता॥

rūpasya sarvasya nidānabhūtā naṣṭā hyahantā nijatattvabodhāt |
rūpāṇyato'santi hi buddhapuṁsastanmugdhataiṣā bata rūpavārtā ||

By the dawn of Right Awareness of the Real Self, the ego, the root cause of the appearance of forms, has been lost. Therefore for the Sage, all forms are unreal and hence this talk of forms is foolishness.

Bhagavan Sri Ramana has made it clear by adopting the simile of the river mingling with the ocean, that the soul as such does not survive the dawn of Right Awareness. The soul itself has been declared to be a false appearance due to confusion of the body with the Self, which cannot survive the extinction of the Ignorance, its parent.

586.   अभूदिदं पूर्वमथ प्रणष्टमित्येवमुक्तिश्च न युज्यते यत् ।
रूपी न कोऽप्यस्ति हि तत्त्वदृष्ट्या रूपी प्रबुद्धो भविता कथं नु ॥

abhūdidaṁ pūrvamatha praṇaṣṭamityevamuktiśca na yujyate yat |
rūpī na ko'pyasti hi tattvadṛṣṭyā rūpī prabuddho bhavitā kathaṁ nu ||

Since it is not proper to say that this (world) existed before (Enlightenment), but was lost afterwards, and since (even in Ignorance) no one has a form from the point of view of the Reality, how can the Sage have a form?

Forms belong to Duality, but Duality, it has been declared is never real, and that Non-Duality is true always.

587.   भावे तुरीये सहजे स्थितस्य बुद्धस्य देहत्रितयं विनैव ।
इच्छाऽपि रूपग्रहणे कथं स्यात् सेयं वृथा पामररञ्जनी वाक् ॥

bhāve turīye sahaje sthitasya buddhasya dehatritayaṁ vinaiva |
icchā'pi rūpagrahaṇe kathaṁ syāt seyaṁ vṛthā pāmararañjanī vāk ||

In the case of the Sage who is established in His own Natural State, free of all the three bodies, how can a desire arise to have a body? This talk of forms is in vain, being merely a concession to the unenlightened.

Even in the Upanishads there are passages suggesting that in salvation there are forms, but they are interpreted as a means of enabling unripe souls to take to sadhana for salvation. The real teaching of the Upanishads appears in texts like the following.

588.   नदी यथा वारिधिमेत्य तस्मिन् हित्वा नदीरूपमुपैत्यभेदम् ।
एवं प्रबुद्धोऽपि विहाय रूपं परात्परे पुंसि भजत्यभेदम् ॥

nadī yathā vāridhimetya tasmin hitvā nadīrūpamupaityabhedam |
evaṁ prabuddho'pi vihāya rūpaṁ parātpare puṁsi bhajatyabhedam ||

As a river reaching the ocean loses its river-form and becomes indistinguishable from it, so too the sage, losing his form as a soul, becomes non-different from that Supreme Being, to whom all else is inferior.

589.   एवं श्रुतिर्वक्ति हि रूपहानादैक्यं परस्मिन् विदुषस्तुरीये ।
जीवन्विमुक्तोऽप्यशरीर एव शरीरिणं स्वं न हि मन्यतेऽसौ ॥

evaṁ śrutirvakti hi rūpahānādaikyaṁ parasmin viduṣasturīye |
jīvanvimukto'pyaśarīra eva śarīriṇaṁ svaṁ na hi manyate'sau ||

Thus Revelation says that the Sage in that Supreme State becomes one with the Supreme Being. Even when alive, the Liberated One is bodiless because He does not think of Himself as having a body.

Bhagavan Sri Ramana defines Liberation as follows.

590.   बुद्धस्य रूपं प्रति योऽहमाख्यो वादी भवेत् तस्य विनाश एव ।
       ब्रवीति मुक्तिं भगवान् गुरुर्यन्निरर्थकोऽयं बत रूपवादः ॥

buddhasya rūpaṁ prati yo'hamākhyo vādī bhavet tasya vināśa eva |
bravīti muktiṁ bhagavān gururyannirarthako'yaṁ bata rūpavādaḥ ||

Sri Bhagavan, our Guru, says that Liberation is just the extinction of the Ego, who becomes a disputant concerning the form of the Sage. So this dispute about forms is meaningless.

It is to be noted that those who raise this controversy, do so without losing their ego-sense. Can they raise this question after getting rid of their ego?

591.   अतो न निर्याति हि देहपाते सूक्ष्मं वपुस्तस्य यथाऽज्ञपुंसाम् ।
       विलीयतेऽत्रैव हि तत् स्वमूले न शिष्यते किञ्चन निर्गमाय ॥

ato na niryāti hi dehapāte sūkṣmaṁ vapustasya yathā'jñapuṁsām |
vilīyate'traiva hi tat svamūle na śiṣyate kiñcana nirgamāya ||

Therefore on the fall of the body His subtle body does not go forth, as in the case of the ignorant; it goes back and merges into its cause, and nothing survives for going forth.

The cause of the subtle body is the unquintuplicated five *bhutas* (materials of creation).

There is an incidental misconception which is next dispelled.

592. प्रबुद्धपुंसां बहुताऽपि मर्त्यैः प्रतीयमाना न भवेद्यथार्था ।
प्रापञ्चिका एव हि सर्वभेदा न निष्प्रपञ्चे खलु ते भवन्ति ॥

prabuddhapuṁsāṁ bahutā'pi martyaiḥ pratīyamānā na bhavedyathārthā |
prāpañcikā eva hi sarvabhedā na niṣprapañce khalu te bhavanti ||

The popular notion that there are many sages, is also not true. All differences belong to the world. In the worldless state they do not exist.

The controversy about the plurality of selves, which has been discussed and settled before, is relevant here also.

593. बुद्धः पुमानेष मयाऽद्य दृष्टो द्रक्ष्याम्यतोऽन्यानपि बुद्धपुंसः ।
इति ब्रुवाणो विदुषां स्वरूपं न वेत्ति सच्चित्सुखरूपमेकम् ॥

buddhaḥ pumāneṣa mayā'dya dṛṣṭo drakṣyāmyato'nyānapi
    buddhapuṁsaḥ |
iti bruvāṇo viduṣāṁ svarūpaṁ na vetti saccitsukharūpamekam ||

He who says, "I have today seen this Sage; I shall see others also," does not know the true nature of sages, which is Reality-Consciousness-Bliss. This is what Bhagavan has told us on this point.

594. अजानतः स्वं बत बुद्धमन्तर्विभान्ति बुद्धा बहवो विभिन्नाः ।
तं स्वात्मभूतं समवैति यस्तु न तस्य नानात्वमिदं यथार्थम् ॥

ajānataḥ svaṁ bata buddhamantarvibhānti buddhā bahavo vibhinnāḥ |
taṁ svātmabhūtaṁ samavaiti yastu na tasya nānātvamidaṁ yathārtham ||

For him that knows not the Sage who is within himself, there appear many sages. For him who knows that One, who is his own Self, this plurality (of sages) is non-existent.

The absurdity of these questions is thus pointed out by Bhagavan Sri Ramana. Questions about the Egoless state cannot be decided by the ego-ridden ones.

The following is the corollary from the above discussion.

595. आद्यो गुरुर्यो मुनिसत्तमानां दिदेश मौनेन परं पदं स्वम् ।
पश्चाच्च यः शङ्करदेशिकेन्द्रः स एव हि श्रीरमणो गुरुर्नः ॥

ādyo gururyo munisattamānāṁ dideśa maunena paraṁ padaṁ svam |
paścācca yaḥ śaṅkaradeśikendraḥ sa eva hi śrīramaṇo gururnaḥ ||

That first Guru (Dakshinamurti), who taught those great Munis by Silence the Truth of His Own Supreme State, and who afterwards appeared as the Great Guru, Sri Sankaracharya, is Himself our Guru, Sri Ramana Bhagavan.

This should be self-evident.

A notion prevails among the people that a sage or a perfected man must be able to perform miracles. These miracle-working powers are called Siddhis. The word literally means 'gain' of something. The sages make a difference between these so called Siddhis and the real Siddhi, whereby the whole of Samsara is transcended, and the Highest State, Egolessness, is reached.

596. यन्नित्यसिद्धं निजतत्त्वमन्तस्तदात्मना सुस्थितिरेव तुर्ये ।
सिद्धिर्यथार्था न तु काचिदन्येत्यस्मद्गुरुः श्रीरमणो ब्रवीति ॥

yannityasiddham nijatattvamantastadātmanā susthitireva turye |
siddhiryathārthā na tu kācidanyetyasmadguruḥ śrīramaṇo bravīti ||

Our Guru, Sri Ramana, tells us that the real Siddhi (to be striven for) is to be firmly established in the Natural State of the Real Self who is Ever-Present in the Heart; nothing else.

And since He is in the Heart, the only thing needed is to seek Him there and enjoy His Bliss.

597. लब्धव्य आत्मेति मतिर्न सत्या नासौ विनष्टः खलु तत्त्वदृष्ट्या ।
वदन्ति बुद्धा अत एव सत्यं तं नित्यसिद्धं निखिलस्य जन्तोः ॥

labdhavya ātmeti matirna satyā nāsau vinaṣṭaḥ khalu tattvadṛṣṭyā |
vadanti buddhā ata eva satyam tam nityasiddham nikhilasya jantoḥ ||

The notion that the Self has to be won is untrue, because really He was never lost, from the point of view of the Truth. The Sages therefore say that the Real Self is ever present.

This fact is illustrated by the simile of the forgotten necklace, which was diligently sought while all the time it was on the neck of the seeker.

Those that go after the vanities of the world are enamoured of the false Siddhis, because they do not know that the Self is the summum bonum (the greatest good).

598. भूमानमात्मानमतोऽन्यदल्पं श्रुतिर्वदन्ती दिशतीममर्थम् ।
विक्रीय तं विश्वमिदं समस्तं क्रीत्वाऽपि मर्त्यः कृपणो हि शोच्यः ॥

bhūmānamātmānamato'nyadalpam śrutirvadantī diśatīmamartham |
vikrīya tam viśvamidam samastam krītvā'pi martyaḥ kṛpaṇo hi śocyaḥ ||

Revelation teaches this truth by saying that Self is Infinite, and all else finite and trivial. He that buys the whole world by selling the Real Self is just a pauper, to be pitied.

The so-called Siddhis are of no value, because they are in the *Samsara* and are therefore mere vanities, unreal, like the world. A saying of the same import is attributed to Jesus, who was a Sage.

599. अतो ह्यकार्पण्यपदं तुरीयं कार्पण्यमन्यच्छ्रुतयो वदन्ति ।
पूर्णो हि सम्राडिव सम्प्रबुद्धो भिक्षामटंश्चापि न दैन्यमेति ॥

ato hyakārpaṇyapadam turīyam kārpaṇyamanyacchrutayo vadanti |
pūrṇo hi samrāḍiva samprabuddho bhikṣāmaṭamścāpi na dainyameti ||

Therefore, that Supreme State is freedom from poverty, and all else is only poverty, says the Revelation. Like an emperor the Sage is above all wants (in a different way). Even when going about begging (his daily meal) He is not cast down.

600. वदन्ति सिद्धीरणिमादिकांस्तु बहिर्मुखा भोगपरा विमूढाः ।
वक्ति श्रुतिर्मन्ददधियां कथञ्चित् प्ररोचनार्थं बत ताश्च सिद्धीः ॥

vadanti siddhīraṇimādikāṁstu bahirmukhā bhogaparā vimūḍhāḥ |
vakti śrutirmandadhiyāṁ kathañcit prarocanārtham bata tāśca siddhīḥ ||

It is the deluded men with outward-turned minds, hankering for worldly enjoyments, who talk of these Siddhis, namely becoming minute, etc. Revelation mentions these 'Siddhis' for attracting the dull-witted ones also to the path for Deliverance.

601. आविद्यकाः स्वप्नसमा यतस्ता न तासु मोहं भजते विवेकी ।
पूर्णस्तुरीये स्थितिमेत्य सत्ये बुद्धो न मुह्येदनृतासु तासु ॥

āvidyakāḥ svapnasamā yatastā na tāsu mohaṁ bhajate vivekī
|pūrṇasturīye sthitimetya satye buddho na muhyedanṛtāsu tāsu ||

Since these are in the realm of the Ignorance, and therefore unreal like dream-gains, no discriminating person will be deluded by them. (Of course) the Sage is not deluded by these unrealities as He has attained the Supreme State, which is the State of Reality.

602. इत्यात्मलाभस्य समोऽन्यलाभो नास्तीति बुद्धेः प्रकटीकृतेऽपि ।
मत्वाऽऽत्मनाशस्य पदं तुरीयं बिभ्यत्यमुष्मादविवेकिनस्तु ॥

ityātmalābhasya samo'nyalābho nāstīti buddhaiḥ prakaṭīkṛte'pi |
matvā''tmanāśasya padaṁ turiyam bibhyatyamuṣmādavivekinastu ||

Though thus it has been made clear that there is no gain equal to the gain of the Self, undiscriminating ones are afraid of the Supreme State, believing that therein the Self will be lost.

That the Self is not lost therein is next demonstrated by citation of the meaning of a verse in the Yoga Vasishtham.

603.   प्रयान्ति वृद्धिं विदुषस्तुरीये स्थितस्य तेजो धिषणा बलं च ।
यथा वसन्तस्य समागमेन सौन्दर्यमुख्याः सुगुणास्तरूणाम् ॥

prayānti vṛddhiṁ viduṣasturīye sthitasya tejo dhiṣaṇā balaṁ ca |
yathā vasantasya samāgamena saundaryamukhyāḥ suguṇāstarūṇām ||

"Just as, by the oncoming of spring, excellences like beauty and so on come to trees, so, to the Sage, who abides in the Supreme State, come lustre, keen intelligence and strength (of all kinds).

Even a common man, without education, if he becomes somehow aware of the Real Self, becomes a centre of attraction for others and is worshipped as a Perfected One. Also other perfections are seen in the Sage.

604.   शमादिका ये सुगुणा मुमुक्षोर्यत्नेन सम्पाद्य च रक्षणीयाः ।
स्वाभाविकास्ते विदुषो भवन्ति स निर्गुणः सद्गुणशेवधिश्च ॥

śamādikā ye suguṇā mumukṣoryatnena sampādya ca rakṣaṇīyāḥ |
svābhāvikāste viduṣo bhavanti sa nirguṇaḥ sadguṇaśevadhiśca || 604

Peace of mind, and other good qualities, which aspirants to Deliverance have to acquire and retain with effort, are natural to the Sage. He is beyond the (three) qualities (Sattva, Rajas and Tamas) and at the same time is the abode of all good qualities.

So the conclusion reached is as follows.

605. नाशोऽहमस्तन्न हि काऽपि नष्टिर्नैवात्मनाशस्य पदं तुरीयम् ।
अहन्तयाऽऽत्माऽस्ति तु नष्टकल्पो नाशोऽहमो नश्यति नष्टिरेषा ॥

nāśe'hamastanna hi kā'pi naṣṭirnaivātmanāśasya padaṁ turīyam |
ahantayā''tmā'sti tu naṣṭakalpo nāśe'hamo naśyati naṣṭireṣā ||

So, when the Ego is lost, there is no real loss. The Supreme State (won by the loss of the ego) is not one in which the Self is lost. But the self is as good as lost due to the ego-sense, and when this is lost, there is a loss of this loss.

It is like a creditor unexpectedly receiving payment of a debt, which he had written off as irrecoverable.

This loss of the ego is indeed an enormous gain, as shown below.

606. एषोऽन्ततोऽहङ्कृतिनाश एव धर्मार्थकामा अपि सत्यवाणी ।
सन्न्यासमौने च तपोऽपि योगः सत्यं परस्मै स्वनिवेदनं च ॥

eṣo'ntato'haṅkṛtināśa eva dharmārthakāmā api satyavāṇī |
sannyāsamaune ca tapo'pi yogaḥ satyaṁ parasmai svanivedanaṁ ca ||

This complete and final loss of the Ego is itself all these things (and more):— Righteousness, Wealth,

Enjoyment (of all pleasures at once), Truthfulness, True Renunciation, Silence, Tapas, Union with God, and true Surrender of oneself to Him.

Innumerable gains and goodnesses are comprised in Egolessness.

The things having the same names are next shown to be worthless.

607.   भवन्त्यसत्यानि तदाख्यकानि वपुष्यहन्तामलिनीकृतानि ।
स्वाभाविकान्येव भवन्ति तानि स्थितस्य सत्यात्मतया तुरीये ॥

bhavantyasatyāni tadākhyakāni vapuṣyahantāmalinīkṛtāni |
svābhāvikānyeva bhavanti tāni sthitasya satyātmatayā turīye || 607 ||

Those having the same names (which are prized greatly) are tainted and of little worth, because of association with the ego. But these are natural to the Sage, who dwells in the Supreme State (always).

Another unique feature of the Sage is next dealt with.

608.   अलङ्कृती द्वे विदुषो निरुक्ते कर्तव्यहानिः कृतकृत्यता च ।
अज्ञानमूलं ह्युभयं नरस्य कर्तव्यता चाप्यकृतार्थता च ॥

alaṅkṛtī dve viduṣo nirukte kartavyahāniḥ kṛtakṛtyatā ca |
ajñānamūlaṁ hyubhayaṁ narasya kartavyatā cāpyakṛtārthatā ca ||

Two excellences are stated as belonging to the Sage, namely freedom from obligation to perform prescribed actions and at the same time being contented and happy (as having attained the goal of action). For the common man the absence of these, is due to his Ignorance.

The latter is bound by duties and never reaches the goal of action. In the Sage these two rare good features are united and inseparable. The Bhagavat-Pada, Sankaracharya has given prominence to these two unique features of the Sage at the end of a long discourse to establish the truth that Illumination, unaided, confers Deliverance.

609.   न कर्म साध्यं विदुषोऽस्ति यस्मात् किञ्चिन्न कर्तव्यमिहास्ति तस्य ।
कर्तव्यमत्रास्ति तु यस्य किञ्चित् स मोहपाशैर्बत बद्ध एव ॥

na karma sādhyaṁ viduṣo'sti yasmāt kiñcinna kartavyamihāsti tasya |
kartavyamatrāsti tu yasya kiñcit sa mohapāśairbata baddha eva ||

The Sage is not bound to perform actions, because for Him there is nothing to be gained by means of action. He, for whom there is obligation to do actions is not Free, but is bound by the fetters of Delusion.

This shows up well the vast difference between the bound and the free.

Incidentally, a question is dealt with, which shows the ignorance of the questioners.

610.   पृच्छन्ति केचित् किमु बुद्धपुंसो ध्यानं न कार्यं भवतीति मुग्धाः ।
गत्वा विदेशान् ननु शिक्षणीया बुद्धेन मर्त्या इति पृच्छ्यतेऽन्यैः ॥

pṛcchanti kecit kimu buddhapuṁso dhyānaṁ na kāryaṁ bhavatīti mugdhāḥ |
gatvā videśān nanu śikṣaṇīyā buddhena martyā iti pṛcchyate'nyaiḥ ||

Some ask whether the Sage does not need to practise meditation, not knowing the Truth (about sages). By others the question is raised: 'Should not the Sage go to foreign countries and teach the people there?'

611. अहं तदस्मीत्यनुसन्दधानो भवेन्न बुद्धः खलु साधकोऽसौ ।
ध्यानं तदस्मीति तु बुद्धपुंसा ध्यानं नरोऽस्मीति यथा नरेण ॥

ahaṁ tadasmītyanusandadhāno bhavenna buddhaḥ khalu sādhako'sau |
dhyānaṁ tadasmīti tu buddhapuṁsā dhyānaṁ naro'smīti yathā nareṇa ||

He that practices the meditation 'I am That' is not a Sage, but only a Sadhaka. If the Sage meditates 'I am That', it would be like a man meditating 'I am a man'.

612. यद्विस्मृतं तत्स्मृतिरेव युक्ता नाविस्मृतस्य स्मृतिरस्ति लोके ।
न विस्मृतं यद् विदुषाऽऽत्मतत्त्वं तस्य स्मृतिस्तेन कथं घटेत ॥

yadvismṛtaṁ tatsmṛtireva yuktā nāvismṛtasya smṛtirasti loke |
na vismṛtaṁ yad viduṣā"tmatattvaṁ tasya smṛtistena kathaṁ ghaṭeta ||

It is proper for one to remember something he has forgotten. In the world remembrance of something not forgotten cannot occur. Since the Truth of the Self is never once forgotten by the Sage, how can He meditate on It?

613. ध्यानं यथार्थं तु सतः परस्य निष्ठैव चिन्तारहितात्मभावे ।
निरन्तरं ध्यानमिदं न हातुं शक्यं न कर्तुं विदुषा कदाऽपि ॥

dhyānaṁ yathārthaṁ tu satah parasya niṣṭhaiva cintārahitātmabhāve |
nirantaraṁ dhyānamidaṁ na hātuṁ śakyaṁ na kartuṁ viduṣā kadā'pi ||

The true meditation of the Supreme Reality (the Self) is only to remain as the Self, in the thought-free State. This 'meditation' can be neither given up, nor taken up by the Sage.

This is the sense of the latter half of the first Benedictory Verse in the Bhagavan's 'Forty Verses on the Reality'. The Experience of the Self by the Sage in His Natural State is not knowing, but Being the Self. From this State of Being there can never be a relapse to the thought 'I am this body'.

The answer to the question about going about lecturing or teaching the people all over the world, is as follows.

614. क्वचित् प्रदेशे स्थितवत् प्रबुद्धः सन्दृश्यमानोऽपि वियत्समोऽसौ ।
तिष्ठन् सदा स्वे सहजे समाधौ व्याप्नोति शक्त्या भुवनं समस्तम् ॥

kvacit pradeśe sthitavat prabuddhah sandṛśyamāno'pi viyatsamo'sau |
tiṣṭhan sadā sve sahaje samādhau vyāpnoti śaktyā bhuvanaṁ samastam ||

Even though apparently dwelling in some corner of the world, He is really like the Sky. Remaining always (uninterruptedly) in His own Natural State (Samadhi), by His power He pervades the whole world.

This power of the Sage is 'Grace', the power to Bless.

615. अवत्यसौ स्वानतिदूरतश्चाप्यचिन्त्यशक्त्या निजया प्रबुद्धः ।
विनैव चिन्तां सहजे समाधौ स्थितोऽपि सन् सन्ततमस्तचित्तः ॥

avatyasau svānatidūrat, aścāpyacintyaśaktyā nijayā prabuddhaḥ ।
vinaiva cintāṁ sahaje samādhau sthito'pi san santatamastacittaḥ ॥

The Sage, remaining all the time continuously
in the Natural State, with His mind utterly stilled,
protects His own people even from a very great
distance, by His unthinkable power of Grace.

But this protection is automatic, without effort, or even
conscious knowledge of doing this work of Grace.

616. करोति चिन्तां किमु कोऽपि नृणां स्वप्रेक्षितानां मनुजः प्रबुध्य ।
तथाऽज्ञानृणां न करोति चिन्तां स्वाज्ञाननिद्रोत्थित आत्मबोधात् ॥

karoti cintāṁ kimu ko'pi nṝṇāṁ svapnekṣitānāṁ manujaḥ prabudhya ।
tathā'jñanṝṇāṁ na karoti cintāṁ svājñānanidrotthita ātmabodhāt ॥

Does anyone worry about men seen in a
dream, after awakening? So too, the Sage, that
has awakened from the sleep of Ignorance, is not
anxious about those that are still in Ignorance.

From His point of view no one is really ignorant.
The actions of a Sage ought not to be judged from the
ordinary human standpoint.

617. गुणान्सौ त्रीनतिवितते यदतो न दोषाः प्रभवन्ति तस्मिन् ।
किमत्र यद्यत् कुरुते प्रबुद्धस्तत्तद् भविष्यत्यनवद्यमेव ॥

guṇānasau trīnativartate yadato na doṣāḥ prabhavanti tasmin |
karmātra yadyat kurute prabuddhastattad bhaviṣyatyanavadyameva ||

Since the Sage has transcended the three grades of character, there can be no faults in Him. Whatever He does in the world is surely blameless.

618. अत्येति शास्त्राण्यत एव बुद्धो निबध्यते तैर्न हि निर्मनस्कः ।
भवन्त्यविद्वद्विषयाणि तानि ते ह्येव कर्तृत्वधिया विधेयाः ॥

atyeti śāstrānyata eva buddho nibadhyate tairna hi nirmanaskaḥ |
bhavantyavidvadviṣayāṇi tāni te hyeva kartṛtvadhiyā vidheyāḥ ||

For this reason the Sage transcends the sacred books bearing on human conduct, because the Mind-free one is not bound by them. Those books are concerned with ignorant ones; they are subject to regulation by them, because they have the sense of being doers of action.

The conventions of samsara have no place in the state of the Sage.

619. प्रतिष्ठितो यत्र पदे प्रबुद्धो भवन्त्यवेदाः खलु तत्र वेदाः ।
देवा अदेवा इति तस्य भावो निर्दिश्यते हि श्रुतिशीर्षवाचा ॥

pratiṣṭhito yatra pade prabuddho bhavantyavedāḥ khalu tatra vedāḥ |
devā adevā iti tasya bhāvo nirdiśyate hi śrutiśīrṣavācā ||

By Revelation the Sage's state is described as one in which the Vedas are not Vedas, and the Devas (gods) are not Devas.

Incidentally a warning is given to disciples and sadhakas.

620.   बुद्धोपदेशान् मनुजोऽनुतिष्ठेद् बुद्धैः कृतं कर्म तु नानुतिष्ठेत् ।
बुद्धोपदेशाः परमं प्रमाणं न कर्म तेषां तु तथा प्रमाणम् ॥

buddhopadeśān manujo'nutiṣṭhed buddhaiḥ kṛtaṁ karma tu nānutiṣṭhet |
buddhopadeśāḥ paramaṁ pramāṇam na karma teṣāṁ tu tathā pramāṇam ||

One should act upon the teachings of the sages; he must not imitate any act done by a Sage. The teachings of Sages are the highest authority, not so their actions.

A noteworthy passage in the Gita in this contect is the following: "Even if He kills all these people, He is not a killer, nor is He bound."

Nor is the Sage bound to conform to any particular mode of life.

621.   सर्वांश्च योगानतिगत्य तिष्ठन् तुर्येऽच्युतो बुद्धपुमान् भवेऽत्र ।
योगीव वा भोगिवदेव वा स्यात् तौ योगभोगौ भवतो न सत्यौ ॥

sarvāṁśca yogānatigatya tiṣṭhan turye'cyuto buddhapumān bhave'tra |
yogīva vā bhogivadeva vā syāt tau yogabhogau bhavato na satyau ||

In the course of life, the Sage, who has transcended all the Yogas, being established in the Supreme State, may live like a Yogi, or even like a bhogi, but that yoga and that bhoga are not real.

'Bhoga' means enjoyment and a bhogi is one who lives for enjoyment, such as a householder. Some sages, like Ribhu, have been without any ashrama (particular prescribed mode of life). Such a one is called an *athyasrami*. The next topic concerns the pair of opposites, bondage and freedom (on Deliverance).

622.　शिष्योपदेशे समुदीरिते द्वे बन्धो विमुक्तिर्भवतो न सत्ये ।
　　　द्वन्द्वानि सर्वाणि मृषेति सिद्धे द्वन्द्वं तदेतत् कथमस्तु सत्यम् ॥

śiṣyopadeśe samudīrite dve bandho vimuktirbhavato na satye |
dvandvāni sarvāṇi mṛṣeti siddhe dvandvaṁ tadetat kathamastu satyam |

The pair of bondage and freedom, which are spoken of in the course of instruction to disciples, does not really exist. Since it is settled that all pairs of opposites are unreal, how can this pair be real?

623.　आत्मा स्वयं नित्यविमुक्त एव बद्धस्त्वविद्योदित जीव एव ।
　　　तत् तत्त्वतो नास्ति हि काऽपि मुक्तिर्बन्धप्रतीत्यैव हि
　　　मुक्तिचिन्ता ॥

ātmā svayaṁ nityavimukta eva baddhastvavidyodita jīva eva |
tat tattvato nāsti hi kā'pi muktirbandhapratītyaiva hi mukticintā ||

The Real Self is Ever-Free. The bound one is only the soul, the effect of the Ignorance. Therefore in truth there is no Deliverance either. The thought of Deliverance is due only to the belief in bondage.

How to verify this unreality?

624. कस्यास्ति बन्धोऽयमिति स्वतत्त्वं मुमुक्षुरन्विष्यति चेत् तदन्ते ।
आत्माऽनुभूयेत हि नित्यमुक्त इत्यास्ति वाणी भगवत्तमस्य ॥

kasyāsti bandho'yamiti svatattvaṁ mumukṣuranviṣyati cet tadante |
ātmā'nubhūyeta hi nityamukta ityasti vāṇī bhagavattamasya |

"If one makes the Quest, 'Who is he for whom there is bondage?', at the end of the Quest the Ever-Free Self will be experienced." This is what the Most Holy One has said (on this point).

625. अजातिरेव प्रकटीकृता हि श्रुत्याऽपि बुद्धैश्च सतः परस्य ।
तस्यैव सत्यात्मतया स्थितत्वात् स बन्धमापेति कथं नु वाच्यम् ॥

ajātireva prakaṭīkṛtā hi śrutyā'pi buddhaiśca sataḥ parasya |
tasyaiva satyātmatayā sthitatvāt sa bandhamāpeti kathaṁ nu vācyam ||

Since the Non-Becoming of the Supreme Reality has been made clear by both Revelation and the sages, and since it is that Reality that is the Real Self, how can it be said that that One became bound?

Whoever does not accept the perfect supremacy of the Reality is unfit to be a disciple. He disqualifies himself by not accepting this as true.

626. सत्यो हि बन्धो यदि नान्तमीयादनादिरङ्गीक्रियते हि बन्धः ।
सान्तादिमत्वाच्च भवेद्विमुक्तिर्बन्धस्य मिथ्यात्वमतोऽनिवार्यम् ॥

satyo hi bandho yadi nāntamīyādanādiraṅgīkriyate hi bandhaḥ |
sāntādimatvācca bhavedvimuktirbandhasya mithyātvamato'nivāryam ||

If bondage were real, it would never indeed end. Bondage is accepted as having no beginning. Also, Deliverance would arise (only) on account of (bondage) having a beginning with an end. Thus, the unreality of bondage is irresistible.

It is an axiom of the Advaita-Vedanta that whatever is real has neither beginning nor an end, and that whatever has a beginning must have an end, and is therefore unreal, as set forth already.

627. बद्धोऽभवम् पूर्वमथास्मि मुक्त इत्येवमुक्तिं शृणुमो न बुद्धात्।
कालातिगा सा पदवी हि तुर्या चिन्त्यं भवेज्जन्म कथं तदीयम्॥

baddho'bhavam pūrvamathāsmi mukta ityevamuktiṁ śṛṇumo na buddhāt |
kālātigā sā padavī hi turyā cintyaṁ bhavejjanma kathaṁ tadīyam ||

We do not hear from the Sage the saying: "I was bound before, but now I am free". That supreme State is beyond Time. How can Its beginning be imagined?

What Bhagavan Sri Ramana did say is next recorded.

628. नैवागतं किञ्चन मत्स्वरूपे सदैकधैवास्मि विकारहीनः।
इत्येवमूचे भगवान् हि पृष्टो लब्धा विमुक्तिर्भवता कदेति॥

naivāgataṁ kiñcana matsvarupe sadaikadhaivāsmi vikārahīnaḥ |
ityevamūce bhagavān hi pṛṣṭo labdhā vimuktirbhavatā kadeti ||

Bhagavan Sri Ramana, when asked 'When did your holiness attain Deliverance'; replied:

"Nothing has happened to Me; I am the same always, unchanged."

To make this teaching intelligible Bhagavan Sri Ramana used the following two similies.

629. पुर्यां सतां पण्ढरिनामिकायां यामः कदा तामिति गीतमादौ ।
प्राप्ता वयं तामिति गीतमन्ते यद्वत् तथैवेह विमुक्तिवार्ता ॥

puryāṁ satāṁ paṇḍharināmikāyāṁ yāmaḥ kadā tāmiti gītamādau |
prāptā vayaṁ tāmiti gītamante yadvat tathaiveha vimuktivārtā ||

This talk of Deliverance is just like the singing, by dwellers in Pandharpur, of songs to the effect, 'When shall we go to that place', and finally singing 'We have reached the place.'

630. स्वप्ने भ्रमित्वा स्वगृहं निवृत्य भूयोऽपि तत्रैव गतः सुषुप्तिम् ।
प्रबुध्य पश्येत् स्वगृहे यथा स्वं मुक्तिस्तथैवेति गुरुर्जगाद ॥

svapne bhramitvā svagṛhaṁ nivṛtya bhūyo'pi tatraiva gataḥ suṣuptim
|prabudhya paśyet svagṛhe yathā svaṁ muktistathaiveti gururjagāda ||

Just as one in his dream, after wandering (abroad), returning home, goes to sleep there, and, waking, finds himself in his own home, so is Deliverance, said our Guru.

So Deliverance is only a change in the understanding, as shown below.

631. नित्यानुभूते मम सत्स्वरूपे स्थितोऽस्मि मिथ्या ह्यनुभूतयोऽन्याः ।
इति प्रबोधेन मतिप्रसादो भवेद्विमुक्तिर्न किमप्यपूर्वम् ॥

nityānubhūte mama satsvarūpe sthito'smi mithyā hyanubhūtayoo'nyāḥ |
iti prabodhena matiprasādo bhavedvimuktirna kimapyapūrvam ||

Deliverance is just the clarification of the mind in this form: "I am (ever) in My own Real Nature, all other experiences are illusory." It is not something that has newly come about.

Another very notable feature of the Sage's Being is next taken up.

632. बुद्धस्य नित्यो महिमाऽस्ति सोऽयं वृद्धिक्षयौ तस्य न कर्मणेति ।
अनिष्टमिष्टं च फलं कृतस्य न कर्मणः स्याद्विदुषः कदाऽपि ॥

buddhasya nityo mahimā'sti so'yaṁ vṛddhikṣayau tasya na karmaṇeti |
aniṣṭamiṣṭaṁ ca phalaṁ kṛtasya na karmaṇaḥ syādviduṣaḥ kadā'pi ||

The Eternal Greatness of the Sage consists in this, that He neither waxes, nor wanes, by actions done or not done. For Him there will never accrue any result from actions whether unpleasant or pleasant.

This is a necessary corollary from the teaching that the Sage, being only the Real Self, is egoless, and therefore not an actor, but at the most only a witness, or not even a witness.

Some sectarians identify the Real Self with the sheath of intellect (the Vijnanamaya-kosha). But they are not Advaitis.

This is explained further by Bhagavan Sri Ramana himself.

633.	यथा कथासंश्रवणे सुदूरं धिया गतो नैव कथां शृणोति ।
	कर्माणि कुर्वन्नपि बुद्ध एवम् निर्वासनत्वान्मनसो न कर्ता ॥

yathā kathāsaṁśravaṇe sudūraṁ dhiyā gato naiva kathāṁ śṛṇoti |
karmāṇi kurvannapi buddha evam nirvāsanatvānmanaso na kartā ||

Just as one engaged in listening to a story, does not really hear it, his mind having wandered far away, so the Sage, though (apparently) doing actions, is really not an actor, because of his mind not being full of its (previous) habitual modes of functioning.

It has been shown before that the mind is just a bundle of habits of activity, which means that when those habits have been extinguished it ceases to bind. The actions of the Sage are not due to His personal will, as will be shown later.

But the condition of one whose mental vasanas are active is different, as shown below.

634.	सवासनत्वान्मनसस्तु कर्ता भवत्यकुर्वन्नपि चाज्ञमर्त्यः ।
	स्वप्ने यथाऽद्रेः शिखरादधस्तात् पतेच्छरीरे सति निश्चलेऽपि ॥

savāsanatvānmanasastu kartā bhavatyakurvannapi cājñamartyaḥ |
svapne yathā'dreḥ śikharādadhastāt pateccharīre sati niścale'pi ||

But the ignorant man, because his mind is subject to vasanas, becomes an actor, even without actively doing any action, just as a man, in his dream, may fall from the cliff of a mountain, though his body is lying motionless (in his bed).

The fact is, the mind is the real agent in action, not the body which by itself is inert and actionless.

The following is from the Vasishtham:

635.　शरीरमात्रेण कृतं न कर्म मनःकृतं यत् तु तदेव कर्म।
नाचेतनं कर्तृ भवेच्छरीरं मनो भवेत् कर्तृ तु चेतनत्वात्॥

śarīramātreṇa kṛtaṁ na karma manaḥkṛtaṁ yat tu tadeva karma |
nācetanaṁ kartṛ bhaveccharīraṁ mano bhavet kartṛ tu cetanatvāt ||

Action is not what is done by the body alone.
That alone is action which is done by the mind.
The body, being insentient, cannot be an actor.
The mind, being sentient, can be an actor.

636.　प्रारब्धवेगेन चरन्ति कर्म देहेन्द्रियप्राणमनांसि यद्यत्।
न लिप्यते तेन पुमान् प्रबुद्ध इत्युक्तवान् श्रीभगवान् गुरुर्नः॥

prārabdhavegena caranti karma dehendriyaprāṇamanāṁsi yadyat |
na lipyate tena pumān prabuddha ityuktavān śrībhagavān gururnaḥ ||

Whatever the body the senses, life and the mind do by the force of the Prarabdha Karma the Sage is not affected by it. So said Bhagavan, our Guru.

This is further sustained by comparison of the Sage with God in His personal aspect.

637.　न लिप्यते सृष्ट्यवनादि कर्म कुर्वन्नपीशः खलु तद्वदेव ।
　　　न लिप्यते कर्मभिरत्र बुद्धो भिदा तयोर्नास्ति हि तत्त्वदृष्ट्या ॥

na lipyate sṛṣṭyavanādi karma kurvannapīśaḥ khalu tadvadeva |
na lipyate karmabhiratra buddho bhidā tayornāsti hi tattvadṛṣṭyā ||

God is unaffected by His activities in creation, protection, etc.; just in the same way the Sage remains unaffected by (His) actions, since there is no real difference between them, from the standpoint of the Truth.

It is taught that God is not Himself the doer of all that work, the work being done in His presence by His power called Maya, as said before.

638.　अश्नंश्च गच्छंश्च वदन् स्मरंश्च कर्माणि कुर्वन्निव लक्ष्यतेऽज्ञैः ।
　　　कर्ताऽपि भोक्ता न तु तत्त्वतोऽसौ स हीश्वराधीनसमस्तवृत्तिः ॥

aśnaṁśca gacchaṁśca vadan smaraṁśca karmāṇi kurvanniva lakṣyate'jñaiḥ |
kartā'pi bhoktā na tu tattvato'sau sa hīśvarādhīnasamastavṛttiḥ ||

He appears to the ignorant as acting — eating, walking, talking and remembering, — but in truth He is neither an actor nor a recipient of the fruits of action, because all His activity is entirely subject to God.

The following is what Bhagavan Sri Ramana says on this topic.

639.　कर्ता यदि स्वः स भवेद्धि भोक्ता कर्तृत्वनाशे निजमार्गणेन ।
साकं विनश्येत् त्रिविधं च कर्म विमुक्तिमेतां समवेहि नित्याम् ॥

karta yadi svaḥ sa bhaveddhi bhokta kartṛtvanāśe nijamārgaṇena |
sākaṁ vinaśyet trividhaṁ ca karma vimuktimetāṁ samavehi nityām ||

If the Self were the actor, then He would receive the fruits of actions. But when by the Quest of the Real Self the sense of doership is lost, therewith will be lost all the three kinds of actions. Understand that this Deliverance is eternal.

The following also was said by Bhagavan Sri Ramana.

640.　भुङ्क्ते यथा निद्रितबालकोऽन्नं स्वमातृदत्तं न तु वेत्ति भुक्तम् ।
एवं प्रबुद्धोऽपि हि कर्मजन्यं भुङ्क्ते फलं भोक्तृतया विनैव ॥

bhuṅkte yathā nidritabālako'nnaṁ svamātṛdattaṁ na tu vetti bhuktam |
evaṁ prabuddho'pi hi karmajanyaṁ bhuṅkte phalaṁ bhoktṛtayāa vinaiva ||

Just as a sleepy child eats the food given by his mother, but does not know the eating, so too the Sage receives the fruits of actions, without being an enjoyer or sufferer.

But that is not all.

641.　कर्ता न कोऽप्यस्ति हि तत्त्वदृष्ट्या स्वज्ञाज्ञयोरस्ति भिदेयमेव ।
कर्ताऽहमस्मीत्यभिमन्यतेऽज्ञो बुद्धस्य नोदेति तु कर्तृताधीः ॥

karta na ko'pyasti hi tattvadṛṣṭyā svajñājñayorasti bhideyameva |
kartā'hamasmītyabhimanyate'jño buddhasya nodeti tu kartṛtādhīḥ ||

In Truth no one is an actor. The difference between the knower and the non-knower of the Self is only this: The ignorant man believes himself to be the actor, but to the Sage the thought of being an actor does not arise (at all).

Here is an incidental problem, due to difference of views.

642. आगामिकर्माण्यपि सञ्चितानि नश्यन्ति बुद्धस्य पुनर्न जन्म ।
प्रारब्धकर्म त्ववशिष्टमस्तीत्युक्तिर्न सत्या परमार्थतः ॥

āgāmikarmāṇyapi sañcitāni naśyanti buddhasya punarna ja |
prārabdhakarma tvavaśiṣṭamastītyuktirna satyā paramārt   yā ||

The saying: "The future actions and the stored up ones are lost for the Sage, and so He is not born again; but the current actions (prarabdha karma) remain over," is not true, from the standpoint of the Supreme Truth.

This Bhagavan Sri Ramana illustrates with a simile from life.

643. यथा मृते भर्तरि सत्यमुष्य शिष्येत भार्याऽविधवा न काऽपि ।
एवं मृते कर्तरि नैव कर्म फलप्रदं किञ्चन शिष्टमस्ति ॥

yathā mṛte bhartari satyamuṣya śiṣyeta bhāryā'vidhavā na kā'pi |
evaṁ mṛte kartari naiva karma phalapradaṁ kiñcana śiṣṭamasti ||

Just as, when a husband dies, none of his wives remains unwidowed, so when the actor (the ego) dies, no actions remain over, which could yield results (to the Sage).

Another simile is also available.

644. यथा प्रबोधे सति नैव कर्म स्वप्ने कृतं किञ्चन शिष्टमस्ति ।
कर्माज्ञतायां चरितं तथैव सत्यात्मबोधे सति नास्ति शिष्टम् ॥

yathā prabodhe sati naiva karma svapne kṛtaṁ kiñcana śiṣṭamasti |
karmājñatāyāṁ caritaṁ tathaiva satyātmabodhe sati nāsti śiṣṭam ||

Just as actions done in dream do not survive on waking, so actions done during the prevalence of Ignorance do not survive on the True Nature of the Self being experienced.

When Ignorance dies, all its products also cease to be. But the survival of Prarabdha Karma is stated in the Vedantic lore. The answer to this is given.

645. प्रारब्धमस्तीति वचः श्रुतीनां भवेदिदं त्वज्ञधियोऽनुरोधः ।
तदीयदृष्ट्या फलमस्ति तस्य बुद्धः शरीरी बत तन्मतेन ॥

prārabdhamastīti vacaḥ śrutīnāṁ bhavedidaṁ tvajñadhiyo'nurodhaḥ |
tadīyadṛṣṭyā phalamasti tasya buddhaḥ śarīrī bata tanmatena ||

The statement in Revelation that Prarabdha Karma survives is only in comformity with the view of the ignorant. From their point of view those actions have results, because in their view the sage is embodied.

But this is only in some stray contexts. More emphatically in many places the Vedantas support the teaching of the sages.

646.   प्रियाप्रिये न स्पृशतो हि बुद्धं देहं विनैव स्थितमात्मभावे ।
नैष्फल्यमेवं विदुषः कृतीनां वेदान्तवाचैव निरुक्तमस्ति ॥

priyāpriye na spṛśato hi buddhaṁ dehaṁ vinaiva sthitamātmabhāve |
naiṣphalyamevaṁ viduṣaḥ kṛtīnāṁ vedāntavācaiva niruktamasti ||

The Vedantic text, 'the pleasant and unpleasant effects (of actions) do not affect the Sage, who dwells as the Self, bodiless', shows the unfruitfulness of actions of the Sage.

This is also confirmed by the following from the Yoga Vasistham.

647.   कृत्तेऽपि दग्धे विदुषः शरीरे च्युतिर्न तस्यास्ति निजस्वरूपात् ।
यथा गुडं चूर्णितमग्नितप्तं त्यजेन्न माधुर्यरसं स्वकीयम् ॥

kṛtte'pi dagdhe viduṣaḥ śarīre cyutirna tasyāsti nijasvarūpāt |
yathā guḍaṁ cūrṇitamagnitaptaṁ tyajenna mādhuryarasaṁ svakīyam ||

Even when a sage's body is cut or burnt, there is no swerving for him from His Real Nature, just as jaggery (raw sugar) does not lose its natural sweetness even when powdered or boiled over fire.

A practical instance of this occurred when Bhagavan Sri Ramana, who had been having cancer of the left arm for some years, finally submitted to an extensive operation, which was insisted upon by the surgeons and doctors sent for by the Ashram authorities. Bhagavan Sri Ramana did not have any anaesthetic, and the operation lasted for nearly three hours. If He felt the pain, He did not show it. Later, when asked about the pain, He quoted the verse from the 'Yoga Vasishtham' whose meaning has been given above.

There were other instances in His life which showed His unlimited power of endurance of pain. The Bhagavad Gita has this line, यस्मिंस्थितो न दुःखेन गुरुणापि विचाल्यते (yasmimsthito na duḥkhena guruṇāpi vicālyate) "Remaining wherein, He is not shaken (from His Natural State) even by great pain."

All this would suffice to show that the Sage is really bodiless, that thus He is truly *Asanga* (असंगः - asaṅgaḥ), unattached, as the Self is said to be in the Upanishads.

This raises the question of the apparent distinction between the two kinds of Deliverance spoken of, Deliverance with the body and deliverance without the body, the former being supposed to be the state while the body continues alive, and the latter after the body's death. To this the Bhagavan's answer is given.

648.   सदेहमुक्तिश्च विदेहमुक्तिरुक्ते उभे ह्यज्ञधियोऽनुवृत्त्या ।
      देही भवेन्नैव हि कोऽपि मुक्तो भवेद्धि मुक्तिः सकलैकरूपा ॥

sadehamuktiśca videhamuktirukte ubhe hyajñadhiyo'nuvṛttyā |
dehī bhavennaiva hi ko'pi mukto bhaveddhi muktiḥ sakalaikarūpā ||

In conformity with the beliefs of the ignorant, two kinds of Deliverance are stated, one with the body and another without the body. Really no Free One is with body; All Deliverance is bodiless.

What is meant is that though the body remains alive, the Sage is unattached, because His causal body, which is Ignorance, has been destroyed, without which there is nothing to connect the Real Self, which the Sage is, with the subtle and the gross bodies.

Now the question of the Prarabdha Karma is resumed.

649.   प्रारब्धशक्तिर्भविता हि देहे नात्मस्वरूपेऽस्ति तु शक्तिरस्य ।
तस्मै स्वदेहो विदुषाऽर्पितो यत् कथं नु बाध्येत स तेन बुद्धः ॥

prārabdhaśaktirbhavitā hi dehe nātmasvarūpe'sti tu śaktirasya |
tasmai svadeho viduṣā'rpito yat katham nu bādhyeta sa tena buddhaḥ ||

The power of the Prarabdha Karma extends only to the body; it does not affect the Self. Since His body has been surrendered to the Prarabdha by the Sage, how can He be affected by the Karma?

650.   प्रारब्धकर्मार्पितदेहकोऽसौ बुद्धोऽस्ति देहे ममतां विनैव ।
एवं स्फुटं शङ्करदेशिकेन दिष्टं मनीषाभिधपञ्चकेऽस्ति ॥

prārabdhakarmārpitadehako'sau buddho'sti dehe mamatām vinaiva |
evam sphuṭam śaṅkaradeśikena diṣṭam manīṣābhidhapañcake'sti ||

"The Sage, having given over His body to the Prarabdha Karma, remains in His Own State without the sense of mineness in the body", thus the great Guru Sankara has shown the truth of this in His 'Manisha Panchakam'.

The truth that the Real Self is unattached is further elucidated.

651.　सूक्ष्मं शरीरं विदुषोऽस्ति शिष्टमित्युच्यते चेदिह कारणाख्यम् ।
अज्ञानरूपं निधनं गतं यत् सूक्ष्मेण सङ्गो विदुषः कथं स्यात् ॥

sūkṣmaṁ śarīraṁ viduṣo'sti śiṣṭamityucyate cediha kāraṇākhyam |
ajñānarūpaṁ nidhanaṁ gataṁ yat sūkṣmeṇa saṅgo viduṣaḥ kathaṁ syāt ||

If it be said that the subtle body of the Sage survives, (the answer is that) since the causal body consisting of the Ignorance, has been extinguished, how can there be attachment of the Sage (the Self) to the subtle body?

652.　ब्रह्मास्त्यसङ्गं हि तथैव बुद्धो भवत्यसङ्गो हि भवे यथा खम् ।
वपुर्विकारा उत मानसाश्च बुद्धं कथञ्चिन्न हि संस्पृशन्ति ॥

brahmāstyasaṅgaṁ hi tathaiva buddho bhavatyasaṅgo hi bhave yathā kham |
vapurvikārā uta mānasāśca buddhaṁ kathañcinna hi saṁspṛśanti ||

Since the Brahman is unattached, so is the Sage also, in Samsara, like the Sky; and hence the changes in the body and in the mind do not touch the Sage.

653.　जागर्ति यो नैजपदे प्रबुद्धो याने सुषुप्तस्य समः स उक्तः ।
यानस्य तुल्यं गदितं शरीरं तुरङ्गवच्चापि दशेन्द्रियाणि ॥

jāgarti yo naijapade prabuddho yāne suṣuptasya samaḥ sa uktaḥ |
yānasya tulyaṁ gaditaṁ śarīraṁ turaṅgavaccāpi daśendriyāṇi ||

The Sage, who is wide-awake in His own Natural State (as the Self), is said to be like one soundly asleep in a carriage. The body is likened

to a carriage, and the ten sense-organs are likened
to the horses (of the carriage).

654.　गतिं स्थितिं वाजिवियोजनं च यानस्य नो वेत्ति हि तत्र सुप्तः।
एवं सुषुप्तश्च शरीरयाने न वेत्ति बुद्धो हि शरीरभावान्॥

gatiṁ sthitiṁ vājiviyojanaṁ ca yānasya no vetti hi tatra suptaḥ |
evaṁ suṣuptaśca śarīrayāne na vetti buddho hi śarīrabhāvān || 654 ||

The sleeper in the carriage does not know
the going, the stoppage and the unyoking of the
horses (of the carriage). Just so, the Sage who is
asleep (to the world) in the carriage, the body,
does not know its changing conditions.

655.　बुद्धस्तु तिष्ठन् सहजे समाधौ कर्माणि कुर्वन्निव लक्ष्यतेऽज्ञैः।
नानाऽप्यवस्था भजतीव भाति ता वीक्ष्य मुह्यन्त्यविवेकिनस्तु॥

buddhastu tiṣṭhan sahaje samādhau karmāṇi kurvanniva lakṣyate'jñaiḥ |
nānā'pyavasthā bhajatīva bhāti tā vīkṣya muhyantyavivekinastu ||

But the Sage, being immersed in His Natural
Samadhi, is seen by the ignorant as if He were
doing actions and going through various (bodily
or mental) conditions, and, seeing these, the
undiscriminating ones are confused.

656.　सुप्तिः समाधिश्च शरीरचेष्टा इति त्रिधा भान्ति हि तस्य भावाः।
एनांश्च भिन्ना इति मन्यतेऽज्ञो विलोक्य बुद्धस्य शरीरमात्रम्॥

suptiḥ samādhiśca śarīraceṣṭā iti tridhā bhānti hi tasya bhāvāḥ |
enāṁśca bhinnā iti manyate'jño vilokya buddhasya śarīramātram ||

It appears to the ignorant that He has three distinct states, namely sleep, samadhi and bodily activities, and the ignorant one thinks that these are distinct from one another, looking only at the body of the Sage.

657. सदैकधैवास्ति तु संप्रबुद्धस्तस्य स्थितिर्नित्यसमाधिरेव ।
न कर्मभिस्तस्य विरोधलेशो न कर्मणां तेन विरोधलेशः ॥

sadaikadhaivāsti tu samprabuddhastasya sthitirnityasamādhireva |
na karmabhistasya virodhaleśo na karmaṇāṁ tena virodhaleśaḥ ||

But the Sage is always the same. His State is one of eternal Samadhi. This Samadhi (of His) is not in any way hindered in the least by actions. Nor are actions hindered in the least by the Samadhi.

Samadhi is the state of Awareness of the Self alone.
If the Sage remains in Samadhi all the time, how can actions be performed? The answer is given in the verses that follow:

658. द्वे निर्विकल्पे हि समाधिनिष्ठे स्यात् केवलैका सहजाभिधाऽन्या ।
न केवलां प्राप्य भवेत् प्रबुद्धः स एव बुद्धः सहजस्थितो यः ॥

dve nirvikalpe hi samādhiniṣṭhe syat kevalaikā sahajābhidhā'nyā |
na kevalāṁ prāpya bhavet prabuddhaḥ sa eva buddhaḥ sahajasthito yaḥ ||

There are two throught-free Samadhis; one is called the Kevala, the other is called the Sahaja

(Natural). By attaining the Kevala one does not become a Sage. He alone is a Sage, who is firmly established in the Sahaja.

These two are further distinguished and explained in the verses that follow.

659.　यः केवलो नाम समाधिरुक्तः स योगिनः स्यान्मनसो लयेन ।
समाधिरुत्थानमिति प्रसिद्धे स्थिती विभिन्ने भवतोऽस्य लोके ॥

yaḥ kevalo nāma samādhiruktaḥ sa yoginaḥ syānmanaso layena |
samādhirutthānamiti prasiddhe sthitī vibhinne bhavato'sya loke ||

The Kevala Samadhi mentioned here is one that comes to a Yogi by the mind going into latency. For him, it is well-known that there are two distinct states, Samadhi (introvertedness) and coming back (to the common waking of samsara).

It has been shown before that mental quiescence is of two kinds as latency and complete and final extinction, and that the latter alone leads to sagehood. This makes all the difference, therefore, as shown below.

660.　मनः समाधौ बत योगिनोऽस्य सवासनं ह्येव भवेद्विलीनम् ।
स्थित्वा समाधौ सुचिरं च सोऽयं व्युत्थाप्यते वासनया भवाय ॥

manaḥ samādhau bata yogino'sya savāsanaṁ hyeva bhavedvilīnam |
sthitvā samādhau suciraṁ ca so'yaṁ vyutthāpyate vāsanayā bhavāya ||

The Yogi's mind, in his Samadhi, remains latent with all its vasanas; after so remaining for a very long time, it is brought out to samsara by a vasana.

661. यदा समाधेरयमुत्थितः स्यात् पूर्वोज्झितां संसृतिमाददाति ।
सम्मोहनद्रव्यविनष्टबोधः कर्मासमाप्तं प्रतिबुध्य यद्वत् ॥

yadā samādherayamutthitaḥ syāt pūrvojjhitāṁ saṁsṛtimādadāti |
sammohanadravyavinaṣṭabodhaḥ karmāsamāptaṁ pratibudhya yadvat ||

When he is thrown out from the Samadhi, he resumes the Samsara just where he left it off, just as an anaesthetised person (on recovering consciousness) resumes the work left unfinished before.

This was illustrated by Bhagavan Sri Ramana by the story of a yogi. He had awakened from Samadhi and being thirsty asked his disciple to bring water to drink. But before the water was brought he again went into Samadhi and remained in it for about three centuries during which the Muslim Raj had come and gone, being superseded by the British raj. When he awoke he called out addressing his disciple — (Who had long ago died) 'Have you brought water?'

662. संसारमेवं प्रतिपद्य योगी भूयः समाधिं प्रविशेत् प्रयत्नात् ।
बुद्धस्त्वयत्नः सहजस्थितत्वान्न तं विमुञ्चत्यपि नाददाति ॥

saṁsāramevaṁ pratipadya yogī bhūyaḥ samādhiṁ praviśet prayatnāt |
buddhastvayatnaḥ sahajasthitatvānna taṁ vimuñcatyapi nādadāti ||

The Yogi, thus returning to Samsara, again enters Samadhi with effort. But the Sage, being established in the Natural State (Sahaja Nirvikalpa Samadhi) neither loses it nor gets it back, (but remains in It uninterruptedly).

663.   न संसृतिं याति कदाऽपि बुद्धः समाधिरेव प्रकृतिर्हि तस्य ।
विना समाधिं स कदाऽपि नास्तीत्यतः समाधिः सहजाभिधोऽयम् ॥

na saṁsṛtiṁ yāti kadā'pi buddhaḥ samādhireva prakṛtirhi tasya |
vinā samādhiṁ sa kadā'pi nāstītyataḥ samādhiḥ sahajābhidho'yam ||

The Sage never comes back to Samsara. Samadhi is His Natural State. There is no moment when he is without Samadhi and hence it is called Sahaja (Natural).

This Samadhi is different from the Kevala of the Yogi, in that it does not prevent the Sage being (seemingly) active in the world, while remaining in His Samadhi.

664.   अप्रच्युतोऽसौ निजसत्यभावात् स्थितः सदा स्वे सहजे समाधौ ।
जीवन् विमुक्तो व्यवहर्तुमिष्टे लोके यथा शङ्करदेशिकाद्याः ॥

apracyuto'sau nijasatyabhāvāt sthitaḥ sadā sve sahaje samādhau |
jīvan vimukto vyavahartumiṣṭe loke yathā śaṅkaradeśikādyāḥ ||

The Sage, remaining uninterruptedly in His Natural State of Samadhi, never swerving from It, as a Jivan Mukta, is able to be active in the world, just as the sage of old, Sri Sankaracharya and others did.

665. योगी यदा केवलभावमग्नस्तदा न शक्नोति हि कर्म कर्तुम् ।
यदोत्थितोऽसौ भविता समाधेः करोति कर्माज्ञतया तदानीम् ॥

yogī yadā kevalabhāvamagnastadā na śaknoti hi karma kartum |
yadotthito'sau bhavitā samādheḥ karoti karmājñatayā tadānīm ||

The Yogi, while he is immersed in his Kevala Samadhi is unable to do any work. When he comes out of the Samadhi, then he does work subject to the Ignorance.

666. तत्त्वोपदेशेऽपि मुमुक्षुपुंसां भवेत् समर्थो न स योगिमर्त्यः ।
तिष्ठन् सदैवाच्युत एव तुर्ये शास्ता समर्थोऽस्ति तु बुद्ध एव ॥

tattvopadeśe'pi mumukṣupuṁsām bhavet samartho na sa yogimartyaḥ |
tiṣṭhan sadaivācyuta eva turye śāstā samartho'sti tu buddha eva ||

The Yogi is not equal to the task of teaching the Truth of the Real Self (and the Sadhana for realising It) to disciples. The Sage alone, remaining always, unswervingly, in the Supreme State, is perfectly competent to teach and guide disciples.

667. नाङ्गीकृताऽसौ सहजा स्थितिश्चेद्
गीतादिशास्त्राणि मृषेति सिद्ध्येत् ।
बुद्धोपदेशैर्भरितत्त्वहेतोः शास्त्रं प्रमाणं हि मुमुक्षुपुंसाम् ॥

nāṅgīkṛtā'sau sahajā sthitiśced gītādiśāstrāṇi mṛṣeti siddhyet |
buddhopadeśairbharitatvahetoḥ śāstram pramāṇam hi mumukṣupuṁsām ||

If this Sahaja Samadhi be not accepted, it will follow that the sacred books, like the Gita, etc. are false. Sacred books are authoritative for the aspirants to Deliverance, as being filled with the teachings of sages.

668.   परम्पराऽसौ खलु बुद्धपुंसां मुमुक्षुलोकोद्धरणार्थमेव ।
रक्षत्यविच्छिन्नतया सदैव सुज्ञानशास्त्रस्य सुसम्प्रदायम् ॥

paramparā'sau khalu buddhapuṁsāṁ mumukṣulokoddharaṇārthameva |
rakṣatyavicchinnatayā sadaiva sujñānaśāstrasya susampradāyam ||

The succession of sages is it that preserves the correct tradition of the Science of Right Awareness of the Real Self for the benefit of the aspirants to Deliverance.

669.   अन्त्यं प्रमाणं हि निजानुभूतिर्न संशयानामुदयोऽस्ति यत्र ।
तावत् प्रमाणानि हि बुद्धवाचो लभ्येत यावन्न तथानुभूतिः ॥

antyaṁ pramāṇaṁ hi nijānubhūtirna saṁśayānāmudayo'sti yatra |
tāvat pramāṇāni hi buddhavāco labhyeta yāvanna tathānubhūtiḥ ||

The final proof is one's own Experience of the Truth, wherein doubts can no more arise. And until such Experience is attained the utterances of sages are authority for the aspirants.

The difference between the two kinds of Nirvikalpa (thought-free) Samadhis was explained by the Bhagavan as follows.

670. गत्वाऽंबुधिं तन्मयतां गताया नद्याः समो बुद्ध उदीरितोऽस्ति ।
कूपे निमग्नस्य घटस्य तुल्यो रज्ज्वा निबद्धस्य तु केवलस्थः ॥

gatvā'mbudhiṁ tanmayatāṁ gatāyā nadyāḥ samo buddha udīrito'sti |
kūpe nimagnasya ghaṭasya tulyo rajjvā nibaddhasya tu kevalasthaḥ ||

The Sage (who is in Sahaja Samadhi) is like
the river that has joined the ocean and becomes
merged in it. The Yogi in the Kevala state is like a
bucket let down into a well, by means of a rope
tied to it.

671. घटः सरज्जुर्हि विकृष्यमाणो रज्ज्वा बहिर्याति पुनश्च कूपात् ।
एवम् मनः केवलभावमग्नं विकृष्यते वासनया भवाय ॥

ghaṭaḥ sarajjurhi vikṛṣyamāṇo rajjvā bahiryāti punaśca kūpāt |
evam manaḥ kevalabhāvamagnaṁ vikṛṣyate vāsanayā bhavāya ||

The bucket, when drawn up by the rope,
comes out of the well. Just so the mind immersed
in the Kevala Samadhi, is pulled out of it by
vasanas back to the Samsara.

672. नैष्कर्म्यमेवं सहजस्थितस्य स्फुटीकृतं नो भगवत्तमेन ।
विद्वानकर्तॉपि भवन् स्वभावात् कर्ता महांश्चापि भवत्यसङ्गः ॥

naiṣkarmyamevaṁ sahajasthitasya sphuṭīkṛtaṁ no bhagavattamena |
vidvānakartā'pi bhavan svabhāvāt kartā mahāṁścāpi bhavatyasaṅgaḥ ||

Thus it has been shown by the Most Holy One
that the Sage in the Natural Samadhi has no
activity. But though by Nature the Sage is no actor,

yet He is also a great actor, without being attached (or bound).

The Sage has the whole potency of God in doing His appointed work, and hence there is no limit to His Power, because, being egoless, the Power Divine works through His subtle and gross bodies.

The great blessing that disciples and devotees of the Sage derive from associating with Him is next expounded.

673. सत्सङ्गतिर्नाम निगद्यते या बुद्धस्य पुंसः खलु सङ्गतिः सा ।
अर्थो भवेद् ब्रह्म हि सत्पदस्य तदात्मकोऽसौ भविता हि बुद्धः ॥

satsaṅgatirnāma nigadyate yā buddhasya puṁsaḥ khalu saṅgatiḥ sā |
artho bhaved brahma hi satpadasya tadātmako'sau bhavitā hi buddhaḥ ||

What is called association with the Holy is the association with a sage. The term 'Sat' means the Brahman, and the Sage is identical with That

674. ब्रह्मैव सर्वोऽपि हि को विशेषः प्रबुद्धपुंसीति न शङ्कनीयम् ।
अहन्तयाऽन्यत्र हृतप्रभं सत् पूर्णप्रभं तत्तु विभाति बुद्धे ॥

brahmaiva sarvo'pi hi ko viśeṣaḥ prabuddhapuṁsīti na śaṅkanīyam |
ahantayā'nyatra hṛtaprabhaṁ sat pūrṇaprabhaṁ tattu vibhāti buddhe ||

It must not be doubted, 'Since all alike are Brahman, what is there special in the Sage?'. In others the Real, (Brahman) is eclipsed by the ego, but in the Sage the Brahman shines in its fullest Effulgence.

675.　सङ्गं प्रबुद्धस्य भजन् मुमुक्षुः सङ्गात् समस्तादपि मुक्तिमेति ।
निस्सङ्गभावेन निरस्तमोहो यात्येकतां निश्चलचित्स्वरूपे ॥

saṅgaṁ prabuddhasya bhajan mumukṣuḥ saṅgāt samastādapi muktimeti |
nissaṅgabhāvena nirastamoho yātyekatāṁ niścalacitsvarūpe ||

Being associated with the Sage, the aspirant is freed from all attachments. Being free from attachments, he is freed from delusion and thereby becomes one with the Moveless Consciousness (which is the Brahman).

676.　सत्सङ्गसञ्जातनिजस्वरूपान्वेषेण लभ्यं परमं पदं यत् ।
शास्त्रार्थबोधाच्छ्रवणादिभिर्वा साध्यं न तन्नेतरसाधनैर्वा ॥

satsaṅgasañjātanijasvarūpānveṣeṇa labhyaṁ paramaṁ padaṁ yat |
śāstrārthabodhācchravaṇādibhirvā sādhyaṁ na tannetarasādhanairvā ||

That Supreme State, which will be attained by the Quest of one's own Self, which automatically comes to be made by the power of association with the Holy One, cannot be won by acquiring theoretical knowledge from books, by listening to discourses (by learned men) etc. nor by any other means.

677.　सत्सङ्गतिं चेद् भजते मुमुक्षुश्चरेत् किमर्थं नियमान् यथाऽन्ये ।
शीतो वहेद् दक्षिणमारुतश्चेत् किमर्थमिच्छेद् व्यजनं तदानीम् ॥

satsaṅgatiṁ ced bhajate mumukṣuścaret kimarthaṁ niyamān yathā'nye |
śīto vahed dakṣiṇamārutaścet kimarthamiccched vyajanaṁ tadānīm ||

If an aspirant associates with a Sage, why should he practise the disciplinary courses of action like other men? If the cool south wind blows, why should one take up a fan?

678. तापं शशी कल्पतरुश्च दैन्यं हरेच्च गङ्गा बत पापमात्रम् ।
वीक्षा सतां नाशयति त्रयं च न तत्समं किञ्चन विद्यतेऽन्यत् ॥

tāpaṁ śaśī kalpataruśca dainyaṁ harecca gaṅgā bata pāpamātram |
vīkṣā satāṁ nāśayati trayaṁ ca na tatsamaṁ kiñcana vidyate'nyat ||

The moon relieves only heat; the celestial wishing tree removes only poverty; the holy Ganges removes only sin. But the sight of sages destroys all three. There is nothing else in the world equal to the association with holy ones.

679. समानि सद्भिर्न जलात्मकानि तीर्थानि देवाश्च मृदादिमात्राः ।
पुनन्ति तानि ह्यतिदीर्घकालात् सन्दर्शनादेव पुनन्ति बुद्धाः ॥

samāni sadbhirna jalātmakāni tīrthāni devāśca mṛdādimātrāḥ |
punanti tāni hyatidīrghakālāt sandarśanādeva punanti buddhāḥ ||

The holy bathing places, which are only water, and the deities, which are made of clay or the like, are not equal to the sages. These purify the mind after a long time. But by sight alone the sages purify one.

680. गङ्गाम्भसि स्नानफलं विनाशः पापस्य पुंसो न तु पापकर्तुः ।
सङ्गात् सतां नश्यति पापकर्ता न तत्समं पावनमस्ति लोके ॥

gangāmbhasi snānaphalaṁ vināśaḥ pāpasya puṁso na tu pāpakartuḥ |
sangāt satāṁ naśyati pāpakartā na tatsamaṁ pāvanamasti loke ||

Bathing in the Ganga removes the sins of the man, not the sinner in him (the ego). But association with a Sage destroys the sinner also. There is nothing so powerful to purify the mind like the association with a Sage.

The Sage's greatness is further set forth as follows.

681. मृत्युञ्जयोऽसौ त्रिपुरान्तकोऽसौ स्मरान्तकोऽसौ नरकान्तकश्च ।
स हीश्वराणामपि चात्मभूतस्तमेव सर्वेऽपि हि पूजयन्ति ॥

mṛtyuñjayo'sau tripurāntako'sau smarāntako'sau narakāntakaśca |
sa hīśvarāṇāmapi cātmabhūtastameva sarve'pi hi pūjayanti || 681 ||

He is the Conqueror of Death, of the Demon of Three Cities, of Cupid, and of the Demon Naraka. He is the Self of all the great Gods, and all alike worship only Him.

How He is the killer of the Demon Tripura, and of the Demon Naraka, is next explained.

682. नीतं यदन्तं वपुषां त्रयं च ज्ञानेन तेन त्रिपुरान्तकोऽसौ ।
नीतोऽहमाख्यो निधनं च तेनेत्यतः स बुद्धो नरकान्तकश्च ॥

nītaṁ yadantaṁ vapuṣāṁ trayaṁ ca jñānena tena tripurāntako'sau |
nīto'hamākhyo nidhanaṁ ca tenetyataḥ sa buddho narakāntakaśca ||

Since by Him the three bodies (encompassing the Self) have been destroyed by knowledge, therefore He is the killer of Tripura. Because He has put an end to the Ego, therefore He is also the killer of Naraka.

The three bodies are the gross, subtle and causal, already stated. Naraka is the personification of the Ego.

683.　अहं स्वयं बुद्ध इति ब्रवीति गीतासु कृष्णो भगवान् स्वयं यत्।
　　　 न कोऽपि तस्यास्ति समोऽधिको वा न मीयते तन्महिमा कथञ्चित्॥

aham svayam buddha iti bravīti gītāsu kṛṣṇo bhagavān svayam yat |
na ko'pi tasyāsti samo'dhiko vā na mīyate tanmahimā kathañcit ||

Since in the Gita Bhagavan Sri Krishna Himself says, 'I Myself Am the Sage,' therefore it follows that there is none equal to or greater than He. His greatness is immeasurable.

684.　यतः प्रबुद्धः पर एव साक्षात् तस्योपदेशाः परमं प्रमाणम्।
　　　 ततः परं तस्य वचोभिरेव प्रामाण्यमस्ति श्रुतिशीर्षवाचाम्॥

yataḥ prabuddhaḥ para eva sākṣāt tasyopadeśāḥ paramam pramāṇam |
tataḥ param tasya vacobhireva prāmāṇyamasti śrutiśīrṣavācām ||

Since the Sage is God Himself, His teachings are of the highest authority. Thereafter and by His words alone the Upanishads also have authority.

685.　परात्मशक्तेः करुणाभिधाया रूपं द्वितीयं हि गुरुः प्रबुद्धः।
　　　 अतः सुभक्त्या स्वगुरुं प्रबुद्धं भजन् मुमुक्षुर्भविता कृतार्थः॥

parātmaśakteḥ karuṇābhidhāyā rūpaṁ dvitīyaṁ hi guruḥ prabuddhaḥ |
ataḥ subhaktyā svaguruṁ prabuddhaṁ bhajan mumukṣurbhavitā kṛtārthaḥ ||

Since the Guru, if He be a Sage, is the second Form of God's Grace, therefore the aspirant practising devotion to Him (as to God), will reach his Goal.

Divine Grace has three forms in three stages, first as God, then as Guru and finally as the Real Self. The above verse is, based upon this ancient teaching, repeated by Bhagavan Sri Ramana.

686. शक्तिः शुभा काचन सन्निधाने बुद्धस्य पुंसोऽस्ति सुदूरतश्च ।
त्यज्येत नो कोऽपि तया गृहीतः परं तु नीयेत विमुक्तिमेव ॥

śaktiḥ śubhā kācana sannidhāne buddhasya puṁso'sti sudūrataśca |
tyajyeta no ko'pi tayā gṛhitaḥ paraṁ tu nīyeta vimuktimeva ||

In the Sage's presence and even far away there is a mysterious power. Whoever is caught hold of by It will not be let go, but will surely be taken to the State of Deliverance.

Therefore those that are positively determined not to obtain Deliverance, being greatly in love with samsara, should beware of sages!

687. व्याघ्रेण यद्वद्धरिणो गृहीतो तदन्नतामेति तथैव साधुः ।
ध्रुवं प्रबुद्धेन दृशा गृहीतस्तद्भावमेतीति गुरुर्जगाद ॥

vyāghreṇa yadvaddhariṇo gṛhīto tadannatāmeti tathaiva sādhuḥ |
dhruvaṁ prabuddhena dṛśā gṛhitastadbhāvametīti gururjagāda ||

The Guru has said: Just as a fawn caught by
a tiger becomes its food, so, if a good man is caught
by the gracious look of the Sage, he will surely
attain the State wherein the Sage dwells.

688. बहिः स्थितोऽन्तर्मुखतां विधायाप्यन्तः स्थितोऽन्तश्च
विकृष्य चित्तम् ।
परे पदे स्वे विदधाति निष्ठां साधोः प्रबुद्धो हि गुरुः स्वशक्त्या ॥

bahiḥ sthito'ntarmukhatāṁ vidhāyāpyantaḥ sthito'ntaśca vikṛṣya cittam ।
pare pade sve vidadhāti niṣṭhāṁ sādhoḥ prabuddho hi guruḥ svaśaktyā ॥

Being outside He turns the mind of the
Sadhaka inwards, and from inside (being in the
Heart) He pulls the mind (in to the Heart) and
then fixes him, by His power, in the Supreme state.

689. अगोचरोऽसौ वचसो धियोऽपि निष्ठा हि बुद्धस्य पदे परस्मिन् ।
बोधाय साधोस्तु यथाकथञ्चित् किञ्चित् प्रबुद्धैरिदमुक्तमस्ति ॥

agocaro'sau vacaso dhiyo'pi niṣṭhā hi buddhasya pade parasmin ।
bodhāya sādhostu yathākathañcit kiñcit prabuddhairidamuktamasti ॥

That Supreme State of the Sage transcends
both words and intellect. What has been set forth
here is just a little which has been vouchsafed by
the sages for the sadhaka.

690. व्याख्यात एवं सहजात्मभावः ससाधनोऽसौ गुरुणोपदिष्टः ।
अथोपदेशेष्विह सार एष निरुच्यते साध्ववधारणाय ॥

vyākhyāta evaṁ sahajātmabhāvaḥ sasādhano'sau guruṇopadiṣṭaḥ |
athopadeśeṣviha sāra eṣa nirucyate sādhvavadhāraṇāya ||

Thus has been expounded the Natural State of the Self, along with the Means of Attainment (Sadhana). Hereafter is set forth the essence of the teachings for reflection by Sadhakas.

What is hereinafter set forth is Bhagavan Sri Ramana's own commentary on the First Benedictory Verse of the Forty Verses on Reality.

691. विश्वं स्वदृश्यं च तदीक्षकं स्वं जानाति लोके सकलोऽपि जन्तुः ।
स्वतश्च सत्यं द्वयमप्यवैति मोहस्त्वयं संसृतिहेतुरस्य ॥

viśvam svadṛśyaṁ ca tadīkṣakaṁ svaṁ jānāti loke sakalo'pi jantuḥ |
svataśca satyaṁ dvayamapyavaiti mohastvayaṁ saṁsṛtiheturasya ||

Every creature is aware of its own spectacle, the world, and its seer himself (the individual soul) and understands these two as real in their own right. This delusion is the cause for its samsara.

692. सत्यं स्वतश्चेदुभयं तदेतद् भायादविच्छिन्नतया सदैव ।
कदाऽपि भातं च कदाप्यभातं भवेत् तु यत् तत् कथमस्तु सत्यम् ॥

satyaṁ svataścedubhayaṁ tadetad bhāyādavicchinnatayā sadaiva |
kadā'pi bhātaṁ ca kadāpyabhātaṁ bhavet tu yat tat kathamastu satyam ||

If the two were real in their own right, they would appear continuously. How can something

 Sri Ramanaparavidyopanishad

that appears at sometimes and does not appear at other times, be real (in its own right)?

693. प्रकाशते मानसचेष्टयैव स्वप्नेऽपि जाग्रत्युभयं तदेतत् ।
भाति द्वयं नैव सुषुप्तिभावे ततो मनोमात्रमिदं द्वयं च ॥

prakāśate mānasaceṣṭayaiva svapne'pi jāgratyubhayaṁ tadetat |
bhāti dvayaṁ naiva suṣuptibhāve tato manomātramidaṁ dvayaṁ ca ||

This pair shines, in dream and waking only by the functioning of the mind. In deep sleep both of them fail to shine. Therefore both are mental.

694. यस्मिन् मनो याति लयं च यस्मादुदेति भूयोऽपि तदेव सत्यम् ।
लयोदयाभ्यां रहितं तदेतत् सत्यं स्वतो मुक्तिपदं मुमुक्षोः ॥

yasmin mano yāti layaṁ ca yasmādudeti bhūyo'pi tadeva satyam |
layodayābhyāṁ rahitaṁ tadetat satyaṁ svato muktipadaṁ mumukṣoḥ ||

That, wherein the mind goes into latency, and wherefrom it rises again, is alone Real. That One, being without settings and risings, is Real, in its Own Right, and is the Home of Deliverance for the aspirant.

695. सत्ताप्रदं तज्जगतोऽखिलस्य ब्रह्माभिधानं परिपूर्णमेकम् ।
चैतन्यदीप्तिं मनसे तदेव ददाति चैतन्यविवर्जिताय ॥

sattāpradaṁ tajjagato'khilasya brahmābhidhānaṁ paripūrṇamekam |
caitanyadīptiṁ manase tadeva dadāti caitanyavivarjitāya ||

That Reality, named Brahman, which is only One without a second, and complete in Itself, is the Giver of existence to the whole world. It also gives the light of consciousness to the mind, which in itself is inconscient.

696. अन्तर्हृदि स्वात्मतया तदेव साक्षीव निश्चिन्तनमस्त्यसङ्गम् ।
आच्छाद्यते तत्तु बहिर्मुखत्वे मृषाप्रपञ्चेन मनोमयेन ॥

antarhṛdi svātmatayā tadeva sākṣīva niścintanamastyasaṅgam |
ācchādyate tattu bahirmukhatve mṛṣāprapañcena manomayena ||

That Itself dwells in the Heart (of all creatures) as the Own Self like a Witness, without thoughts and unrelated. But that One is concealed, during the outward-turned state of mind, by the false (appearance of the) world, which is of the stuff of the mind.

697. अतो न तं कश्चन वेत्ति लोके पश्यन्निदं सत्यवदेव मोहात् ।
शरीरमेवात्मतयाऽपि मत्वा भ्राम्यत्यसङ्ख्येषु भवेषु दुःखी ॥

ato na taṁ kaścana vetti loke paśyannidaṁ satyavadeva mohāt |
śarīramevātmatayā'pi matvā bhrāmyatyasaṅkhyeṣu bhaveṣu duḥkhī ||

Therefore no one in the world knows This (Real Self), due to Illusion. Also, being persuaded that the gross body is itself the Self, he wanders in lives innumerable, suffering unhappiness.

698. तेनात्मरूपेण परेण विश्वमाच्छादनीयं तु मनोविनाशात् ।
भायात् तदैव प्रतिबन्धहीनं ह्यात्मस्वरूपं विमलं यथावत् ॥

tenātmarūpeṇa pareṇa viśvamācchādanīyaṁ tu manovināśāt |
bhāyāt tadaiva pratibandhahīnaṁ hyātmasvarūpaṁ vimalaṁ yathāvat ||

This world must be covered over by the Supreme
who is the Real Self, by extinction of the mind. Then
the Pure Real Self will shine unhindered, as He really
is (as the Sole Reality, the Brahman).

699. विवेकवैराग्ययुतो विमुक्त्यै गुरूक्तमार्गेण यदा यतेत ।
मूले निजे ब्रह्मणि जन्म लब्ध्वा विमुच्यतेऽसौ भवबन्धपाशैः ॥

vivekavairāgyayuto vimuktyai guruktamārgeṇa yadā yateta |
mūle nije brahmaṇi janma labdhvā vimucyate'sau bhavabandhapāśaiḥ ||

If and when he makes efforts, equipped with
Discrimination and Detachment, for deliverance
by the means taught by the Holy Guru, then he
becomes Free from the bondage of Samsara by
attaining Birth in his own Source, the Brahman.

700. कृत्वा मनोऽन्तर्मुखमस्तचिन्तं निमज्य चान्तर्निजमार्गणेन ।
मनोविनाशेन विनष्टमोहो भवेद्विमुक्तः स नरः प्रबुद्धः ॥

kṛtvā mano'ntarmukhamastacintaṁ nimajya cāntarnijamārgaṇena |
manovināśena vinaṣṭamoho bhavedvimuktaḥ sa naraḥ prabuddhaḥ ||

Turning his mind inwards, free from
thoughts, and diving into the Heart by the Quest

of his own Real Self, becoming free from delusion by the extinction of the ego-mind, he attains the State of Deliverance. Such One is a Sage.

The following is the concluding verse.

701.　परात्परं यत् सकलात्मभूतमस्मद्गुरुः श्रीरमणो बभूव ।
यावद्भविष्यत्यहमो विनाशः सहस्रशः सन्तु नमांसि तस्मै ॥

parātparaṁ yat sakalātmabhūtamasmadguruḥ śrīramaṇo babhūva |
yāvadbhaviṣyatyahamo vināśaḥ sahasraśaḥ santu namāṁsi tasmai ||

To that Supreme One, the Self in all creatures, which became our Guru, Sri Ramana, let there be thousands of namaskaras until there comes about the extinction of the ego.

There is the possibility of namaskaras only so long as the ego survives. Until then namaskaras are necessary to ensure its extinction.

॥ ॐ नमो भगवते श्रीरमणाय ॥
|| om namo bhagavate śrīramaṇāya ||